GOLDEN HEROES

FIFTY SEASONS OF FOOTBALLER OF THE YEAR

DENNIS SIGNY and NORMAN GILLER

An introduction by
MICHAEL PARKINSON

CHAMELEON

First published in Great Britain in 1997 by Chameleon Books
an imprint of André Deutsch Ltd
106 Great Russell Street
London WC1B 3LJ

www.vci.co.uk

André Deutsch Ltd is a subsidiary of VCI plc

British Library Cataloguing in Publication Data for this book is available from the British Library.

ISBN 0 233 99163 8

Jacket design by Design 23
Book design by Generation Studio

Printed & bound in Great Britain
by Butler & Tanner, Frome and London

A C K N O W L E D G E M E N T S

Authors Dennis Signy and Norman Giller wish to thank David Crowe (DC Publications Ltd) and Paul Sudbury for his design and computer skills, Tim Forrester and his staff at André Deutsch – in particular, Nicky Paris – for their enthusiasm and expertise in helping to get this book to press. Thanks, too, to Mike Scott and Phil McNeill for their editing input, and Michael Giller for his statistical contribution and Mark Peacock, Joe Crowe and Joanne Meeks for their valuable help. We are, of course, indebted to Carling for their support, and thank Richard Thompson for his motivation. You are all selected as members of our dream team. Most of all, a big thank you to all the Golden Heroes who kindly co-operated with us, and to Michael Parkinson for giving us such a splendid kick-off. In return for all the co-operation they have received, the authors are making a donation to the Children in Need Fund.

THE CONTRIBUTIONS FROM THE LATE FOOTBALL MASTERS JOHNNY CAREY, JOE MERCER, HARRY JOHNSTON, BILLY WRIGHT, DON REVIE, DANNY BLANCHFLOWER, AND BOBBY MOORE ARE ALL ADAPTED FROM INTERVIEWS CONDUCTED BY NORMAN GILLER FOR A FOOTBALL LISTS COLLECTION THAT HE COMPILED, AND FROM WHAT THEY SAID WHEN RECEIVING THEIR AWARDS.

PHOTOGRAPH ACKNOWLEDGMENTS

ALLSPORT PICTURE LIBRARY

PAGES : 64-5, 76-7, 84, 86-91, 93-8, 102-10, 116-120.

ALLSPORT HISTORICAL COLLECTION

PAGES : 12-3, 19, 22-4, 26-8, 30-1, 42, 46-51, 62-3, 68, 70, 72.

COLOURSPORT

PAGES : 6, 7, 14, 18, 24-5, 29, 32-4, 38-9, 40, 44, 52-5, 58-61, 67, 69, 71-5, 80-3, 101,

112.

PRESS ASSOCIATION PICTURE LIBRARY

PAGES : 12, 14, 20, 22, 26, 28, 30, 34, 40, 42, 44, 46, 50, 52, 54, 58, 62, 64, 66, 68,

70,

72, 74, 76, 86, 88, 90, 92, 94, 96, 100, 104, 106, 108, 110.

POPPERFOTTO

PAGES : 8, 10, 11, 15-7, 32, 36-8, 41, 43, 48, 50, 56-7, 60, 66, 78-9, 84-5, 98-9, 116.

SOUND STILLS

PAGES : 9-102.

PAGES 20 & 21 BY KIND PERMISSION OF HARRY WOLSTENHOLME

PAGE 35 BY KIND PERMISSION OF RON WASH

PAGES 45 & 46 BY KIND PERMISSION OF BOBBY COLLINS.

JACKET PHOTOGRAPHS:

STANLEY MATTHEWS AND BOBBY MOORE: ALLSPORT HISTORICAL COLLECTION

ALAN SHEARER AND GIANFRANCO ZOLA: ALLSPORT

FOOTBALLER OF THE YEAR TROPHY: SOUND STILL PHOTOGRAPHS

DEDICATIONS

Dedicated to the memories of
Johnny Carey, Joe Mercer, Harry Johnston, Billy Wright,
Don Revie, Danny Blanchflower and Bobby Moore.
Footballing masters for all seasons.

FOOTBALLER
OF THE YEAR

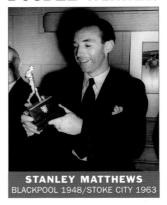

DOUBLE WINNER

STANLEY MATTHEWS
BLACKPOOL 1948/STOKE CITY 1963

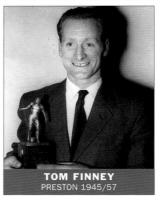

DOUBLE WINNER

TOM FINNEY
PRESTON 1945/57

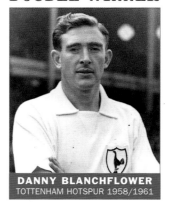

DOUBLE WINNER

DANNY BLANCHFLOWER
TOTTENHAM HOTSPUR 1958/1961

CARLING

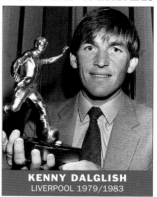

DOUBLE WINNER

KENNY DALGLISH
LIVERPOOL 1979/1983

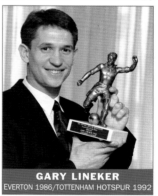

DOUBLE WINNER

GARY LINEKER
EVERTON 1986/TOTTENHAM HOTSPUR 1992

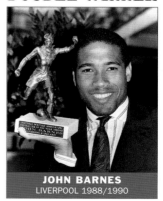

DOUBLE WINNER

JOHN BARNES
LIVERPOOL 1988/1990

My footballing life from Matthews to Zola

Looking at the list I have measured my life with the Footballers of the Year. Stanley Matthews, the first winner, was one of the reasons I became attracted to the game. Gianfranco Zola, the latest, is one of the reasons I remain interested. A lot has happened in the past 50 years, some of it wondrous, much of it worrying. When I first started watching football the only difference between fans and players was one worked down the pit and watched Barnsley and the others worked down the pit and played for Barnsley. One of our players used to wait at the top of the lane in his pit muck and travel with the fans on the Yorkshire Traction bus, his boots in a carrier bag.

Oakwell football ground was the centre of our universe. A trip to Chesterfield was as far afield as we ever went and that was in a foreign country. When we signed Jimmy Baxter from North of the Border, he played against Manchester United on the Saturday and started work at the pit on Monday. Baxter was a magician with a fag in his mouth. When television did a documentary on Tom Finney, Baxter, by then Finney's team-mate at Preston, was seen in the background smoking a Woodbine and finishing a pint.

His partner at Barnsley was Johnny Kelly, a winger of the sort you don't see nowadays, meaning he was two footed, could beat a man inside or outside and used to cross those lovely balls which sat up and begged the centre forward to score. He invented a liquid bleach called Kelzone and used to drive round town selling it to housewives. Beaumont Asquith, who nowadays would be worth a fortune as an all-purpose midfielder, had a milk round, Gordon Pallister, as elegant a full-back as ever I saw, ran a temperance bar which sold saspirilla, Danny Blanchflower studied economics part-time at the local technical college, and when he retired my beloved Skinner Normanton lived in a bungalow and grew sunflowers. God rest his simple soul.

The footballers I grew up with were part of our community. We were bound together by the unique links forged between a football club and the community. When I tell my children about those days I can see them smiling at the quaintness of it all. How could the terraces we stood on be better than the super stadia of today? Well they weren't but they were different; funnier, less threatening, warmer in the sense of being more neighbourly. How could the players of yore compete with today's superstars? Very well, as it happens. And if we are talking about British rather than foreign players, and home grown talent instead of the imported variety, there is no doubt the generation I grew up in had by far the greater riches.

Look at the list. Matthews, Carey, Joe Mercer, Billy Wright, Nat Lofthouse, Tom Finney. Think who is missing: Wilf Mannion, Raich Carter, the incomparable Peter Doherty, Tommy Lawton, Len Shackleton. That the lot? Not even started. What about one of the greatest all round players I ever saw. John Charles. Then there's Jackie Milburn, Stan Mortensen, Jimmy McIlroy. Johnny

Johnny Haynes of Fulham and England would today be voted Footballer of the Year unopposed.

Haynes never gets a mention in the list of Footballers of the Year. Nowadays he would win it unopposed.

When you look at the players who won the award in the 1960s you are as intrigued by the omissions as the selections. No Greaves or John Giles, not to mention Jim Baxter, Denis Law, John White or Rodney Marsh. That's a random list. I am sure more careful research would reveal significant absentees. The point is if you take the past decade from mid-1980s it won't offer too many alternatives. Most significantly of all the choice of Klinsmann, Cantona and Zola in the last three years tells its own story about the state of British football. And if Zola didn't win it this year who were the alternatives? Juninho, Di Matteo, Leboeuf perhaps. Such players are welcome. Of course they are. What we must be careful of is creating a financial free-for-all which neglects the traditional tap roots of our game.

I was reminded of what they are when I watched Barnsley play this season. We won promotion to the Premier League with a team which cost £850,000 over three years. The achievement was as much a victory for good management and common sense as it was a triumph for smaller clubs who could be overwhelmed by the ambitions of the big boys. It was also a reminder of what a football team means to a community, a throwback to those days when players were not separated from fans by limousines with smoked glass windows and screened from reality by business managers and agents.

It was also a reminder of the days when pressure meant working down a pit and playing football was reckoned a bobby's job, when managers and media supped from the same glass and a coach was something the team travelled away in. I am not worried by the game changing. Inevitably it must. I am concerned by what is left behind as it hurtles towards the moon.

I'll give you an example of what I mean. Bobby Charlton won the Footballer of the Year award in 1966. The image I have of him is standing holding the World Cup at Wembley with three lions on his England shirt. The image I have of Alan Shearer is modelling a new England shirt on which the name of the manufacturer is the most prominent feature. If I were a Martian just landed in England without a clue of where I was I would imagine I was living in a land called Umbro. Is it old fashioned to believe there are certain things not for sale. Or doesn't it matter any more? A look at the list of winners should be sufficient to convince even the most insensitive soul this is a game worth preserving.

My two favourite players are there: Tom Finney and George Best. Why Tom has not been knighted is a mystery. Not only would his playing ability guarantee him a place in any world team in any era you care to mention but his impeccable sportsmanship, his conduct both on and off of the field have set the example for all to follow. Tom thinks George

George Best, a bridge between two generations.

Best was on his own and I'm not one to argue with God. It is significant that when the winners of the Footballer of the Year title were canvassed they chose George as the Players' Player. When history comes to judge George Best it might acknowledge his importance went far beyond his talents as a player.

He was the bridge between one generation and the next. More than that, he was the catalyst for change between the wage slaves of my youth and the rich men of today. He was the first footballer to become a pop star, the man who made the headlines both on front and back pages. When I think of him I remember that slight, boyish figure ghosting past defenders as if nailed to the floor, going one on one with the keeper. I used to love that moment. There was never a doubt he would score. One on one and you could bet the house on George scoring. A shimmy, a flick and there he was wheeling away, hand raised in triumph. When I look through the list remember those moments of joy football has given me, and, for all my misgivings, will continue to provide. Realising I have seen all these great players in action is a definition of a very lucky man.

Michael Parkinson.

MICHAEL PARKINSON

Michael Parkinson has donated the fee for this introduction to the Professional Footballers' Association Benevolent Fund.

The original Footballer of the Year trophy, made of bronze and presented to Stanley Matthews in 1948.

The making of the Footballer of the Year

The decision to form a Football Writers' Association was made on board a boat on 22 September, 1947 by a group of journalists returning from an international match in Brussels where they had reported on England's 5-2 beating of Belgium. Stanley Matthews had laid on all five goals for Tommy Lawton (two), Stan Mortensen (two) and Tom Finney. It was a good time to be an English football writer.

Charles Buchan, the old footballing master of Sunderland, Arsenal and England, was one of the founder members in those days preceding jet-set travel around the world who took advantage of a leisurely trip home to set up the Association.

It was writer-publisher Buchan, whose Football Monthly was must reading in the post-war years, who some two and a half months later proposed that the Association should elect an annual Footballer of the Year.

The original minute book records that Buchan suggested an award 'to the professional player who by precept and example is considered by a ballot of members to be the footballer of the year'. It was agreed to award a statuette to be kept by the winner, and the Footballer of the Year was born.

Note the word 'the' in the original minute. Over the past 50 years this has become the most prestigious individual award in soccer.

Others have followed suit with similar awards. But this is *the* Footballer of the Year. A main attraction is that the FWA has always concentrated on the one award and the roll of honour contains some of the great names of the game.

The entrance fee and annual subscription for the original members was five guineas from November, 1947 to May 1948, with a subsequent annual subscription of two guineas. Election to the Association was at the discretion of the committee.

There were 42 members when Stanley Matthews, now of course Sir Stanley, was voted the first Footballer of the Year. Today there are 350, paying £20 a year for full membership and £10 for associate membership embracing radio and television journalists.

Estimates for the first trophy were £45 for silver or £20 for bronze. It was a bronze award that Matthews collected, with Blackpool and England team-mate Stan Mortensen the runner-up and Frank Swift, the Manchester City goalkeeper, in third place.

The venue for the first dinner was the Hungaria Restaurant in London; members had considered using the restaurant at Waterloo Station.

Today the Footballer of the Year dinner, held two days before the FA Cup final, is one of the major events of the soccer social calendar.

For more than 20 years the Cafe Royal, with its plush chandeliered surroundings, was the venue, but so great was the demand that a switch was made to the Royal Lancaster Hotel where 700 sell-out attendances are the norm.

The original members set down that not more than six leading personalities be invited to the dinner. Today a top table of 30-plus are invited and, if there is a good response from former Footballers of the Year to the annual invitation, there is a double-tiered top table.

Writing this book is something of a labour of love for me. I became secretary of the FWA in the late 1960s and have had the enjoyable task since, twice as chairman and today as an Honorary Life Member and national committee man, of notifying each winner of his award before it is announced.

There have been six double winners. The late

Charles Buchan, who masterminded the idea of the Footballer of the Year award, leads out Arsenal in 1927.

50TH FOOTBALLER OF THE YEAR AWARD

50TH FOOTBALLER

Masters past and present line up during the 50th anniversary celebrations of the Footballer of the Year award. Back row, from left, Pat Jennings, Bill Slater, Steve Nicol, Ian Callaghan, Frank McLintock, Tony Book, Emlyn Hughes, Frans Thijssen and Clive Allen. Front row, from left, Dave Mackay, Sir Bobby Charlton, Sir Stanley Matthews (the first recipient), Gianfranco Zola, Gary Lineker and Bobby Collins.

Danny Blanchflower, Sir Stanley Matthews, Tom Finney, Kenny Dalglish, John Barnes and Gary Lineker. There was one historic tie when Dave Mackay and Tony Book each collected an award.

The votes arrived in sealed envelopes at my London home. Voting ended with the arrival of the first post one morning and I took the sealed envelopes to the offices of the national newspaper, where the current chairman worked, for an official count. It finished all-square and we notified the two players and their managers of the result before making the announcement.

When I arrived home later in the day I discovered two votes, both for the same person, that had arrived second post – just missing the agreed deadline. This story has never been told before, and the identity of the player who would have won if the votes had been delivered on time will stay with me.

Only twice has the winner not been present to collect his trophy. Danny Blanchflower was abroad the first time, playing for London in Barcelona in the old Fairs Cup, and he sent a tape eloquently expressing his apologies and grateful acceptance.

On the other occasion I was in the Mayor's Parlour at the town hall in Hendon at lunchtime on the day of the dinner when I received a message saying that Terry McDermott was unable to attend and that he was asking a team-mate to collect the trophy for him.

Hours of fruitless phoning failed to locate McDermott. I asked Trevor Brooking, runner-up to McDermott, to accept the trophy on his behalf but he was not attending the dinner due to a prior engagement. An hour before the dinner Bob Paisley, then the Liverpool manager, agreed to accept the award on behalf of his missing player.

Bert Trautmann became the first player born

overseas to win the trophy. In subsequent years it has gone to Frans Thijssen (Holland), Jurgen Klinsmann (Germany), Eric Cantona (France) and Gianfranco Zola (Italy).

With hindsight you can say there are great players who never won the award. Denis Law, Jimmy Greaves and Peter Shilton are just three who spring immediately to mind.

When I vote I look at the list of previous winners and try to envisage if this year's choice will sit comfortably alongside the likes of great players such as Matthews, Finney, Blanchflower, Moore, Bobby Charlton and co. in ten years time.

One fact is indisputable. The 42 members who took part in the first vote in favour of Matthews certainly got it right. Fifty years on he is still revered and going strong.

So is the Footballer of the Year award.

DENNIS SIGNY

1940s

Football was said to be losing its head when Tommy Lawton became the first £20,000 player in 1947 following his move from Chelsea to Notts County.

Crowd of memories

A footballer from the 1990s arriving in the 1940s would think he had landed on another planet. Everything about the game was different. For a start, the most a player could earn for his talent – whether he was Stanley Matthews or Joe Bloggs – was £10 a week in the season and £7 a week in the summer close season. This had risen to a heady £12 and £10 by the end of the decade.

The wages were ridiculously low, while the attendances were remarkably high. Tired, Victorian-built grounds heaved with record crowds in the immediate post-war years as football cashed in on its biggest boom. The minimum price to stand on the jammed terraces was 1s 6d (7.5p), and you could sit in the stand for half a crown (12.5p). Programmes cost 2d (less than 1p), and there was talk of the game going off its head when Tommy Lawton became the first £20,000 footballer in 1947.

Team formations were the traditional 2-3-5 line-ups, with two full-backs, two wing-halves flanking a 'stopper' centre-half and five forwards. Wingers dribbled and dazzled down the touchlines, with muscular centre-forwards making their presence felt in the middle and two inside forwards providing the goal-making passes.

All wore baggy shorts and heavy ankle-high boots that needed to be sturdy to hoof the laced, leather ball and to withstand the tackles from behind that were not only extremely dangerous but also quite legal.

This was the Age of Austerity, with football as one of the few escapes from a grey world of ration books, and with prosperity only a distant promise. Television was just a metropolitan toy for the rich, and the new Labour Government under Clement Attlee was building the Welfare State against a background of a flourishing blackmarket and high unemployment.

It was football that helped put a smile on the faces of a population weary from war and want. When Dynamo Moscow became the first Russian side to visit England in 1945 a crowd of 85,000 was shoe-horned into Stamford Bridge, with hundreds spilling on to the pitch and taking bird's eye views from the top of the stand. A record 83,260 crammed into Maine Road to see Manchester United play Arsenal in a First Division match on 17 January 1948 (Old Trafford was closed because of bomb damage).

Down in the Third Division South a crowd of 51,621 gathered to watch Cardiff play Bristol City on 7 April 1947. An astonishing 1,269,934 spectators watched the 44-match League programme in a single day on 27 December 1949. The aggregate for the previous season was a record 41,271,414, more than double the average seasonal figure in the 1990s.

The names of the prominent players of that era echo like a roll-call of footballing gods: Stanley Matthews, Tom Finney, Tommy Lawton, Raich Carter, Len Shackleton, Wilf Mannion, Nat Lofthouse, Stan Mortensen, Jackie Milburn, Frank Swift, Billy Wright and Alf Ramsey, along with Scots like Billy Liddell and Billy Steel, Welsh masters such as Ron Burgess and Trevor Ford, and Irish stars Peter Doherty and Johnny Carey.

It was the period in which English football was respected and admired around the world. We were known as the Old Masters. England had not yet entered a World Cup tournament and there was a long, proud unbeaten home record still to protect.

On the domestic scene, Liverpool won the first post-war League championship in 1946-7. Arsenal, captained by the bow-legged, big-hearted Joe

Supporters pack into Stamford Bridge, where an 85,000 crowd was shoe-horned to watch Dynamo Moscow during their visit in 1945 which was part of a bid to put a smile back on the faces of post-war Britain.

Mercer, won it in 1947-8, and in the last two years of the decade, during which the Footballer of the Year Award was launched, Portsmouth won back-to-back championships. With the final shots of the war only recently fired, Pompey were able to attract top players from among the servicemen at the ship-jammed Royal Navy base.

The FA Cup, the only other major competition in these pre-European football days, was captured in 1946 by a Derby County team rich with the individual skills of Raich Carter and Peter Doherty. They beat Charlton Athletic 4-1 after extra time at the end of a competition that was decided on a home-and-away, two-leg basis. Charlton were back the following year, this time beating Burnley 1-0 thanks to a rasping goal from the right boot of the usually left-footed Chris Duffy. Astonishingly, the match ball burst during both these Wembley finals. Not a lot of people know that.

The first of Matt Busby's exceptional Manchester United teams purred to the FA Cup in 1948, beating Blackpool 4-2 in a classic final after trailing at half-time during which Busby issued the priceless instruction: 'Just keep playing football.'

Those were the days, my friends. Yes, those were the days.**–Norman Giller**

Who won what

1945-6
FA Cup final: Derby County 4, Charlton 1 (aet)

1946-7
First Division: Liverpool
Second Division: Manchester City
Third Division (South): Cardiff City
Third Division (North): Doncaster Rovers
FA Cup final: Charlton Athletic 1, Burnley 0
First Division marksman: Derek Westcott (Wolverhampton Wanders), 37 goals
Scottish champions: Rangers
Scottish Cup final: Aberdeen 2, Hibernian 1

1947-8
First Division: Arsenal
Second Division: Birmingham City

Third Division (South): QPR
Third Division (North): Lincoln City
FA Cup final: Man United 4, Blackpool 2
First Division marksman: Ronnie Rooke (Arsenal) 33
Footballer of the Year: Stanley Matthews (Blackpool)
Scottish champions: Hibernian
Scottish Cup final: Rangers 1, Morton 0
(after a 1-1 draw)

1948-9
First Division: Portsmouth
Second Division: Fulham
Third Division (South): Swansea
Third Division (North): Hull City
FA Cup final: Wolves 3, Leicester City 1
First Division marksman: Willie Moir (Bolton), 25
Footballer of the Year: Johnny Carey (Man United)
Scottish champions: Rangers
Scottish Cup final: Rangers 4, Clyde 1

Top ten transfers

PLAYER	FROM	TO	DATE	FEE
Eddie Quigley	Sheffield Wednesday	Preston North End	Dec. 1949	£26,500
Johnny Morris	Manchester United	Derby County	Mar. 1949	£25,000
Bobby Langton	Preston North End	Bolton Wanderers	Nov. 1949	£22,250
Alf Ramsey	Southampton	Tottenham Hotspur	May 1949	£21,000
Len Shackleton	Newcastle United	Sunderland	Feb. 1948	£20,050
Tommy Lawton	Chelsea	Notts County	Nov. 1947	£20,000
Eddie Kilshaw	Bury Town	Sheffield Wednesday	Dec. 1948	£20,000
Bobby Brennan	Luton Town	Birmingham City	July 1949	£20,000
Don Revie	Leicester City	Hull City	Nov. 1949	£20,000
George Lowrie	Coventry City	Newcastle United	Mar. 1948	£18,000

Stanley Matthews

Born: Hanley, Stoke-on-Trent, 1 February 1915. The son of Jack Matthews, a professional featherweight boxer known as The Fighting Barber of Hanley.

Honours: Twice Footballer of the Year, in 1948 and 1963. Twice won Second Division honours with Stoke, in 1933 and 30 years later in 1963. In between he played for Blackpool for 14 years from 1947.

While with the seaside club he appeared in three FA Cup finals (1948, 1951, 1953), but was on the winning side only in 1953 when his stunning performance led to the match being known as the Matthews Final. He won 54 international caps, making his debut in 1934 at the age of 19 and playing his last game for England in 1957 at the age of 41. He also played in 29 unofficial wartime and Victory internationals.

He was the first footballer to be awarded the CBE (1957) and the first to be knighted (1965), and the first European Footballer of the Year (1956).

The Wizard of Dribble made his League debut for Stoke City at the age of 17, and he had passed his 50th birthday when he played his last League game in 1965.

Following his retirement he served as general manager of Port Vale for three years and later coached in Malta and South Africa.

His son, also named Stanley Matthews, played Davis Cup tennis for Britain.

The Wizard of Dribble won his second Footballer of the Year award in 1963 after returning to Stoke following 14 years at Blackpool.

Matthews made his England debut as a 19-year-old in 1934, and went on to win 54 caps – his last in 1957 at the age of 41.

This was my year

Winning the Footballer of the Year award for the second time at the age of 48 was a big moment for me, but could not match my first win in 1948. The original bronze trophy has pride of place in my den at home. To be the first winner was marvellous and still to be around and invited to the 1997 dinner as guest of honour to mark the 50th anniversary underlines what I mean about the significance of that award to me.

I can remember being in Troon on a Friday night before a Scotland-England game when I was told that the Football Writers' Association had elected me the first winner. The award was made at the Hungaria Restaurant in London on the eve of my playing for Blackpool in the FA Cup final against Manchester United.

There were about 100 people there and I can remember Ivan Sharpe, a leading soccer writer of the day, welcoming me.

My good friend Stan Mortensen, who played alongside me at Wembley next day, was runner-up. That Blackpool side had a very good season in the old First Division, but the nearest the club came to winning the championship was in 1955-6 when they finished runners-up. I guess it was getting to Wembley that helped me get the votes in 1948, although I was an England regular. The 1948 final was a classic in which we went 2-1 up against United, who pulled back to win 4-2.

At 46 I returned home to Stoke, where I still live and go to games. Two years later in 1963, playing alongside the likes of Dennis Viollet and Jackie Mudie, we won the Second Division championship and I won my second award.

Today, at the age of 82, I am still involved in the game as President of Stoke City, and when I look back over my career, those two Footballer of the Year awards mean so much to me. They represent what I achieved over a long period, and I am very, very proud of them.

My Dream Team

PAT JENNINGS

GEORGE HARDWICK   **EDDIE HAPGOOD**

DANNY BLANCHFLOWER   **JOHN CHARLES**   **BOBBY MOORE**

GEORGE BEST   **WILF MANNION**   **TOMMY LAWTON**   **JIMMY GREAVES**   **TOM FINNEY**

WHAT THE PLAYERS SAY...

There will never be another like him. He had incredible ball control, and could send an entire defence the wrong way with a shimmy, a sudden surge and clever dribbling. His centres laid on hundreds of goals.   **– TOM FINNEY**

The Wizard of Dribble was the perfect nickname for Stanley. That's just what he was – a wizard who bamboozled defences with his ball control. He could turn any full-back inside out.   **– NAT LOFTHOUSE**

Sir Stanley transcended football. He was the most famous sportsman of his generation, and his name was known right around the world. He truly is a legend in his own lifetime. I had the privilege of playing alongside him in his farewell match, and even at 50 he could dance rings around opponents.

– JIMMY GREAVES

The years in football have flown away and trying to pick a Dream Team has been a near impossible task. In days gone by there were so many more personalities in the game, so many legends. I have had to insist on a full set of substitutes to salvage my conscience when I think of some of those I played with who have not made it to the team or even the squad.

Pat Jennings is, without doubt, my first choice goalkeeper, even though that means making Gordon Banks my alternative. Jennings was the first 'keeper, to me, who really controlled his entire area.

George Hardwick, the immaculate Middlesbrough player who captained England just after the war, gets my vote at right-back even though he won only 13 caps – all as captain, incidentally. Eddie Hapgood, who won 30 caps, was a class left-back in an outstanding Arsenal team.

Bobby Moore gets in on merit, but Neil Franklin, one of England's all-time great centre-halves, can only get on the bench. My skipper is John Charles, the Gentle Giant and an outstanding centre-half or centre-forward.

George Best and Tom Finney would play wide in my team – but even Tom, who is rated one of England's best ever, only gets the vote when I have thought long and hard about 'Boy' Bastin, the legendary Cliff who played for Arsenal and still holds their goal-scoring record to this day even though he played on the wing. Bastin scored 150 League goals for Arsenal and, though statisticians say Ian Wright will replace him in the record books, they are talking about goals in all competitions.

There have been great inside forwards over the years and I edge Wilf Mannion over Raich Carter for my team, which leaves Peter Doherty without a place and he was some player. And what about wee Alex James, another from that era of Arsenal dominance of our game, and Bobby Charlton? There would be more skill on my bench than in most teams of the last decade. Two modern players would sit comfortably alongside them, though: Paul Gascoigne and Alan Shearer.

I go with the powerhouse Tommy Lawton as my centre-forward, with Jimmy Greaves alongside him. The way the game is played today, little Jim would probably earn his team as many penalties as goals.

Having opted for Lawton, I sadly have to put Nat Lofthouse on the bench alongside my old pal Stan Mortensen.

I've seen a few legends in the last 50 years, and I could have selected half a dozen teams that would make your mouth water.

Stanley Matthews, the hero of the hour, lifts the FA Cup with his Blackpool skipper Harry Johnston after the 1953 final that has gone down in history as the 'Matthews Final'.

Johnny Carey

Born: Dublin, 23 January 1919.

Died: 23 August 1995.

Honours: Gentleman John, as he was known throughout football, was one of the most versatile players ever to pull on a pair of football boots.

He joined Manchester United from Irish club St James Gate in 1936 for £200 as an inside forward, and played in virtually every position during his 17 years at Old Trafford. He would have doubled his 304 League appearances but for the outbreak of war.

Johnny, who was most comfortable at right-back, captained United's 1948 FA Cup-winning team against Blackpool, and collected a League championship medal in his last season in 1952.

In 1947 he had the distinction of skippering the Rest of Europe against England, and in 1949 was a key man in the Ireland team that inflicted England's first ever home defeat by a non-British country when Ireland won 2-0 at Goodison Park. In all he won 29 caps for the Republic of Ireland and seven for Northern Ireland. He was voted Sportsman of the Year for 1950.

Carey had a distinguished managerial career, guiding both Blackburn Rovers and Leyton Orient to promotion to the First Division and a three-year spell in charge at Everton. He had a five-year association with Nottingham Forest before returning to Blackburn in 1968-9 for a period in the general manager's chair at Ewood Park.

This was my year

In that season when I was elected Footballer of the Year, United finished runners-up to Portsmouth and we were beaten by Wolves in an FA Cup semi-final replay. We had won the Cup the previous season with a 4-2 victory over Blackpool after we had trailed 2-1 at half-time.

The personal high spot for me was skippering the Irish team that beat England 2-0 at Goodison Park. England included great players such as Tom Finney, Wilf Mannion, Billy Wright and Neil Franklin, and they were stunned by our display. They could not believe it back home in Dublin, and most people thought the announcer had made a mistake when the result was given on the wireless.

I would not have changed a second of my career at Old Trafford. They were the best years of my life. I had some success as a manager, but there is nothing to touch playing the game. My biggest break was having Matt Busby as manager. He preached a policy of always playing football, and that was my philosophy too. I had no time for kick and rush. For me, the game was as much about brain as brawn.

I was happy to play for United in whatever position suited the needs of the team. I wore every shirt except the No. 11, and I recall even playing in goal once against Chelsea after our goalkeeper Jack Crompton had been injured. There was not a lot of money to be earned in my day. In fact the most I picked up as a player was £14 a week plus £2 win bonuses. But people were not motivated by profit. The thrill and satisfaction was in playing the game.

My selection as Footballer of the Year filled me with pride. Just think of the players who were around in the First Division then – Matthews, Finney, Lawton, Lofthouse, Mortensen, Wright, Swift, Ramsey, Carter ... they roll off the tongue like Gods of the game. I was honoured to be mentioned in the same breath as them.

The versatile Irishman Carey played in virtually every position during his successful 17-year career with Manchester United.

My Dream Team

PAT JENNINGS

ALF RAMSEY   ROGER BYRNE

DANNY BLANCHFLOWER   JOHN CHARLES   DUNCAN EDWARDS

PETER DOHERTY   GEORGE BEST

STANLEY MATTHEWS   BOBBY CHARLTON   TOM FINNEY

WHAT THE PLAYERS SAY...

John was a gifted player who could fit into any role. He played in an era when there was a lot of physical contact, yet never ever resorted to rough play. He was a true gentleman and sportsman.

– SIR STANLEY MATTHEWS

I recall his performance for Ireland when they shocked England to defeat at Goodison Park in 1949. He was a magnificent captain, inspiring his team by example. Believe me, he deserved to be on the winning side that day. **– TOM FINNEY**

There have been few players to match Johnny Carey for all-round ability. He was always comfortable on the ball, and got his work done without fuss or frills. There is no doubt that he was a key man in Matt Busby's first excellent Manchester United team.

– SIR ALF RAMSEY

I know I will be accused of bias, but I have both a strong Irish influence and the cream of Manchester United players in my team. For a start, there have been few better goalkeepers in history than Pat Jennings. He has to be exceptional for me to place him ahead of outstanding players of my era such as Frank Swift, Bert Trautmann and Bert Williams.

My full-back pairing has the solidness and reliability of Alf Ramsey at right-back, and the flair and strength of Roger Byrne at left-back. Alf would be my captain. He was known as the General and was a born tactician.

John Charles, the magnificent all-rounder, would hold the centre of the defence together. Big John, a Welsh mountain of a man, has never really been given the recognition he deserves in Britain because his peak years were spent in Italy with Juventus, where he was idolised. Yet despite his size he had the grace of a ballet dancer, and his aerial power was used to his team's advantage in both penalty areas.

The Gentle Giant would be flanked by the cultured Danny Blanchflower and the awesomely powerful Duncan Edwards, who – along with Roger Byrne – died at Munich in that terrible disaster that ripped the heart out of the Busby Babes. We never saw Duncan even approach his peak, yet he had already provided enough evidence for everybody in the game to know that he was a

legend in the making. I was always a believer in having wingers giving width to an attack, and they have never come better than Stanley Matthews and Tom Finney. Matthews with his dribbling skill and Finney with his more direct approach would give defenders nightmares.

Bobby Charlton leads my attack, and it would be left to him whether he wanted to play an orthodox role or drop back into a deep-lying position, in which he was so successful for England's 1966 World Cup-winning team. I would encourage Bobby to let fly with his bombshell long-range shots, and he and Tom Finney would look to swap roles whenever it suited them. People forget that Finney was equally effective coming through the middle as a traditional centre-forward as he was on either wing.

My two inside forwards are arguably the greatest players ever to come out of Ireland. George Best would have a free role at inside right, while Peter Doherty would set up the goal chances with his inch-perfect passes.

Although I would love to manage this team, I will in fact stand down and allow Matt Busby that honour. He would simply tell them: 'Just go out and play football.'

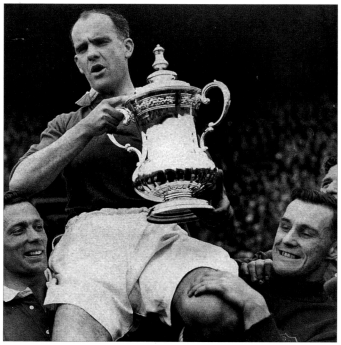

Gentleman Johnny Carey, who always preached a gospel of pure footballing tactics, is carried from the field after leading Manchester United to FA Cup glory in 1948.

Moment of truth

The 1950s started badly for England's footballers . . . and got worse. First there came a devastating kick to English pride on a far-off playing field in Brazil, and then an even more shattering blow to their dignity on their own hallowed turf at Wembley.

Long-held claims that England were the masters of football deflated like a punctured balloon when a team of part-timers and immigrants representing the United States shocked England to a 1-0 defeat in the 1950 World Cup finals in Belo Horizonte, Brazil. England were left horizontal in Horizonte. Unkind jokes linked the defeat with that of British horizontal heavyweights.

It was dismissed as a freak result, and English football went blindly on its way playing stereotyped, blinkered tactics that were shown up as being light years out of date at Wembley in 1953.

A Hungarian team orchestrated by Ferenc Puskas played England off the park on the way to a 6-3 victory, the first ever by a foreign team on English soil apart from a solitary defeat by the Republic of Ireland at Goodison Park in 1949.

This was the moment of truth. England team manager Walter Winterbottom, his hands tied by a committee of interfering amateur selectors, led the inquests into the defeats, and it was accepted that England had fallen behind the times with their tactics and technique.

English teams at club and country level were still playing the old-fashioned 'WM' formation with two wide full-backs, a 'stopper' centre-half in the middle and two defensive wing half-backs feeding the ball to two ball-playing inside forwards. Two wingers patrolled the touchlines and a battering-ram centre-forward led the line down the middle.

The Hungarians played their No 9 Hidegkuti as a deep-lying centre-forward and Blackpool centre-half Harry Johnston had no idea how to mark him. Hidegkuti played hide-and-seek, and nipped in unseen for a hat-trick.

Even the old men who ran our football were forced to pull their heads out of the sand, and leading club managers were called together for their opinions. Winterbottom took careful note of their views, and it all led to a gradual change in training methods, playing tactics and kit.

Out went the heavy boots, bulky shin pads, baggy shorts and shirts, and the thick socks. Appearance money for international players was increased from £30 to £50 (the equivalent of more than two weeks' wages), and the FA selectors at last accepted that they had to start listening to professional opinion.

The English game began to restore its pride, led by the outstanding club sides at Manchester United and Wolves. But everything was torpedoed by the blackest moment of the 1950s – the horrific Manchester United disaster at Munich on February 6, 1958: a date burned into the hearts and minds of anybody involved in football.

Of the eight United players tragically killed in the air crash on the way back from a European Cup victory in Belgrade, three (Roger Byrne, Duncan Edwards and Tommy Taylor) were key men in the England team aiming for the 1958 World Cup finals. To lose three players of their calibre would have knocked any team sideways. England lost all their impetus going into the World Cup finals that were won in startling style by a Brazilian team parading a precocious 17-year-old called Pele.

The decade finished with the smell of mutiny in the air. England's footballers were fed up with being treated like slaves, and going into the 1960s a campaign had started to kick out the maximum £20-a-week wage. This was the era when Prime Minister Harold Macmillan was telling the country, 'You've never had it so good.'

England's footballers wanted it a lot better.

–Norman Giller

Hidegkuti rounds off Hungary's historic 6-3 hiding of Walter Winterbottom's England by firing home the sixth goal.

Alf Ramsey watches as Gaetjens' shot beats England goalkeeper Bert Williams to give the USA a 1-0 win during the 1950 World Cup.

Who won what

1949-50

League champions: Portsmouth
FA Cup final: Arsenal 2, Liverpool 0
First Division marksman: Dick Davis (Sunderland), 25
Footballer of the Year: Joe Mercer (Arsenal)
Scottish champions: Rangers
Scottish Cup final: Rangers 3, East Fife 0
World Cup deciding match: Uruguay 2, Brazil 1

1950-1

League champions: Tottenham Hotspur
FA Cup final: Newcastle United 2 Blackpool 0
First Division marksman: Stan Mortensen (Blackpool) 30
Footballer of the Year: Harry Johnston (Blackpool)
Scottish champions: Hibernian
Scottish Cup final: Celtic 1 Motherwell 0

1951-2

League champions: Manchester United
FA Cup final: Newcastle United 1 Arsenal 0
First Division marksman: George Robledo (Newcastle) 33
Footballer of the Year: Billy Wright (Wolves)
Scottish champions: Hibernian
Scottish Cup final: Motherwell 4 Dundee 0

1952-3

League champions: Arsenal
FA Cup final: Blackpool 4 Bolton Wanderers 3
First Division marksman: Charlie Wayman (Preston) 24
Footballer of the Year: Nat Lofthouse (Bolton Wanderers)
Scottish champions: Rangers
Scottish Cup final: Rangers 1 Aberdeen 0 (after a 1-1 draw)

1953-4

League champions: Wolverhampton Wanderers
FA Cup final: West Bromwich Albion 3 Preston North End 2
First Division marksman: Jimmy Glazzard (Huddersfield) and Johnny Nicholls (WBA) 29
Footballer of the Year: Tom Finney (Preston North End)
Scottish champions: Aberdeen
Scottish Cup final: Celtic 2 Aberdeen 1
World Cup final: West Germany 3 Hungary 2

1954-5

League champions: Chelsea
FA Cup final: Newcastle United 3 Manchester City 1

First Division marksman: Ronnie Allen (WBA) 27
Footballer of the Year: Don Revie (Manchester City)
Scottish champions: Aberdeen
Scottish Cup final: Clyde 1 Celtic 0 (after a 1-1 draw)

1955-6

League champions: Manchester United
FA Cup final: Manchester City 3 Birmingham City 1
First Division marksman: Nat Lofthouse (Bolton) 33
Footballer of the Year: Bert Trautmann (Manchester City)
Scottish champions: Rangers
Scottish Cup final: Heart of Midlothian 3 Celtic 1
European Cup final: Real Madrid 4 Stade de Reims 3
European Footballer of the Year: Stanley Matthews (Blackpool)

1956-7

League champions: Manchester United
FA Cup final: Aston Villa 2 Manchester United 1
First Division marksman: John Charles (Leeds United) 38
Footballer of the Year: Tom Finney (Preston North End)
Scottish champions: Rangers
Scottish Cup final: Falkirk 2 Kilmarnock 1 (after a 1-1 draw)
European Cup final: Real Madrid 2 Fiorentina 0
European Footballer of the Year: Alfredo di Stefano (Real Madrid)

1957-8

League champions: Wolverhampton Wanderers
FA Cup final: Bolton Wanderers 2 Manchester United 0
First Division marksman: Bobby Smith (Tottenham) 36
Footballer of the Year: Danny Blanchflower (Tottenham)
Scottish champions: Heart of Midlothian
Scottish Cup final: Clyde 1 Hibernian 0
European Cup final: Real Madrid 3 AC Milan 2 (after extra time)
European Footballer of the Year: Raymond Kopa (Real Madrid)
World Cup final: Sweden 2 Brazil 5

1958-9

League champions: Wolves
FA Cup final: Nottingham Forest 2 Luton Town 1
First Division marksman: Jimmy Greaves (Chelsea) and Bobby Smith (Tottenham) 32
Footballer of the Year: Syd Owen (Luton Town)
Scottish champions: Rangers
Scottish Cup final: St Mirren 3 Aberdeen 1
European Cup final: Real Madrid 2 Stade de Reims 0
European Footballer of the Year: Alfredo di Stefano (Real Madrid)

Ferenc Puskas, No. 10, scores the fourth of Hungary's six goals against England in 1953 that brought a tactical revolution to English football.

1950

Joe Mercer

Born: Ellesmere Port, Cheshire, 9 August 1914.
Died: 9 August 1990.
Honours: Joe followed his father and grandfather into professional football when he signed for Everton in 1931. Goodison idol Dixie Dean took one look at Mercer's spindly, bandy legs and joked, 'Those legs wouldn't last a postman one morning. You could drive a bus through them.' But the legs and the heart were strong enough to carry Joe through an outstanding 23-year career.

By the outbreak of war in 1939, he had won a League championship medal with Everton and he collected five successive England caps. He played 22 unofficial wartime internationals when he completed an illustrious half-back line with Cliff Britton and Stan Cullis.

Following his demob from the army in 1945 he was handicapped by a recurring knee injury. Arsenal gambled on his fitness, paying £6,000 for his transfer. He became a hero at Highbury, leading them to the League championship in 1947-8 and again in 1952-3, and to two FA Cup finals at Wembley.

His playing career was ended by a broken leg during a First Division match against Liverpool at Highbury in 1954. He then had a distinguished managerial career with Sheffield United, Aston Villa, Manchester City and as general manager of Coventry City.

He also had a successful spell as England caretaker manager, and became football's favourite 'uncle' figure.

Mercer spent the first part of his 23-year playing career as a half-back with Everton, where he won a League championship medal.

Mercer won two League titles and played in two FA Cup finals with Arsenal after his demob in 1945, despite a recurring knee injury.

This was my year

I collected my Footballer of the Year award on the eve of the FA Cup final at the London Press Club. We were playing Liverpool the next day and an Anfield director at the Football Writers' Dinner said: 'All our players are tucked up in bed.'

'Maybe they are,' I said, 'but are they sleeping?'

I left the dinner at nine-thirty and went to the Great Northern Hotel where I was rooming with Arsenal goalkeeper George Swindin. I was on great terms with the Liverpool players because I trained with them for most of the season while joining Arsenal on match days. But I was determined to spoil their party at Wembley, because an FA Cup winner's medal meant so much to me.

An odd thing happened when I met Liverpool skipper Phil Taylor in the middle for the toss-up. I spun the coin and it landed on the soaking wet surface and sat upright, with the edge of the coin stuck in the Wembley turf. It was the only time I ever saw it happen. I had to toss again, and got laughs with the story for years afterwards when I would say that I did it deliberately to put Liverpool in a spin!

We won 2-0 thanks to two goals by Reg Lewis, and I recall that there were tears in my eyes when I went up to collect the FA Cup from Her Majesty the Queen, now the Queen Mother. You have to remember that the FA Cup meant so much more then because it was the only trophy to aim for apart from the League championship.

As I turned away with the Cup, I was summoned back to the Queen. She had given me a runners-up medal by mistake!

Another thing that stands out in my memory is that a bunch of Arsenal supporters pounced on me as I left the after-match banquet at the Café Royal, and they carried me like a trophy all the way back to our hotel at Charing Cross.

Happy days!

My Dream Team

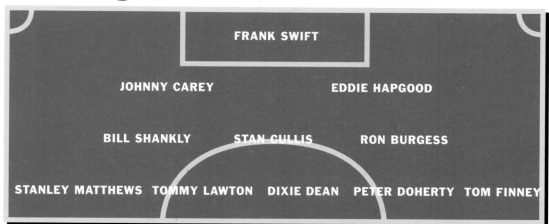

FRANK SWIFT

JOHNNY CAREY   EDDIE HAPGOOD

BILL SHANKLY   STAN CULLIS   RON BURGESS

STANLEY MATTHEWS TOMMY LAWTON DIXIE DEAN PETER DOHERTY TOM FINNEY

WHAT THE PLAYERS SAY...

The England wartime half-back line of Britton, Cullis and Mercer was a magnificent combination. I played against Joe late in his career, and I was in awe of him. Yet never once did I know him to show a shred of arrogance. **– JIMMY HILL**

It is one of my most cherished memories that I played against Joe during the war when he was guesting for Aldershot and I was with Chelsea. He was a fine player but, more important, a wonderful human being. **– RON GREENWOOD**

Joe was an outstanding captain at Arsenal, who really motivated us and inspired by example. I had a marvellous time playing with him, and it was rewarding to see him go on to such great success as a manager. **– DENIS COMPTON**

To make my life easier, I have restricted my selection to footballers I played with or against, otherwise I would have lost sleep trying to get in such modern masters as George Best, Bobby Charlton and Bobby Moore.

My goalkeeper is big Frank Swift, who guarded the Manchester City and England goals like a one-man wall. He had a heart as big as his head, and was unbelievably brave in an era when goalkeepers were the target for battering-ram centre-forwards.

Johnny Carey and Eddie Hapgood are as formidable a pair of full-back partners as you can find. Gentleman Johnny was comfortable in any position for Manchester United and Ireland, but was at his most effective as a thinking right-back. I considered Alf Ramsey for the No. 2 shirt, but Johnny got my vote because he had such polished all-round ability. Eddie Hapgood was a strong and skilful left-back for Arsenal, and helped make me feel at home when I made my debut for England in 1937.

Stan Cullis, with whom I grew up in Ellesmere Port, will be the captain at centre-half where he was a tiger for Wolves and England. He was an extremely effective 'stopper' centre-half, and could hold his own in the air and on the ground. Billy Wright learned a lot from him, but was not as commanding as Stan in the air.

Flanking Stan at wing-half I have Scottish dynamo Bill Shankly and Welsh master Ron Burgess. Shanks used to play for Preston and Scotland with the same passion and commitment that he later brought into management, and Burgess was a colossus in the push-and-run Spurs team that won the League championship in 1950-1.

Scotland's Billy Liddell loomed large in my thoughts, but if you are going to have wingers I don't think you can possibly look past Stanley Matthews and Tom Finney. Matthews was the greatest dribbler who ever breathed, and Finney was a dangerman whether coming down the wing or cutting inside.

Providing the passes I have the old Irish maestro Peter Doherty, who had beautiful ball control and could penetrate the tightest defence with his precise passes.

I could not bring myself to leave out either of my old Everton buddies Dixie Dean and Tommy Lawton, so I have selected them both. They will be unstoppable in the air and their shooting will give goalkeepers nightmares. Dixie's 60 First Division goals in a season will never be beaten, and Tommy's heading power was just unbelievable. Don't forget that he lost his best years to the war, otherwise he would have at least doubled his goals output.

What a fantastic team!

Joe Mercer, who became football's favourite uncle figure, had a successful career in football management, including a spell in charge of England.

Johnston returned to his Blackpool newsagents after seven years as Reading's manager following his retirement from playing in 1955.

Skipper Harry Johnston celebrates with trainer Johnny Lynas after leading Blackpool to victory in the 1953 'Matthews Final'.

Harry Johnston

Born: Manchester, 26 September 1919.

Died: 12 October 1973.

Honours: Henry (Harry) Johnston joined the Blackpool ground staff from Droylsden Athletic, Manchester, at 15 and served the seaside club for 17 years during which he played 386 League matches despite losing his best years to the war.

His was capped ten times by England over a six-year period from 1946, starting with an 8-2 victory over Holland and finishing with a 6-3 defeat in the historic match against Hungary at Wembley in 1953.

Harry started out as a driving wing-half and later switched to the middle of the defence, where he was easily distinguishable because of his thinning hair.

He was noted for his driving leadership, and three times led Blackpool to the FA Cup final at Wembley. In 1948 and 1951 he had to be content with collecting runner's-up medals. Then, in 1953, he led the Blackpool team up the Wembley steps at the end of the unforgettable 'Matthews Final'.

While at his peak, Harry started a business in Central Drive in Blackpool that had a newsagent's, hairdresser's and a general shop under its umbrella. He had seven years in charge at Reading following his retirement in 1955 and was briefly caretaker manager of his beloved Blackpool. His death at the age of 54 was mourned throughout the sport he had served with such distinction.

This was my year

Winning the Footballer of the Year trophy meant a great deal to me because I thought I had lost any chance of that sort of recognition to the war. Like so many in my generation, the war cut into my peak years. I was 20 when war was declared, and 26 before I started playing regular First Division football.

I won my first first cap at the age of 27, and I was 34 when I had the rather harrowing experience of playing against Hungary in my last international appearance in 1953.

I was astonished to be told that I had been voted Footballer of the Year. After all, this was the era of Stanley Matthews, Raich Carter, Stan Mortensen, Tommy Lawton, Jackie Milburn and Len Shackleton. I was still playing at right-half for Blackpool, and had made an England comeback, only to be on the losing side against Scotland after we lost Wilf Mannion with a fractured cheekbone.

In the League, Blackpool had finished third behind Arthur Rowe's superb push-and-run Spurs and Manchester United. It was in the FA Cup that Blackpool had shone, and I accepted my award the evening before the final against Newcastle on behalf of the team. I was so lucky to be playing in a side that had the magic of Stanley Matthews and the speed and power of Stan Mortensen.

There was disappointment next day at Wembley. Newcastle, who had been struggling in the League, played to the peak of their form while we could not get into our stride. We were beaten by two Jackie Milburn goals, and for the second time in three years went home with runners-up medals.

Two years later we were back at Wembley for the most memorable match in FA Cup history. I had now switched to centre-half. Matthews ran the Bolton defence dizzy, and Morty helped himself to the first hat-trick in an FA Cup final as we came from behind to win 4-3. It became known as the 'Matthews Final', but we called it 'Stanley's Final'.

My Dream Team

FRANK SWIFT

ROY GOODALL   ERNIE BLENKINSOP

ALEX JAMES   NEIL FRANKLIN   RONNIE BURGESS

STANLEY MATTHEWS   STAN MORTENSEN   TOMMY LAWTON   PETER DOHERTY   TOM FINNEY

WHAT THE PLAYERS SAY...

Harry was an excellent captain and an outstanding tactician who understood the finer points of the game. I had a lot to thank Harry for, because it was his accurate passes from right-half that made my life easier on the wing. **– SIR STANLEY MATTHEWS**

It was the play of the two Stanleys, Matthews and Mortensen, that took the eye with Blackpool, but Harry Johnston was every bit as important to the team. He was a great competitor, but always sporting.
– TOM FINNEY

I had some great duels with Harry, and admired his tenacity. He could be physical when it was necessary, but he preferred to play a constructive game and make use of the ball with a neatly placed pass rather than belting it out of defence.
– NAT LOFTHOUSE

I have only picked players from my era, which was the Golden Age for outstanding forwards. Just look at the names of some of the players I have left out: Raich Carter, Wilf Mannion, Ted Drake, Nat Lofthouse, Jimmy Hagan, Cliff Bastin, Billy Liddell and Len Shackleton. They would adorn any team.

There was little opposition to Frank Swift as my goalkeeper. He used to really dominate his goalmouth, and had an excellent pair of hands. Frank could more than hold his own in physical confrontations and was a master at positioning.

My full-backs are two pre-war players from Yorkshire – Roy Goodall from Huddersfield and Ernie Blenkinsop from Sheffield Wednesday. Both were poised and purposeful players, and totally reliable under pressure. Goodall captained England eleven times and Blenkinsop was skipper in four internationals. It is their leadership qualities that helps win them places in my team. They just got my vote ahead of Alf Ramsey and Sam Barkas.

I play Alex James in a midfield role as the conductor of the attack, with Neil Franklin and Ronnie Burgess side by side at the heart of the defence. James was a maestro for Arsenal and Scotland, while Franklin was a cultured centre-half who would fit in perfectly alongside the dynamic Burgess.

It goes without saying that I will have Stanley Matthews and Stan Mortensen in my team. They were magnificent partners for Blackpool and England, and I felt privileged to have them feeding on my passes.

Tommy Lawton will lead my attack because he was simply the best centre-forward I ever played against. He won the No. 9 shirt by a head from Manchester United's Tommy Taylor, Arsenal's Ted Drake and Bolton's Nat Lofthouse.

Tom Finney was an automatic choice for the left wing. It used to infuriate me to hear so many debates about whether the England selectors should choose Matthews or Finney, when the simply answer was to select Matthews *and* Finney. They went together like bacon and eggs.

Sharing the scheming duties with Alex James will be the Irish master Peter Doherty, whose body swerve, ball control and non-stop energy makes him a must for my team.

Peter just got into my side ahead of Raich Carter, who was an outstanding general but too much in the Alex James mould. They would have not made such a good balance as James and Doherty.

I also considered the Clown Prince, Len Shackleton, but he was so unpredictable that none of his team-mates would have known what he was going to try next. He was without doubt the greatest of all the entertainers.

What a team, and to manage it I would have the one and only Matt Busby.

Johnston, who won the last of his ten England caps in the 6-3 defeat against Hungary in 1953, is put through his paces by Blackpool's trainer Johnny Lynas.

Billy Wright

Born: Ironbridge, Shropshire, 6 February 1924.

Died: Barnet, Hertfordshire, 3 September 1994.

Honours: Billy started with Wolves as a groundstaff boy in 1938 after being sent home because he was considered too small to make the grade. He went on to play 491 League games for Wolves, first as an inside forward, then as a powerhouse half-back and, finally, as a rock-steady centre-half. His motivational leadership was a key factor in the 1950s when gold-shirted Wolves pioneered evening floodlit matches against European opposition. His England career stretched to 105 England caps (1946-1959), 90 as captain, and he skippered Wolves to three League championships in 1954, '58 and '59; also to the FA Cup in 1949.

Stan Cullis, England's pre-war centre-half and manager of Wolves, was a major influence on him and it was Billy who helped nurse along the Cullis Cubs.

He was England's first-choice half-back before switching to centre-half for his 60th cap following the defection of pay rebel Neil Franklin to Colombia, and played a record 70 successive internationals.

Billy was the first player to win a century of caps, and was awarded the CBE for his service to football. Later, he had a short spell as England Under-23 and Arsenal manager before becoming a TV sports executive in the Midlands. He was memorably married to Joy, of the singing Beverley Sisters.

This was my year

Funnily enough, I was voted Footballer of the Year in what was one of my less successful years. It was in the 1951-2 season when Matt Busby captured the first of his championships with Manchester United. Wolves finished down in 16th place and went out in the fourth round of the FA Cup, and so it came as a pleasant shock when I was told that I had been elected Footballer of the Year.

It was a tremendous privilege because the First Division was absolutely jam packed with wonderful players who I thought would have got the vote ahead of me. Shrewd judges realised that Wolves were laying the foundations for some great years ahead, and over the next eight or so seasons we rivalled and sometimes surpassed United as the best side in the country.

I saw my award as recognition of what was being achieved at Molineux, and it belonged as much to the team and manager Stan Cullis as to me. They were wonderful days for me at Wolves,

and throughout the 1950s we felt we were a match for anybody.

Stan Cullis put a great emphasis on fitness, and I doubt if there has been a team in history to match us for stamina and strength. We played a straightforward game in which the idea was to get the ball into the opposition penalty area as quickly and as often as possible. I admit it was not always pretty to the eye, but it was extremely effective and brought great success.

Just a couple of weeks after I had the honour of collecting the treasured Footballer of the Year trophy I skippered England against Austria in Vienna. That was the extraordinary match in which Nat Lofthouse had a storming game and was knocked out scoring our winning goal for a 3-2 victory. It earned him the nickname the Lion of Vienna, and if the match had been played a month earlier I know there would have been only one candidate for Footballer of the Year!

Billy Wright led out the England side in 90 of his 105 international appearances, a record he shares with the great Bobby Moore.

My Dream Team

GORDON BANKS

JIMMY ARMFIELD   ROGER BYRNE

DANNY BLANCHFLOWER   NEIL FRANKLIN   DUNCAN EDWARDS

STANLEY MATTHEWS WILF MANNION JOHN CHARLES BOBBY CHARLTON TOM FINNEY

WHAT THE PLAYERS SAY...

Billy was Mr Dependable. He was not a particularly big man, but when he pulled on the shirt of Wolves or England he seemed to visibly grow in size. He had the heart of a lion, and never knew when he was beaten. — **TOM FINNEY**

It was a tremendous boost to your confidence to look back down the pitch to see Billy rolling up his sleeves and brandishing a fist. He was a captain who led by marvellous example. — **SIR STANLEY MATTHEWS**

I started my international career under Billy's captaincy, and he went out of his way to make me feel part of the team. He was a really smashing bloke, and a player of iron discipline and total dedication. He later became my boss at Central TV, and was just as nice, modest, and friendly as he had always been. — **JIMMY GREAVES**

I found selecting the Dream Team a nightmare. It was really painful having to leave out so many exceptional players. I tortured myself over whether to put the great Frank Swift in goal, but finally gave the nod to Gordon Banks because of his remarkable consistency.

At right-back I was torn between Jimmy Armfield and Alf Ramsey, my vote going to Jimmy because he was a more accomplished attacking player.

I had no hesitation in picking Roger Byrne at left-back. The Manchester United skipper, tragically killed in the Munich air disaster, was a beautifully balanced full-back with excellent ball control and a biting tackle. Ray Wilson is the only left-back I have seen approaching his class.

Neil Franklin was my first choice at centre-half, although I toyed with the idea of playing John Charles in the middle of the defence. Neil was a superb stylist with an instinctive positional sense. His international career ended when he was suspended for becoming a mercenary in the outlawed Bogota league, and I eventually took his place after the selectors had tried ten different players in the No. 5 shirt.

If Neil had been satisfied with the maximum £20 he was earning at Stoke City, he would have played for England for at least another four years and I often wonder what difference that would have made to my career.

On the right side of midfield, or at right-half as we used to call it, I have picked a poet of a player in Danny Blanchflower. He was all silken skill and made Spurs' outstanding Double team tick. He would be the captain of my team.

Danny was not the fiercest of tacklers, but that does not concern me because alongside him in midfield I have the most complete footballer I ever saw in Duncan Edwards. He could tackle like a clap of thunder, had a crashing shot and was equally effective in defence or attack. Playing with him was a joy.

Pulling the strings between Danny and Duncan would be Wilf Mannion, an artist of a ball player who was deadly accurate with his passes.

Playing just ahead of Wilf I would have the one and only Bobby Charlton, whose bullet shots and positive passing would cause trouble in any defence.

I gave a lot consideration as to how I could fit George Best into my team, but I just could not leave out either Stanley Matthews or Tom Finney. Their crosses will be tailor-made for John Charles, who just got the nod over Tommy Lawton because of his physical presence.

I know that I have left out a lot of marvellous players such as Raich Carter, Stan Mortensen, Jimmy Greaves and Bobby Moore, but you will struggle to find a better balanced team. It would be a dream to manage it.

Captain Wright is carried from the Wembley pitch in 1959 after a 1-0 win over Scotland, having become the first England player to win 100 caps.

Bolton skipper Nat Lofthouse is paraded after his two goals had beaten Manchester United in the 1958 FA Cup final.

Lofthouse proved a bargain following his £10 signing-on fee for Bolton in 1946, scoring 256 goals in 14 years at Burnden Park.

Nat Lofthouse

Born: Bolton, 27 August 1925.

Honours: Nathaniel Lofthouse was the youngest of four sons of the head horsekeeper of Bolton Corporation and attended the same Castle Hill School as Tommy Lawton, his predecessor as England centre-forward. Lofty has served Bolton for more than 50 years, first as a player and later as coach, scout and, briefly, manager.

He scored a club record 256 goals in 452 League matches for Bolton between 1946 and 1960. In 33 England matches he netted 30 goals.

It was fitting that Rocky Marciano was ruling as the world heavyweight champion when Nat was at his mightiest. He was the Marciano of football, playing with clenched fists and crashing through defences with brute force and little concern for his or anybody else's physical welfare. And, like The Rock, Lofthouse away from the sporting arena was a gentle person who was never boastful or arrogant.

Lofty was the captain of the Bolton team that beat Manchester United 2-0 in the 1958 post-Munich FA Cup final. He refused to let sentiment get in his way as he hammered the two goals that gave Bolton victory.

The second came when he charged goalkeeper Harry Gregg and the ball into the net. It was a physical gesture that summed up his approach to the game: 'Get out of the way… Nat Lothouse is here!'

This was my year

Winning the Footballer of the Year trophy in that year of 1953 was a highlight of my career, even though I earned the tag of the Lion of Vienna as an England goalscorer and went on to win an FA Cup medal in 1958.

To be honest, I have only a blurred recollection of the match in Vienna with which I have always been linked. The game was deadlocked at 2-2 with about eight minutes to go when I raced half the length of the pitch with the ball and with a pack of Austrian defenders on my heels. Goalkeeper Gil Merrick had thrown the ball out following a corner, and Tom Finney pushed it ahead of me and I set off for goal.

The Austrian goalkeeper was in two minds and hesitated about coming out. He was a split-second too late to stop me shooting as he finally raced off his line. We collided head on and I went out like a light. Our trainer Jimmy Trotter brought me round with the magic sponge, and it was Jimmy who told me that I had scored. I had a splitting headache, but it was well worth it!

I cost Bolton a £10 signing-on fee when I joined them. In fact, the team that went to Wembley in 1958 and beat Manchester United 2-0 against the odds and against the feelings of everyone in the country outside Bolton cost a modest £110,000 in signing-on fees. They did not buy from another club but believed in breeding their own players.

I was proud to grab the two goals that beat United on a day when sympathy had to take a back seat. In the modern game I admit the goal when I shoulder-charged goalkeeper Harry Gregg into the net would not be allowed. But in those days it was every man for himself, and it made for a great spectacle.

I am still associated with Bolton as president, have an office at the ground and am thrilled to be having a stand named after me.

My Dream Team

GORDON BANKS

ALF RAMSEY   ROGER BYRNE

BILLY WRIGHT   NEIL FRANKLIN   DUNCAN EDWARDS

BOBBY CHARLTON   GEORGE BEST

STANLEY MATTHEWS   ALAN SHEARER   TOM FINNEY

I am sure that my choice of Alan Shearer to lead the attack in my Dream Team will cause a few raised eyebrows, because I have had to look beyond some of the greatest centre-forwards in the history of the game who were in action when I was playing.

I always thought that Tommy Taylor was the best I had ever seen. He had a mixture of skill and strength and was a magnificent leader of the Busby Babes, who were so cruelly cut down in their prime in the Munich air crash of 1958.

Tommy Lawton, of course, was outstanding and led the England attack with driving power. If I had to pick a player purely for heading ability, then Tommy would have no rival for the No 9 shirt.

There is also a firm case for picking another modern player in Gary Lineker. He had a tremendous goal scoring record.

But it is Shearer who gets my vote without resorting to picking a name from a hat. There is one word that sums him up . . . phenomenal. Shearer is the nearest I've seen to the old-style centre-forward who really makes his physical presence felt. He has got two good feet, and his right-foot shot is a real snorter. His power in the air troubles any defence and he has excellent positional sense. In fact, the lad has got everything.

Gordon Banks got my vote as the goalkeeper, a fingertip ahead of Frank Swift. I have never seen a goalkeeper so composed as Gordon at his peak.

Billy Wright would be the skipper of my team, as he was in so many games for England in collecting 105 caps, and he and the rest seem natural choices to me.

He would be the motivating force alongside the cultured Neil Franklin in a defence in which Alf Ramsey and Roger Byrne would be a perfect balance at full-back.

Duncan Edwards was a powerhouse of a half-back, and could be influential in defence and attack.

Who can argue with Stan Matthews and Tom Finney as two of the all-time great English players, and Bobby Charlton and George Best were undoubtedly the tops in their generation. It is an attack that makes your mouth water just looking at the names on paper. On the pitch it would be a dynamic combination.

It was the magical Matthews who stole the show the day after I picked up my award from the football writers in 1953. That year's FA Cup final is always referred to as the Matthews Final after Blackpool came out on top 4-3 through his brilliance after we had led 3-1.

It was a masterly performance of trickery and it is interesting that Stan thinks he unfairly won the plaudits and the headlines when Stan Mortensen got three goals. Stanley won't even watch replays of the game on TV or video and I know he always turns away from the screen when it is shown and blown up as the Matthews Final.

WHAT THE PLAYERS SAY...

Nat was perfectly named as The Lion. He roared through every game, giving defenders a nightmare with his non-stop probing and tremendous power. Nat never knew when he was beaten, and continually popped up with vital goals.

– TOM FINNEY

Nat was not all muscle, like his reputation suggested. He also had a lot of method. His positional sense made him an ideal centre-forward who was always finding room so that his colleagues could pick him out with passes.

– JOHNNY HAYNES

The courage that Nat Lofthouse showed in the match against Austria in Vienna was typical of him as a man and as a player. He lifted the heart of every Englishman in the stadium, and made us redouble our efforts to keep the Austrians out.

– SIR ALF RAMSEY

Lofthouse, scorer of 30 goals in 33 games for England, shows the determination that earned him the nickname the Lion of Vienna.

Tom Finney

Born: Preston, Lancashire, 5 April 1922.

Honours: Tom remained at Preston for his entire career, scoring a club record 187 goals in 433 League matches between 1946 and 1960. He played for Preston in the 1941 wartime FA Cup final, and spent the next four years on Army service. His one peace-time FA Cup final appearance ended with a surprise 3-2 defeat by West Bromwich Albion in 1954, the day after he had received his first Footballer of the Year award.

He collected a second Footballer of the Year award, in 1957 to add to his 76 England caps (1946-58). Tom won his caps in three different positions: outside-right (40), outside left (33), centre-forward (three), and he also played much of one game at inside-forward. His 30 goals was then a record haul for an England player.

Injury cost Finney another 11 caps, and he would have won even more but for the selectors dithering as to whether to play both him and Stanley Matthews in the same attack. When they finally played together in Portugal in 1947, England won 10-0. They scored a goal each and laid on four for both Tommy Lawton and Stan Mortensen. Gentleman Tom was never ever booked, and was respected everywhere for his sportsmanship.

Awarded the OBE in 1961 and the CBE in 1992, he combined his football career with running a family plumbing and electrical business which continues to this day.

This was my year

Winning the Footballer of the Year trophy on two separate occasions was among the biggest thrills of my playing career. I was dubbed the Preston Plumber by the newspapers, and I was proud to be a one-club man with my hometown team Preston North End. I maintain my connections with Deepdale to this day as club president.

It might have been so different and I might never have stepped up to collect my awards. For, after playing for England in Italy in 1952, I was approached after the game with an offer to go to Palermo.

The signing-on fee was £10,000 – enormous money in those days – and the weekly pay packet on offer was £100. Mind-boggling for a player, albeit an England international, earning just £14 a week at Preston. I went to see the chairman and told him about my chance to go to Italy to better myself. 'If you don't play for us, you don't play for

anyone,' was his reply. And that was that. So I stayed at Deepdale – my wages soaring to a heady £20 a week – and I had the consolation of becoming the first double winner of the Footballer of the Year award.

The first time I won, in 1954, Preston reached the FA Cup final, but lost at Wembley 3-2 against West Bromwich Albion. And, just a day after being crowned Footballer of the Year, I had a stinker. But I think perhaps I warranted my win because I had enjoyed a reasonably good season, although I felt at the time that many had voted for me because Stanley Matthews had been a previous winner and we were often compared.

When I won again in 1957 I had moved to a centre-forward role at the age of 35. A bit late in life for that maybe, but I scored 28 of our 80 goals and felt the second award was perhaps harder earned. They were wonderful days, and I would not have changed them for the world.

Tom Finney was the epitome of consistency during his 14-year career at Preston, scoring 187 goals in 433 appearances.

My Dream Team

GORDON BANKS

GEORGE YOUNG   RAY WILSON

BOBBY MOORE   NEIL FRANKLIN   DAVE MACKAY

STANLEY MATTHEWS   WILF MANNION   ALAN SHEARER   PETER DOHERTY   GEORGE BEST

My Dream Team is selected in the old 2-3-5 formation we played in my day. Having picked my side, I can only apologise that I haven't chosen Bobby Charlton, my first substitute, John Charles, Danny Blanchflower, Joe Mercer, Matt Busby or Duncan Edwards, although we did not see the best of him. Perhaps I could name myself as a reserve.

Gordon Banks was, of course, an outstanding goalkeeper, and Scottish lionheart George Young, who would be my captain, was a colossus in the centre of the defence or at right-back. He was very quick for a big guy and so hard to play against. Johnny Carey was another in mind for right-back and Jimmy Armfield, too, was outstanding.

Eddie Hapgood was a classy player I considered for left-back, but Ray Wilson had that extra bite to his game and just got the nod ahead of Roger Byrne.

I go for Neil Franklin at centre-half as the best I have ever played with, but John Charles merits attention as a versatile player who could play equally well at the back or up front. I was also always impressed by the composure of Alan Hansen at the heart of the Liverpool defence.

I just have to fit Bobby Moore into my team and that driving, determined Scot Dave Mackay is in on the left side of midfield as a balance to the cultured play of Franklin and Moore.

Stanley Matthews, the man with whom I was linked throughout my career, was the best ball player I ever saw, an artist and an entertainer. Perhaps he lacked a bit on scoring ability – he was not a good finisher – but he was happier making goals for others. Nobody could match him for dribbling.

Wilf Mannion edges Raich Carter for the No. 8 shirt and I choose Peter Doherty as my inside-left. He could play anywhere and was a complete inside-forward. I saw him when I was a young lad in wartime football and later playing for Ireland. He had tremendous skill, but was able to match the physical side of the game.

Tommy Lawton was the best centre-forward I played with and Nat Lofthouse's 30 goals in 33 internationals says so much for him. But I have to go for Alan Shearer in the No. 9 shirt. He is the complete striker, as they are called today. Alan is brave, strong, good in the air, moves about well, shows intelligence on the wing and gets in accurate crosses – and the way he finishes!

You have to include George Best in any Dream Team. Just imagine Shearer between him and Stan Matthews. Now that would be the stuff of which dreams are made.

WHAT THE PLAYERS SAY...

Tom Finney was so good that he could have gone through any defence while wearing a heavy overcoat. He had pace, incredible ball control, was two-footed and as brave as they come. There have been few better players in history.

– TOMMY DOCHERTY

The press built up a rivalry thing between Tom and myself, but we had no problems at all. He was a great, great footballer and one of the most versatile players ever to grace a football field. It was a joy to play with him. **– SIR STANLEY MATTHEWS**

There were few players in the world who could touch Tom at his peak. Whether on the right wing, left wing, at inside forward or wearing the No. 9 shirt he was a handful for any defence. I felt privileged to be on the same pitch as him. **– NAT LOFTHOUSE**

He made life very difficult for us goalkeepers, but even in those days when we were targets for the shoulder charge he never took liberties. I remember him with awe for his skill and with fondness for his sportsmanship.

– BERT TRAUTMANN

Tom Finney, who made 76 England appearances between 1946 and 1958, combined his football with a career as a plumber.

Revie, a master of positioning, capped a distinguished playing career by winning the Footballer of the Year award in 1955.

Revie had a successful career as first player-manager and then manager of Leeds United after hanging up his boots.

Don Revie

Born: Middlesbrough, 10 July 1927.

Died: 26 May 1989.

Honours: Don Revie's distinguished playing career reached its peak when he was voted Footballer of the Year in 1955 while playing a revolutionary deep-lying centre-forward role with Manchester City. He also played for Leicester, Hull, Sunderland and, finally, Leeds where he was player-manager for a spell before hanging up his boots to concentrate full-time on building the team of his dreams.

His skilful, intelligent football was rewarded with six England caps and an FA Cup winner's medal in 1956.

Don was awarded the CBE for his services to the game in 1970, after twice being named Manager of the Year. He was voted Manager of the Year again in 1972 and when he took over from Sir Alf Ramsey as manager of the England team two years later, it seemed as if the future of our international football team could not be in better hands. But he was less than happy in the job, falling out with the Football Association and deserting his post for a money-motivated move to the United Arab Emirates in 1977.

He died tragically of motor neurone disease at 61, and the tributes that poured in from his former Leeds players was testimony to the fact that he had been one of the most respected managers in football during his time at Elland Road.

This was my year

Along with every thinking footballer, I was motivated by the performance of the Ferenc Puskas-inspired Hungarian team that took England apart and beat them 6-3 at Wembley in 1953. The player who really took my eye was the centre-forward Nandor Hidegkuti, who wore a No. 9 shirt but played a withdrawn role. He came through from midfield to steal a hat-trick, and the England defenders could not cope with him. Until then we always thought of centre-forwards as battering-ram types who led from the front.

We decided to try the system at Manchester City, with me playing the Hidegkuti role. The press called it the Revie Plan, but I could not really claim it as my copyright. It worked well enough to win me my first England cap in that memorable 1954-5 season, and I had the great satisfaction of being elected Footballer of the Year.

The day after receiving my award, we went to Wembley where we were favourites to beat Newcastle in the FA Cup final. But we never functioned against a United team that sprang the offside trap every time I was in possession. We never recovered from being a goal down to a Jackie Milburn header in the first minute, and were then reduced to ten men after Jimmy Meadows had damaged a knee. We eventually lost 3-1, but vowed to return the following year.

I was quite superstitious and began to believe the whispers that the Footballer of the Year award was some sort of jinx. Four of the previous winners had gone to Wembley the next day and lost, and I was the fifth to suffer.

Our goalkeeper Bert Trautmann won the following year and collected the trophy. I wondered if the jinx would strike again, but this time we beat Birmingham City 3-1. Mind you, it was not the happiest of games for Bert. He played through the last 15 minutes with a damaged neck, and an X-ray later revealed that he had broken it!

CARLING

My Dream Team

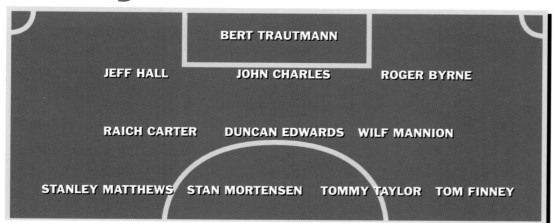

BERT TRAUTMANN

JEFF HALL JOHN CHARLES ROGER BYRNE

RAICH CARTER DUNCAN EDWARDS WILF MANNION

STANLEY MATTHEWS STAN MORTENSEN TOMMY TAYLOR TOM FINNEY

Rather than torture myself trying to choose between players from all those I was lucky to manage, I have confined my selections to footballers from my playing era.

My goalkeeper would be Bert Trautmann, who was my team-mate at Maine Road. He played a procession of extraordinary games for Manchester City and made impossible saves look easy. There was a bravery about his work that just took your breath away. Considering he had been a German prisoner of war, he performed wonders to win over the City fans and was one of the most idolised players in the country.

I am playing just three across the back, with the one and only John Charles looking after the centre of the defence. He was a magnificent player, and it is a pity for English football that he spent his peak years with Juventus, where he was a hero for all seasons.

Flanking him at full-back I have Jeff Hall and Roger Byrne. Both lost their lives tragically while still at their peak. Jeff became a victim of polio, and Roger died in the Munich air crash. They played 17 successive matches together for England before the double tragedy, and were as good a pair of full-backs as have represented England.

Duncan Edwards will be the ball-winner in midfield between the two ball-playing maestros Raich Carter and Wilf Mannion. Edwards was a phenomenal player, and was already a legend when he died at the age of just 22 following the Munich air disaster. He made his England debut in a match in which I played against Scotland at Wembley in 1955. We annihilated the Scots 7-2, with Dennis Wilshaw scoring four goals. Nat Lofthouse netted twice and I got the other goal, but it was the barnstorming performance by Edwards that stays etched in my memory. It was astonishing to think that he was only 18.

Anybody from my generation cannot possibly leave Stanley Matthews and Tom Finney out of their team. Their fame transcended football, and they put thousands on the gate wherever they played.

I have picked Stan Mortensen at inside right because he always brought the best out of his Blackpool team-mate Matthews.

I have gone for Tommy Taylor, another who died at Munich, as my centre-forward. It was a toss-up between him, Nat Lofthouse and Tommy Lawton. Taylor was accomplished in the air and on the ground, and was still only 25 and at his peak when he was taken from us.

I would give John Charles orders to come up into the opposition penalty area for dead-ball kicks. The combination of Charles and Taylor together would mean they would murder any defence in the air.

Roger Byrne would be skipper, but this is a team that does not need a captain. They were all born leaders.

WHAT THE PLAYERS SAY...

I made my debut alongside Don when he was player-manager at Leeds. Even in the veteran stage he oozed class, and was a master of positioning. I doubt if there has been anybody to touch him as a thinking footballer. **– BILLY BREMNER**

Don was one of the first to realise that we had to change our approach to football after the defeat by Hungary, and he led the way with his deep-lying centre-forward play. He had excellent ball control, and was a fine finisher. **– BILL NICHOLSON**

Five of Don's England caps were won alongside me. He was a constructive sort of player who was equally effective whether making or taking goals. I was not surprised that he became an outstanding manager because he put so much thought into the game. **– NAT LOFTHOUSE**

Revie, winner of six England caps, demonstrated his skilful, intelligent style at five clubs including Manchester City and Leeds.

Bert Trautmann

Born: Bremen, Germany, 22 October 1923.

Honours: Bert Trautmann is one of English football's most unlikely folk heroes. He was a German paratrooper during the Second World War, and when captured was sent to a prisoner-of-war camp in Lancashire.

He stayed on in what was to become his adopted country at the end of the war and started to play amateur football for St Helens Town. Then Manchester City, in the teeth of considerable hostility from several quarters, spotted him and decided he was the ideal goalkeeper to replace retiring England goalkeeper Frank Swift.

He joined Maine Road as a professional on 6 October 1949, and made his first-team debut on 19 November at Bolton. It was the first of a then club record 508 League appearances.

Bert had the character to overcome the initial storm of anti-German feeling, and he soon established himself as one of the most popular players in the country. He played for City in both the 1955 and 1956 FA Cup finals, playing on with a broken neck in the second one. He also captained both his club and the Football League side.

He became a coach in the Far East before dividing his time between Ruedesheim, where his third wife, Marlies, has a print works, and a retirement home in Spain. A film is planned of his incredible life story.

This was my year

It was my great honour to be the first foreign player to be elected Footballer of the Year. How could I forget it? Just two days after receiving the award I broke my neck in the FA Cup final at Wembley.

I dived at the feet of Birmingham City forward Peter Murphy with 17 minutes to go, and that was the last thing I remembered. His knee hit my neck, and the next thing I knew I was being revived by the trainer pushing smelling salts under my nose.

I played for the rest of the game in a daze, with my head tilted to one side to try to ease the pain. Of course, I had no idea then just how serious the injury was. I joined in the lap of honour and even went to the banquet after the match to celebrate our 3-1 victory before going to St George's hospital for an x-ray.

This showed nothing, but the pain became so bad that four days later I went to Manchester Royal Infirmary where Professor David Lloyd Griffiths, the orthopaedic surgeon, told me quite bluntly that according to all medical know-how I should have been dead! The second vertebra in my neck had cracked in two, and another five vertebrae were dislocated.

I returned to action halfway through the next season and continued to play for City for another eight years.

I had watched the Hungarians beat England 6-3 in 1953 along with several of my City team-mates, and we decided we should try the Hidegkuti style of a deep-lying centre-forward. Don Revie played the role to perfection, and we reached two successive FA Cup finals and I followed Don as Footballer of the Year.

I have so many wonderful memories of my happy years in Manchester at Maine Road, none greater than when an incredible crowd of 47,000 fans turned up for my farewell testimonial match in 1964.

A former German paratrooper, Bert Trautmann made 508 League appearances for Manchester City, then a club record.

CARLING

My Dream Team

GORDON BANKS

ALF RAMSEY **BILLY WRIGHT** **DUNCAN EDWARDS** **ROGER BYRNE**

DANNY BLANCHFLOWER **BOBBY CHARLTON**

STANLEY MATTHEWS **NAT LOFTHOUSE** **DENIS LAW** **TOM FINNEY**

I have chosen from the footballers I played with and against during my 15 years at Manchester City. Firstly, the team needs a strong leader, and that is why I have selected Billy Wright who was an outstanding captain for both Wolves and England.

Billy will play alongside the extraordinary Duncan Edwards at the centre of the defence. Duncan was going to become a giant of the game and was already a magnificent young player when taken from us in the Munich air disaster. His Manchester United team-mate Roger Byrne is another I select from those tragic Busby Babes, with the polished Alf Ramsey as his full-back partner. Ramsey and Byrne would balance each other perfectly, and bring intelligence as well as power to the defence.

Gordon Banks was with Leicester City and just starting out on his England career when I retired. It was obvious he was going to be an exceptional player, and I was flattered to hear I was his schoolboy hero. Everything about him was right for a goalkeeper. He had natural athleticism, good, safe hands, lightning reflexes and a great awareness of his angles.

Pulling the strings for my team in midfield will be two fine users of the ball in Danny Blanchflower and Bobby Charlton, whose career I saw blossom from close range in Manchester. I had an even closer view of Denis Law, who was my team-mate at Manchester City when he was still a teenager

after joining us from Huddersfield. It was obvious to me that United would win everything in sight when Denis teamed up with Bobby at Old Trafford on his return from Italy after leaving City for Turin. That wise judge Matt Busby knew they would bring the best out of each other, and he had a young lad called George Best in the wings. George does not get into my team because I never played against him, but I was a great admirer of his skill.

Stanley Matthews and Tom Finney are automatic choices as my wingers. Matthews is one of the world's legendary figures, and there has never been anybody to touch him for dribbling the ball. Sadly, this has become a lost art. There were few more exciting sights than Matthews taking on and beating a full-back with his shuffling style. Finney's was simpler but just as effective, and he could also finish powerfully with either foot.

Waiting in the middle to take full advantage of their wing work will be Nat Lofthouse, who was a great competitor and a fine all-round centre-forward. I had many duels with Nat in an era when goalkeepers did not have referees protecting them like mother hens. They were memorable times and just looking through the names of the players in my team fills me with nostalgia.

WHAT THE PLAYERS SAY...

When I was a youngster just starting out as a goalkeeper I used to model myself on my boyhood hero, Bert Trautmann. I saw him play several times for Manchester City and used to wonder at his flying saves and incredible bravery. **- GORDON BANKS**

Bert was just about the only goalkeeper big enough to fill Frank Swift's boots. Manchester City fans were lucky to have two of the greatest goalkeepers of all time following each other into the Maine Road team. **- TOM FINNEY**

Goalkeeping was a different game to what it is these days. Bert used to give as good as he got with his powerful shoulders, and I bounced off him many times. He was a magnificent player, with great reflexes and a giant heart. **- NAT LOFTHOUSE**

Trautmann, who beat anti-Germany hostility to become a hero at Manchester City, gives a demonstration of his safe handling against Arsenal.

Danny Blanchflower

Born: Belfast, 10 February 1926.

Died: 9 December 1993.

Honours: One of the most creative and authoritative players ever to set foot on a football pitch, he was a born leader who, as well as skippering Spurs through their 'Glory Glory' years, also captained the Northern Ireland team that reached the quarter-finals of the 1958 World Cup. He won 56 international caps and played 337 League games for Tottenham between 1954 and 1963 after service with Glentoran, Barnsley and Aston Villa.

A recurring knee injury forced his retirement in 1963, after which he became a respected broadcaster and journalist with an acid wit and something fresh to say on every subject. He managed the Northern Ireland team and had a brief but unsatisfactory spell as Chelsea manager. For many years he wrote a column in the *Sunday Express* that was always readable and perceptive.

Danny was considered the poet of Tottenham. He gave the team style and panache and was a captain in every sense of the word, inspiring the players around him with his almost arrogant performances and lifting them with words of wisdom. His contribution to the team was as important as manager Bill Nicholson's. He was the dressing-room tactician and training-ground theorist.

His brother and fellow Irish international, Jackie, survived the 1958 Manchester United air crash but never played again.

This was my year

The first of my two Footballer of the Year awards, in 1958, gave me the greatest satisfaction because it was as much for what I achieved with Northern Ireland as with Tottenham. This was the year that we reached the World Cup quarter-finals in Sweden, much to the surprise of everybody who had written us off – even though we had accounted for Italy to qualify. In the League Tottenham finished strongly to take third place behind Wolves and Preston, and all the signs were there that we were on the verge of greater things.

My second award came the year Tottenham became the first team this century to achieve the FA Cup and League double. This time I felt the statuette was presented to me as much as a representative of that outstanding Spurs side as for my personal contribution.

I was so convinced that we were going to have an exceptional season that I predicted before a ball was kicked that we were going to win the Double. It was not an idle boast. I honestly felt that we had a perfect blend of skill and strength in our team.

We won the first 11 League matches of the season, dropped a point to Manchester City, then won the next four. Even though I was part of it, I found it hard to believe our level of skill and consistency. We finished with a record-equalling 66 points despite a hiccup in the closing weeks when we were tuned to the FA Cup final against Leicester City.

We were introduced to the Duchess of Kent before the kick-off at Wembley, and I recall her asking, 'Why do the Leicester players have their names on the backs of their tracksuits, but Tottenham do not?'

'Well ma'am,' I replied in my best Irish accent, 'we know each other.'

Our performance against Leicester did not show us at our best, but we did enough to deserve our 2-0 victory and clinch what many had thought was the 'impossible' Double.

A born leader, Blanchflower captained Tottenham during the 'Glory, Glory' years and Northern Ireland at the 1958 World Cup finals.

CARLING

My Dream Team

PAT JENNINGS

ROGER BYRNE   JOHN CHARLES   DUNCAN EDWARDS   ALF McMICHAEL

JIMMY McILROY   DAVE MACKAY

GEORGE BEST   DENIS LAW   JIMMY GREAVES   CLIFF JONES

My first selection was not a player but a manager. I wanted somebody who I knew would approach every game with a spirit of adventure and able to motivate the players with his words of wisdom. I did not have to look any further than my old Northern Ireland mentor Peter Doherty.

He talked about the game the way he played it, with flair and passion. I would have my former Tottenham manager Bill Nicholson as his right-hand man. They would make a perfect pair to get the best out of my team.

I had no doubts about selecting Pat Jennings as the goalkeeper. There has rarely, if ever, been a goalkeeper to match him for consistency, and his safe handling would spread confidence right through the team.

I have decided on an attacking 4-2-4 formation, with two of my favourite partners – Jimmy McIlroy for Northern Ireland, and Dave Mackay for Tottenham – at the hub of things. Mackay will win the ball before feeding it to McIlroy, who will light up the attack with imaginative and accurate passes.

I was tempted to make Peter Doherty player-manager. He was in the autumn of his career when I used to watch him play, but even on ageing legs he was a class above everybody else around him. In the end I decided to leave the major orchestrating role to the Burnley ball master McIlroy. Peter can save his energy for the half-time pep talk. My back four has Roger Byrne playing out of place at right-back, with my former Irish team-mate Alf McMichael filling his usual No. 3 shirt. Roger was a majestic player at left back for Manchester United, and was talented enough to play at right-back without weakening the team. He would also be my choice as captain.

Standing rock solid in the middle of the defence will be John Charles and Duncan Edwards, who would both be encouraged to go forward as auxiliary attackers when the situation seems right to them. I have selected intelligent players who will be expected to think on their feet and not get stuck in any stereotyped pattern.

I have always been a supporter of wingers, and in George Best and Cliff Jones I have selected two of the best. My first thought was Matthews and Finney, but I think Best and Jones will give me a little more thrust and speed. George was far and away the greatest British footballer of his generation, while Cliff Jones was fast enough to catch pigeons.

Jimmy Greaves was simply the best finisher I ever played with or against, and it would be fascinating to see him operating alongside Denis Law, whose reactions were always razor sharp. I think they would bring the best out of each other, and their best was the very best.

WHAT THE PLAYERS SAY...

Danny was a great reader of a game, and he had the courage and intelligence to make tactical decisions in the heat of battle that most people are happy to sort out in the dressing-room inquest when it is too late.

– JIMMY GREAVES

I doubt if there has been a more committed captain than Danny. He considered it a role far above just carrying out the ball and tossing up. As well as being a constructive player, he could motivate the players with well-chosen words.

– BILL NICHOLSON

Danny was so vital to the team in our historic Double year of 1960-61. It was his linking with John White in midfield that dictated the tempo of matches, and he always found the right things to say to inspire us. **– DAVE MACKAY**

Blanchflower, who played 337 League games for Spurs, celebrates their 1961 FA Cup victory . . . and the first Double this century.

FOOTBALLER OF THE YEAR 1959

Syd Owen

Born: Birmingham, 29 September 1922.

Honours: Footballing fame came late to Syd Owen, who was not selected for the first of his three caps as England centre-half until he was 31. He made his international appearances in the summer of 1954 before making way in the middle of the defence for the reign of Billy Wright.

His entry into League football was delayed until the end of the Second World War when he was 23. He played just five League matches for his local club Birmingham City before transferring to Luton Town in the summer of 1947.

He quickly established himself as a favourite at Kenilworth Road where he had the greatest days of his playing career. It was his inspiring leadership that motivated Luton on the road to Wembley in 1959 when they shocked the football world by going all the way to the FA Cup final.

It was 36-year-old Owen who led them out against Nottingham Forest, who won 2-1 despite the handicap of losing goal-scoring hero Roy Dwight (Elton John's uncle) with a broken leg.

Syd hung up his boots after the final and switched to a successful coaching career which reached its peak when he teamed up with Don Revie at Leeds United, where his tactical know-how was an important factor in the Elland Road successes of the 1960s and 1970s.

Syd Owen, who won the first of his three England caps at 31, became Footballer of the Year in what he called his 'extra-time'

Owen led Luton Town to the 1959 FA Cup final where they were beaten 2-1 by ten-man Nottingham Forest.

This was my year

I doubt if anybody has had a more memorable final season in football than the one in which I featured with Luton Town. I had decided to hang up my boots at the end of the 1957-8 campaign, but the football gods were certainly smiling down on me when the Luton directors persuaded me to play on until they could find a replacement.

By the time this extra season was over, I was not only the Footballer of the Year but also the Luton manager.

My very last match was in the FA Cup final when we were beaten 2-1 by Nottingham Forest. Roy Dwight scored for Forest before being carried off with a broken leg. This was in the days before substitutes, and Forest having ten men put us out of our stride more than it did them.

We had got to Wembley by conquering Leeds – for whom Don Revie was a key player – 5-1 in the third round, followed by Leicester City, Ipswich Town, Blackpool and, in the semi-final, Norwich City. We did it the hard way, beating Leicester, Blackpool and Norwich in replays. My 36-year-old legs were really feeling the strain by the end of that season!

We were solid in defence, and enterprising in attack. Our right-wing pair of Billy Bingham and Allan Brown was as potent a combination as there was in the League, and Bob Morton led the attack with great enthusiasm after switching from right-half following Jesse Pye's move to Derby.

I had a good understanding with our goalkeeper Ron Baynham, who, like me, was an England international while with Luton. Pulling the strings for us in midfield was Irish international George Cummins, whose passes were always precise.

When I collected my Footballer of the Year award I gave my team-mates much of the credit because it was their performances that had helped bring such a fairy-tale end to my playing career. I had just a brief run as Luton manager before accepting the job of chief coach at Leeds.

My Dream Team

FRANK SWIFT

ALF RAMSEY   JOHN CHARLES   NORMAN HUNTER   ROGER BYRNE

BILLY BREMNER   DUNCAN EDWARDS   JOHNNY GILES

STANLEY MATTHEWS   TOMMY LAWTON   TOM FINNEY

WHAT THE PLAYERS SAY...

Syd was a great inspiration to everybody in the team with his determined performances at the heart of our defence. He never knew when he was beaten, and this never-say-die attitude rubbed off on the players around him. **– BILLY BINGHAM**

Like Syd, I switched from wing-half to centre-half and I admired the way he adapted to his new role as a linchpin in the middle of the Luton defence. He was unlucky that his chance at international level came so late in his career. **– BILL SLATER**

Luton really captured the imagination with their Cup run to Wembley, and Syd Owen typified their spirit. He was a good tactical thinker in the thick of the action, and he took this skill into his coaching after he had retired. **– TOMMY DOCHERTY**

Not surprisingly, there is a strong Leeds influence on my team. I have Billy Bremner and Johnny Giles in the midfield engine room, and John Charles is my automatic choice at centre-half. John came back to Leeds after I had been appointed chief coach at Elland Road. He had lost a little of the pace that had made him such a favourite with Juventus, but he still oozed class and at his peak was one of the untouchables. Playing alongside him I will have the redoubtable Norman Hunter, who gave Leeds outstanding service. You could count his bad games on the fingers of one hand. The combination of Charles and Hunter at the centre of the defence will give my team steel as well as skill.

My goalkeeper will be Frank Swift, who was a giant of the game in the eyes of anybody from my generation. He was surprisingly agile for such a huge man, and could give as good as he got in an era when goalkeepers used to take physical punishment from shoulder-charging forwards.

The full-back partners are Alf Ramsey and Roger Byrne. Alf was a thinking man's right-back who always used the ball with intelligence. Roger was an exceptional player, who was at left-back in the three matches in which I played for England. He was skilful and could also tackle with authority.

It was, of course, a great tragedy when Roger and his team-mates perished in the Munich air disaster. Duncan Edwards was in the foothills of what was going to be one of the great careers at the time of his untimely death at Munich, and he comes into my team as a balance between Bremner and Giles, who used to make the outstanding Leeds United team tick. With Billy's energy, the perfection of Johnny's passing and the sheer dynamic power of Duncan, I see them bossing the midfield from the first whistle.

Stanley Matthews and Tom Finney will play down the touchlines for me, with Tommy Lawton waiting in the middle to convert their crosses. I was lucky to play with as well as against Matthews and Finney, and both could turn defences inside out with just a shrug of their shoulders. Finney was the better all-rounder who could finish with either foot or with his head, but when it came to dribbling there was nobody in Stanley's league. I have seen him beat two or three players in the space of a few yards without breaking sweat before crossing with pin-pointed accuracy.

As a member of the centre-half union, I was always in awe of Tommy Lawton who was unlucky to lose his peak years to the war. He was an incredibly positive player who could head the ball harder than some players could kick it. I will be looking for big John Charles to come forward to support Tommy. What a pair in the air! I certainly would not like to be the centre-half with the responsibility of trying to beat them to the crosses from Matthews and Finney.

Owen, who found fame late in his playing career at Luton Town, went on to use his tactical know-how as a coach at Leeds.

1960s

Alf Ramsey's wingless wonders

The Swinging Sixties were about Beatlemania, colourful fashion and youth culture. And it was all mirrored on the playing fields of England where footballers were transformed into folk heroes. The decade started with a wages revolution that saw the end of the maximum wage, and by the dawn of the 1970s England had won the World Cup, Celtic had become the first British winners of the European Cup and were followed by Matt Busby's Manchester United as the first English winners.

It was a golden era for British football at both club and country level, but tarnished by the gradual swing towards more violent play and the emergence of the first soccer hooligans. Even during England's finest hour – the winning of the 1966 World Cup – there was a price to pay. Wingers, those specialist players who brought excitement to football, all but disappeared.

Manager Alf Ramsey was wrongly blamed for making wingers redundant. He was merely playing to England's strengths by settling for a 4-3-3 formation without recognised flank players. It was not his intention to turn wingers into a dying breed, but England's World Cup success spawned an army of imitators and suddenly most clubs were playing 4-3-3 with the emphasis on defence.

Penalty areas became packed and goals, the lifeblood of the game, were suddenly much harder to come by. Tackling was too often spiteful, the tackle from behind having yet to be banned, and the ankle-tap and the boot in the calf were two of the nastier fouls that became commonplace.

It was during the 1960s that new phrases crept into the game, such as work-rate, the overlap, tackling back, running off the ball, centre-backs, sweepers, ball-watching and midfield anchormen. Coaches were in charge, and their tactics began squeezing the goals out of football.

Jock Stein refused to allow his amazing Celtic team to be drawn into the defensive web. The former Celtic centre-half and captain had always passionately believed football should be played with a positive attitude. Celtic's record under his mesmerising management was unparalleled in British football. In his first six full seasons in charge from 1965, the Parkhead club won six Scottish League titles and lost only 17 of 204 League games while scoring 597 goals. They reached five Scottish Cup finals, winning three; and they won five out of six League Cup finals. Celtic perfected their team-work in a Scottish League where they were so dominant that even Rangers fans had to applaud their achievements.

Celtic stormed into the 1967 European Cup final in which they dismantled Inter Milan, the great architects of defence-dominated football who had won the European Cup in 1964 and 1965.

A year later Manchester United became the first English winners of the European Cup by beating Benfica 4-1 after extra time on an emotion-charged night at Wembley.

Busby and his skipper Bobby Charlton were survivors of an air crash ten years earlier that had cost the lives of eight United players. It was the day a team died, and Busby had silently vowed one day to win the premier prize of the European Cup in memory of those who had perished in Munich. He built his new team around three shining jewels – Charlton, Denis Law and George Best – each of whom was voted European Footballer of the Year during the 1960s.

Ramsey and Busby were both knighted following their triumphs. Many thought Jock Stein should have joined them. Bill Shankly, Stein's great friend who during the 1960s lit the flame to the Red Revolution at Anfield, summed it up when he said, 'Jock never bowed the knee to anybody!'-

–Norman Giller

Bobby Moore celebrates English football's greatest moment after winning the World Cup in 1966 with victory over West Germany.

CARLING

Who won what

1959-60

League champions: Burnley
FA Cup final: Wolves 3 Blackburn Rovers 0
First Division marksman: Dennis Viollet (Man United) 32
Footballer of the Year: Bill Slater (Wolves)
Scottish champions: Heart of Midlothian
Scottish Cup final: Rangers 2 Kilmarnock 0
European Cup final: Real Madrid 7 Eintracht Frankfurt 3
European Nations Cup final: USSR 2 Yugoslavia I (aet)
European Footballer of the Year: Luis Suarez (Barcelona)

1960-1

League champions: Tottenham
FA Cup final: Tottenham 2, Leicester City 0
League Cup final: Aston Villa 3, Rotherham 2 (0-2, 3-0 aet)
First Division marksman: Jimmy Greaves (Chelsea) 41
Footballer of the Year: Danny Blanchflower (Tottenham)
Scottish champions: Rangers
Scottish Cup final: Dunfermline 2, Celtic 0 (after a 0-0 draw)
European Cup final: Benfica 3, Barcelona 2
Cup Winners' Cup final: Fiorentina 4, Rangers 1 (2-0, 2-1)
Fairs Cup final: Birmingham City 2, AS Roma 4 (2-2, 0-2)
European Footballer of the Year: Omar Sivori (Juventus)

1961-2

League champions: Ipswich Town
FA Cup final: Tottenham 3, Burnley 1
League Cup final: Norwich City 4, Rochdale 0 (3-0, 1-0)
First Division marksmen: Ray Crawford (Ipswich Town) and
Derek Kevan (WBA), 33
Footballer of the Year: Jimmy Adamson (Burnley)
Scottish champions: Dundee
Scottish Cup final: Rangers 2, St Mirren 0
European Cup final: Benfica 5, Real Madrid 3
Cup Winners' Cup final: Atletico Madrid 3, Fiorentina 0 (after 1-1)
Fairs Cup final: Valencia 7, Barcelona 3 (6-2, 1-1)
European Footballer of the Year: Josef Masopust (Dukla Prague)
World Cup final: Brazil 3, Czechoslovakia 1

1962-3

League champions: Everton
FA Cup final: Manchester United 3, Leicester City 1
League Cup final: Birmingham City 3, Aston Villa 1 (3-1, 0-0)
First Division marksman: Jimmy Greaves (Tottenham), 37
Footballer of the Year: Stanley Matthews (Stoke City)
Scottish champions: Rangers
Scottish Cup final: Rangers 3, Celtic 0 (after 1-1 draw)
European Cup final: AC Milan 2, Benfica 1
Cup Winners' Cup final: Tottenham 5, Atletico Madrid 1
Fairs Cup final: Dynamo Zagreb 1, Valencia 4 (1-2, 0-2)
European Footballer of the Year: Lev Yashin (Moscow Dynamo)

1963-4

League champions: Liverpool
FA Cup final: West Ham United 3, Preston North End 2
League Cup final: Leicester City 4, Stoke City 3 (1-1, 3-2)
First Division marksman: Jimmy Greaves (Tottenham), 35
Footballer of the Year: Bobby Moore (West Ham United)
Scottish champions: Rangers
Scottish Cup final: Rangers 3, Dundee 1
European Cup final: Inter Milan 3, Real Madrid 1
Cup Winners' Cup final: Sporting Lisbon 1, MTK Budapest 0
(after 3-3 draw)
Fairs Cup final: Real Zaragoza 2, Valencia 1
European Nations Cup final: Spain 2, USSR 1
European Footballer of the Year: Denis Law (Manchester United)

1964-5

League champions: Manchester United
FA Cup final: Liverpool 2, Leeds United I (after extra time)
League Cup final: Chelsea 3, Leicester City 2 (3-2, 0-0)
First Division marksmen: Jimmy Greaves (Tottenham) and
Andy McEvoy (Blackburn), 29
Footballer of the Year: Bobby Collins (Leeds United)
Scottish champions: Kilmarnock
Scottish Cup final: Celtic 3, Dunfermline 2
Scottish Player of the Year: Billy McNeill (Celtic)
European Cup final: Inter Milan I, Benfica 0
Cup Winners' Cup final: West Ham United 2, Munich 1860 0
Fairs Cup final: Ferencvaros 1, Juventus 0
European Footballer of the Year: Eusebio (Benfica)

1965-6

League champions: Liverpool
FA Cup final: Everton 3, Sheffield Wednesday 2
League Cup final: West Brom 5, West Ham 3 (1-2, 4-1)
First Division marksman: Roger Hunt (Liverpool), 30
Footballer of the Year: Bobby Charlton (Manchester United)
Scottish champions: Celtic
Scottish Cup final: Rangers 1, Celtic O (after a 0-0 draw)
Scottish Player of the Year: John Greig (Rangers)
European Cup final: Real Madrid 2, Partizan Belgrade 1
Cup Winners' Cup final: Borussia Dortmund 2, Liverpool 1 (aet)
Fairs Cup final: Barcelona 4, Real Zaragoza 3 (0-1, 4-2)
European Footballer of the Year: Bobby Charlton
(Manchester United)
World Cup final: England 4, West Germany 2 (aet)

1966-7

League champions: Manchester United
FA Cup final: Tottenham 2, Chelsea 1
League Cup final: Queens Park Rangers 3, West Brom 2
First Division marksman: Ron Davies (Southampton), 37
Footballer of the Year: Jack Charlton (Leeds United)
Scottish champions: Celtic
Scottish Cup final: Celtic 2, Aberdeen 0
Scottish Player of the Year: Ronnie Simpson (Celtic)
European Cup final: Celtic 2, Inter Milan I
Cup Winners' Cup: Bayern Munich 1, Rangers 0 (aet)
Fairs Cup final: Dynamo Zagreb 2, Leeds 0 (2-0, 0-0)
European Footballer of the Year: Florian Albert (Ferencvaros)

1967-8

League champions: Manchester City
FA Cup final: West Bromwich Albion 1, Everton 0 (aet)
League Cup final: Leeds United 1, Arsenal 0
First Division marksmen: George Best (Manchester United)
and Ron Davies (Southampton), 28
Footballer of the Year: George Best (Manchester United)
Scottish champions: Celtic
Scottish Cup final: Dunfermline 3, Heart of Midlothian 1
Scottish Player of the Year: Gordon Wallace (Raith Rovers)
European Cup final: Manchester United 4, Benfica 1 (aet)
Cup Winners' Cup final: AC Milan 2, SV Hamburg 0
Fairs Cup final: Leeds United 1, Ferencvaros 0 (1-0, 0-0)
European Championship final: Italy 2, Yugoslavia 0 (after 1-1)
European Footballer of the Year: George Best
(Manchester United)

1968-9

League champions: Leeds United
FA Cup final: Manchester City 1, Leicester City O
League Cup final: Swindon Town 3, Arsenal I (aet)
First Division marksman: Jimmy Greaves (Tottenham), 27
Footballers of the Year: Dave Mackay (Derby County) and
Tony Book (Manchester City)
Scottish champions: Celtic
Scottish Cup final: Celtic 4, Rangers O
Scottish Player of the Year: Bobby Murdoch (Celtic)
European Cup final: AC Milan 4, Ajax I
Cup Winners' Cup final: Slovan Bratislava 3, Barcelona 2
Fairs Cup final: Newcastle United 6, Ujpest Dozsa 2 (3-0, 3-2)
European Footballer of the Year: Gianni Rivera (AC Milan)

*Manager Matt Busby shows off the European Cup following
Manchester United's famous 4-1 victory over Benfica in 1968.*

Bill Slater

Born: Clitheroe, Lancashire, 29 April 1927.

Honours: A university lecturer, Bill had the distinction of playing amateur and professional football for England and represented Great Britain in the 1952 Olympics. He started his career as an amateur with Blackpool, for whom he played in the 1951 FA Cup final and, while still studying at university, had a short spell with Brentford before turning professional with Wolverhampton Wanderers.

He played 310 League matches for Wolves between 1954 and 1962. In the 1958 World Cup finals he formed an all-Wolves half-back line with club-mates Eddie Clamp and Billy Wright. He won a total of 12 caps.

He was a composed and cultured inside-forward who later switched with great success to wing-half and then to centre-half as successor to Billy Wright. He won three League championship medals and skippered the side that won the FA Cup in 1960.

A superior mind was at work when Bill was in action, but while he brought brain to the game he was quite capable of adding considerable brawn and was a firm and authoritative player. He had great strength and stamina to go with his skill, as you would expect of somebody who later became Director of Physical Education at Liverpool University and then Birmingham University. His daughter, Barbara, is a former international gymnast and now a BBC TV sports producer.

Slater won three League championship medals with Wolves and captained them to victory against Blackburn in the 1960 FA Cup.

This was my year

Not only am I the only part-time player to have been chosen as Footballer of the Year, I guess I am the only one who got roasted on the night he went to collect his award.

Bob Lord, who was the Burnley chairman and also a top FA man at the time, stood up at the dinner and told the football writers, 'The Press have got it wrong this time.'

Lord advocated that Jimmy McIlroy, the skilful Irishman who skippered his team, should have been voted winner because, he said, Burnley were going to win the championship.

He put forward a convincing case in his typically forthright way but, in the event, the impact of his words on the football writers proved to be a way of rallying them and, when I stood up to collect the statuette, I got the biggest cheer you can imagine.

Wolves were playing in the FA Cup final against Blackburn Rovers that weekend and, on the night of the dinner, were top of the First Division table after two years of being championship winners. Burnley had to play Manchester City, and win, the week afterwards to pip us for the title – and they did it.

I had already played at Wembley, for Blackpool as an amateur in 1951 alongside Stanley Matthews and Stanley Mortensen, and been on the losing side. Jackie Milburn got both goals in a 2-0 Newcastle victory. The record books show that W J Slater was in the team. My first game for them was when I was a student in 1948.

I had a letter of introduction to Stan Cullis, the legendary Wolves manager, knocked on his door, asked if I could join – and signed as an amateur.

The players used to buy me a present at Christmas, as I was not being paid to play. Later I became a part-timer. I was a teacher throughout my footballing career and enjoyed some fabulous years at Molineux.

Winning the Footballer of the Year award was just one of many wonderful highlights.

My Dream Team

PETER SHILTON

DON HOWE RAY WILSON

BILLY WRIGHT JOHN CHARLES DUNCAN EDWARDS

STANLEY MATTHEWS RAICH CARTER TOM FINNEY GARY LINEKER BOBBY CHARLTON

My Dream Team lines up in the old 2-3-5 formation. It is as much out of loyalty as anything that I have chosen my old skipper Billy Wright as the team captain, but there were so many players to consider for that No. 4 shirt.

I have reluctantly relegated my old friend Danny Blanchflower to the substitutes' bench. Skippering Wolves against Blackburn in the FA Cup final completely revised my thinking about the introduction of substitutes. I had always felt that subs were not something football should embrace. Rovers lost defender Dave Whelan, who was carried off with a broken leg. It took the edge off our 3-0 victory. It would have been more satisfying playing against 11 men.

Whelan, of course, went on to become a millionaire businessman. These days he is chairman of Wigan, but I am sure he would still have settled for a Wembley win for his side and some glory.

Dave Mackay is another exceptional player I have had to put on stand-by. I decided on a half-back line of Wright, John Charles and Duncan Edwards. I doubt if anybody could select a more powerful combination, and both Charles and Edwards had the ability to become auxiliary attackers.

Peter Shilton got my vote for the goalkeeping jersey, but I agonised at having to leave out such notable goalkeepers as Gordon Banks, Frank Swift and my old Wolves club-mates Bert Williams and Malcolm Finlayson.

The full-backs were the hardest to choose. I played alongside Don Howe and know he was a class act. He was a thinking player who was always looking for the opportunity to turn defence into attack. Ray Wilson was outstanding in England's 1966 World Cup campaign, and would make an ideal partner for Don.

Raich Carter gets the edge over Wilf Mannion as my scheming inside-forward. Both could pull apart any defence with their probing passes and clever ball control. It was difficult to make the final choice, but I decided that room had to be found on the crowded substitutes' bench for Wilf.

Gary Lineker gets the striker's role because he has proved himself at the highest level at home and abroad. He would dovetail nicely with Bobby Charlton, and the wing work of Stanley Matthews and Tom Finney would make me confident that this attack could dismantle any defence.

I played in an era when wingers reigned, and at Wolves we had Johnny Hancocks and Jimmy Mullen and, later, Norman Deeley performing wonders down the touchline. It was exciting stuff to watch, but Matthews and Finney were a class above every other winger and would give my team a touch of magic.

WHAT THE PLAYERS SAY...

Bill Slater was an intelligent player, but he could play the hard man if the situation called for it. He was composed on the ball, and was a natural leader of men. I wonder what he might have achieved had he ever become a full-time professional!
– DON HOWE

Bill was one of the players who made that outstanding Wolves team tick. He was a powerful man with a good, solid tackle and he always played the game in true sporting spirit. **– JIMMY McILROY**

The Wolves team of the 1950s was a formidable machine, and Bill Slater was an important cog. Like all Stan Cullis players, he was immensely strong and fit, and accomplished on the ball. Like me, he always had a job to go to off the pitch.
– TOM FINNEY

Slater, a composed player, blended brains with brawn during an eight-year spell at Wolverhampton Wanderers, for whom he made 310 League appearances.

Jimmy Adamson

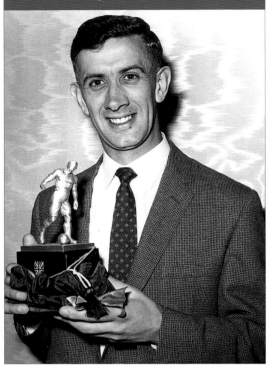

Born: Ashington, 4 April 1929.

Honours: Jimmy was football's Mr Reliable, and acknowledged by his contemporaries as the best uncapped player in the land. He spent his entire career with Burnley, joining them in 1947 and playing 426 League matches between 1950 and 1963.

From the same district as Bobby and Jack Charlton, he carried on the proud North East traditions of playing thoroughbred football. He was the thinking man's wing-half, always a composed and authoritative figure as a defensive anchorman. His job was to win the ball and then pass it to playmaker Jimmy McIlroy, who would in turn feed it to the striking force that included England internationals Ray Pointer, John Connelly and Gordon Harris. The system worked so well under Adamson's thoughtful captaincy that Burnley captured the League championship in 1959-60 and two seasons later finished runners-up to Tottenham in the FA Cup final.

Jimmy was so highly rated as a tactician that he was appointed England coach for the 1962 World Cup finals while still a Burnley player. He declined the chance to take over as England manager from Walter Winterbottom, so leaving the way for Alf Ramsey to be appointed. The rest, as they say, is history.

Jimmy had six years in charge at Burnley where he failed to find the success that he enjoyed on the Turf Moor pitch.

Football's Mr Reliable, an international coach at the 1962 World Cup finals, was widely regarded as England's best uncapped player.

This was my year

Three things made the 1961-2 season particularly memorable for me. There was the honour of skippering Burnley in the FA Cup final, the Footballer of the Year award and then my appointment as coach to the England team for the World Cup finals in Chile. It then all fell a bit flat because we were beaten at Wembley, and failed to perform as well as we might have done in the World Cup.

But nobody could take away from me the Footballer of the Year statuette, nor the fact that we had made it to the FA Cup final. Mind you, we had some scares along the way. We beat Queens Park Rangers 6-1, then had to go to a replay before beating Leyton Orient.

Our finest performance was eliminating an excellent Everton team in the fifth round. We accounted for Sheffield United in the quarter-finals and then had a close call with Fulham in the semi-finals, winning 2-1 in another replay. We were fighting an uphill battle against a magnificent Tottenham team in the final after the ace of goal-poachers Jimmy Greaves had scored in the third minute. I have to say that the 3-1 scoreline at the end of our match flattered them a little.

It was a season of near misses for Burnley. We finished runners-up to Alf Ramsey's Ipswich team in the League, playing with much the same side that captured the championship in 1959-60.

I had claret and blue blood after all my years at Burnley, and it is very sad to see them no longer contesting the main prizes. Our success was built on team-work, with individual stars like Jimmy McIlroy, Ray Pointer, John Connelly and Gordon Harris functioning within a well constructed formation.

We were essentially a footballing team, and concentrated on skill ahead of brute force. They were wonderful years at Turf Moor, and I was content to spend all my playing days there.

My Dream Team

GORDON BANKS

JOHNNY CAREY   JOHN CHARLES   DUNCAN EDWARDS   ROGER BYRNE

DANNY BLANCHFLOWER   JIMMY McILROY

STANLEY MATTHEWS   JIMMY GREAVES   DENIS LAW   BOBBY CHARLTON

I have stuck with players who I either played with or against, and so the likes of George Best, Kevin Keegan, Kenny Dalglish, Bryan Robson, Glenn Hoddle, Gary Lineker and Alan Shearer did not come into my consideration.

Gordon Banks is my choice as goalkeeper because of his incredible consistency. I cannot recall seeing him have a bad game at either club or country level, and he always seemed in command of his area. His handling was clean, and his distribution thoughtful and aimed at putting the opposition under pressure.

There is a strong strand of the Busby Babes team running through my side. Roger Byrne partners his predecessor as Manchester United captain, Johnny Carey, at full-back, while Duncan Edwards will play a free role just in front of the back line of the defence. He can operate alongside John Charles or come forward as a ball winner, as the circumstances demand. I would expect both John and Duncan to move upfield for set piece situations. John would win everything in the air, and Duncan could cause any goalkeeper problems with his powerful shooting.

Two Irishmen who always seemed to be around at key moments during my career are in command in midfield. Danny Blanchflower was a beautifully composed player for Tottenham, while Jimmy McIlroy was majestic as the schemer in our Burnley team. Both played a prominent part in steering Northern Ireland through to the 1958

World Cup quarter-finals. Neither Danny nor Jimmy were particularly strong tacklers, but they will have the dynamic Duncan Edwards winning the ball for them. Once either of the two Irish conductors has the ball at his feet, he will control the pace and the pattern of the game with passes that would be positive and deadly accurate.

Stanley Matthews was a giant of the game for so long that his fame transcended football, and his dribbling wizardry would be a vital element in attack. Waiting to pounce on his passes would be two of the sharpest finishers I ever saw in Jimmy Greaves and Denis Law. Jimmy was a thorn in the side of the Burnley defence in many games when he was poaching goals for Chelsea and Tottenham. Denis had incredibly quick reflexes and could turn a half chance into a goal in the blinking of an eye.

I had the torture of choosing between two gentlemen of the game for the No.11 shirt in Tom Finney and Bobby Charlton. My vote finally went to Bobby because I watched his career with interest from the moment he first emerged as a prodigy while growing up in my home North East territory of Ashington. He was outstanding for England and Manchester United whether bombing on the wing, playing an orthodox inside-forward role or as a deep-lying schemer who was always looking to strike from long range. Our game has rarely had a better ambassador, and his knighthood was a fitting reward for his services to football. My team would be a delight to watch and a joy to manage.

WHAT THE PLAYERS SAY...

It was ridiculous that Jimmy did not win any England caps. He was a magnificent player who had great poise and composure. He never shirked his responsibilities and always had time for a word of encouragement to his team-mates.

– JIMMY McILROY

Jimmy had the respect of everybody in the game, and speaking as a Scot I just could not fathom how the England selectors failed to pick him throughout his career.
– DAVE MACKAY

There are players who have won a dozen or more caps who were not in Jimmy's class. The Burnley team he captained was as good a club side as I played against.
– JIMMY GREAVES

A great ball winner and master tactician, Adamson led Burnley to the League title in 1960 and the FA Cup final two years later.

Bobby Moore

Born: Barking, Essex, 12 April 1941.
Died: 24 February 1993.
Honours: Pele called him simply the greatest defender in the world. He won 108 caps for England, and equalled Billy Wright's record of captaining the team in 90 matches.

Bobby skippered the England youth team while winning a record 18 caps. He made his West Ham debut in 1958, replacing his pal Malcolm Allison, whose career was cut short by tuberculosis. In 1962 he succeeded Bobby Robson in the England team and followed Jimmy Armfield as captain in 1963-4.

In 1966 he completed a remarkable hat-trick of climbing the Wembley steps to collect a trophy for a third successive year: 1964, the FA Cup with West Ham; 1965, the European Cup Winners' Cup; and 1966, the World Cup as captain of England after the 4-2 victory over West Germany.

Moore played 545 League matches for West Ham before switching to Fulham late in his career. In his first season at Craven Cottage he played a major part in steering Fulham to their only FA Cup final. Ironically they were beaten at Wembley by West Ham.

Bobby was following a career in broadcasting after flirting with managerial jobs at Oxford and Southend when he died from cancer at 51. The whole of English football mourned the loss of one of its greatest players.

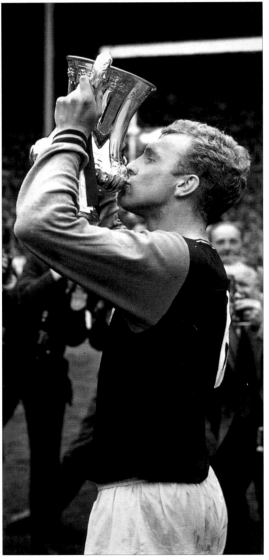

Bobby Moore kisses the FA Cup after leading West Ham to victory in 1964, the first part of a remarkable Wembley hat-trick.

This was my year

One match stands out above all others in my memory of the 1963-4 season. West Ham were drawn to face Manchester United in the FA Cup semi-final at Hillsborough. We were supposed just to play a walk-on part against Cup-holders United, who had the likes of Bobby Charlton, Denis Law and a young Irishman called George Best in their team.

It was an atrocious afternoon, with non-stop rain turning the pitch into a quagmire. We managed to produce the greatest form of our lives, and won 3-1 to book a place in the final at Wembley.

A few weeks later I was named Footballer of the Year, and I am convinced that it was being in the spotlight in that semi-final that clinched it for me. I had to go to collect the award on my own, 48 hours before the final, because of a curfew set by manager Ron Greenwood.

The final against Second Division Preston, including 17-year-old Howard Kendall, was a big anti-climax. We failed to play to anything like our best, and we struggled to beat Preston 3-2. I have to admit we were a little fortunate to clinch victory with a late headed goal by that great West Ham loyalist Ronnie Boyce.

What a pity the game against Manchester United was not the final. People would then have seen us produce the sort of storming form that carried us to the European Cup Winners' Cup final in a classic match against Munich 1860 a year later.

Another personal highspot of that season was establishing myself in the England team to the point where Alf Ramsey invited me to take over from Jimmy Armfield as the captain. No footballer can have a greater honour.

I remember the first game in which I led out England coincided with the first victory under Alf Ramsey's management. We beat Czechoslovakia 4-2 in Bratislava, and that was when we first started to believe that we could win the World Cup. Two years later that dream also came true.

My Dream Team

GORDON BANKS

JOHN GREIG   **MIKE ENGLAND**   **DAVE MACKAY**   **RAY WILSON**

JIM BAXTER   **BOBBY CHARLTON**   **JOHNNY HAYNES**

GEORGE BEST   **DENIS LAW**   **JIMMY GREAVES**

WHAT THE PLAYERS SAY...

Of the hundreds of defenders that played against me during my career, I pick Bobby Moore as the greatest of them all. He was very determined but always fair, and a wonderful ambassador for English football. **– PELE**

The word 'great' is much over-used in football, but where Bobby Moore was concerned it was an understatement. Nobody could read the game better, and he was an absolute master at being in the right place at the right time. **– ALAN MULLERY**

Bobby was weak in the air and pretty slow. Yet his positional sense and composure under pressure were such that he became a defensive master. I'm proud to have been on the same pitch as him, and to have had him as a close pal. **– JIMMY GREAVES**

It was harder deciding which players to leave out than which to select. I have confined myself to footballers I played with or against, which explains why past masters like Stanley Matthews, Tom Finney, Duncan Edwards and John Charles have not made the team.

The first thing I had to decide on was a formation, and I plumped for the 4-3-3 system that brought England the World Cup in 1966. I had no problems picking Gordon Banks between the posts. In all the games we played together for England I can count his mistakes on one hand. Pat Jennings and Peter Shilton would have been my stand-by goalkeepers.

Right-back gave me a lot of trouble, and in the end I went for Scotland's versatile John Greig. He always impressed me with his composure, and he made his presence felt in whichever position he played. I have paired him with Ray Wilson, who was a real class act.

My central defenders are Welshman Mike England and dynamic Scot Dave Mackay. England stood like a Welsh mountain in the middle of Tottenham's defence. He was powerful in the air, and had delicate skills for such a big man. I appreciate that I do not have a ball-winner in midfield, but I will be looking for the mighty Mackay to drive forward and win the ball for us. He will also have the captain's armband.

I have a trio of majestic passers of the ball in midfield in 'Slim' Jim Baxter, Bobby Charlton and Johnny Haynes. In his peak years with Rangers, Baxter was as skilful a player on the ball as I have ever seen. Bobby Charlton could frighten the life out of any defence with his long-range power shooting, and Johnny Haynes could land a ball on a handkerchief from 40 yards. He was a magnificent servant for Fulham, and would have been a world star if he had gone to Italy when he had the chance.

I considered having my old Fulham mate Alan Mullery in midfield as a ball-winner, but elected instead to leave that job to Mackay so that Haynes can patrol in the middle and open up the defence with those inch-perfect passes of his.

It will amaze me if anybody can leave George Best out of any post-war British selection. He was the greatest British player of my generation, and gave me a few chasings in my time. He was fast, brave, two-footed and could make the ball sit up and talk.

I have paired my two favourite strikers to grab the goals, Denis Law and Jimmy Greaves. On their own, they were untouchable. Together, they would be impossible to contain.

Moore, who captained England in a record-equalling 90 matches, made 545 League appearances for West Ham before finishing his playing days across London at Fulham.

Collins, a giant of a player despite standing at just 5ft 3in, helped Leeds reach the 1965 FA Cup final at the age of 34.

Wee Bobby, who made 31 appearances for Scotland, was like a pocket battleship in the Leeds United midfield.

Bobby Collins

Born: Glasgow, 16 February 1931.

Honours: Wee Bobby, just 5ft 3in tall, was a giant in football boots. He won a full house of Scottish medals in ten years with Celtic before joining Everton in 1958-9.

Don Revie signed him as his midfield general for Leeds in 1962, and he had his most memorable season in 1964-5 when, at the age of 34, he helped Leeds reach the FA Cup final, was recalled to the Scottish team after an absence of six years and was elected Footballer of the Year.

He made a total of 31 appearances for Scotland after the selectors blindly ignored him in what seemed almost a punishment for crossing o'er the border to display his skills.

Bobby later played for Bury and Morton, and during a career that spanned 22 seasons he scored 154 League goals. At the end of his career at the age of 41, he started coaching with Oldham and had a spell in Australian football.

He was like a pocket-battleship in midfield, fiercely competitive and a master tactician. His career seemed finished in October 1965, when a tackle by a Torino defender broke his thigh bone. But it was typical of his fighting spirit that he was back in action seven months later. He was a remarkably accurate passer of the ball, and could land it to a team-mate's feet from 40 yards.

This was my year

There was a lot of heartache mixed in with the glory of my season as Footballer of the Year. Leeds went so close to a League and FA Cup double, but finally finished up with nothing. That was very hard to take after all the effort we had poured into the season.

Don Revie had bought me from Everton three years earlier to act as a sort of minder and motivator for his young prospects, such as Billy Bremner, Norman Hunter and Paul Reaney. Don called me his Little General. I was determined to prove Everton wrong in letting me go.

We got a lot of criticism as we battled our way out of the Second Division. Our determination was interpreted as dirty play, but we were just very competitive. Manchester United pipped us to the League championship in 1965 on goal difference, but we had the consolation of beating them in an FA Cup semi-final replay and booking our place at Wembley for a meeting with Bill Shankly's Liverpool.

I was proud to be the first Scot to collect the Footballer of the Year award two days before the final, but then had the disappointment of not performing at my best. We did not really get into top gear throughout the game, and it proved too big an occasion for some of our more inexperienced players. We managed to cling on for extra time, but then an Ian St John goal gave Liverpool a victory that, in truth, they deserved. I have to be honest and admit that Wembley was never my favourite ground. It was something of a jinx place as far as I was concerned.

Later that year I thought my playing days were over when I was scythed down by a diabolical tackle in Turin. My left thigh was broken, but just seven months later I was back in the First Division with Leeds thanks to a career-saving operation in Italy by Professor Re.

I had been written off, but managed to extend my career by another six years.

My Dream Team

GORDON BANKS

GEORGE YOUNG   JOHN CHARLES   RAY WILSON

BILLY BREMNER   BOBBY CHARLTON

KENNY DALGLISH

STANLEY MATTHEWS   TOMMY LAWTON   DENIS LAW   GEORGE BEST

My formative years in football were spent at Celtic, where we were taught that skill counted above all else and that once you combined inspiration with perspiration you were on the right road for success. The team I have selected here is packed with players who were all immensely skilled.

To prove I'm not a biased Scot, my British team is made up of five Englishmen, fours Scots, one Welshman and one Irishman.

Gordon Banks, Bobby Charlton and Ray Wilson were all members of the victorious England 1966 World Cup team, each of them with exceptional talent and capable of performing at their best on the greatest stage. I also gave serious consideration to the late Bobby Moore, but finally decided on my ex-Leeds pal, Welshman John Charles, for the centre-half position. Big John was a player of outstanding ability whether in the No. 5 or No. 9 shirt, and could score goals, make goals and was a magnificent defender. He was one of the greatest headers of the ball I have seen.

I had to have a Scot in my defence, and had no hesitation in selecting George Young at right-back, even though he played for the 'auld enemy', Rangers! I played against George on many occasions. It was difficult for any player to get past him. His tackling was stunning, and he was a wonderful captain for both Rangers and Scotland.

My old Leeds partner Billy Bremner is included in the midfield alongside Bobby Charlton. I saw

Billy develop from being a raw youngster at Elland Road into a tremendous all-round midfielder. He was noted for the competitive edge to his game and his ability to win the ball, but he was also a fine positional player and was often in the right place at the right time to snatch crucial goals.

Kenny Dalglish was not only one of the best goalscorers to come out of Scotland, but also one of the best providers and, therefore, I would play him just behind my front four. And what a front four! There would be the magic of Stanley Matthews and the brilliance of George Best on the wings, and waiting in the middle would be two of the greatest finishers of all time in Tommy Lawton and Denis Law. I first saw Matthews play when I was ten years old in 1941. It was an unforgettable experience, and I then had the pleasure of playing against him in the 1958-9 season in England. He was absolutely brilliant even though nearing 50. He would provide perfect crosses for Lawton and Law, both powerful in the air and on the ground.

Then there's George Best on the left wing. He could turn full-backs inside out with his twisting, jinking runs, could score goals, create goals, get back and defend when necessary and could look after himself. George was the complete player.

My final selection is that of Jock Stein as manager. What he achieved with Celtic, winning nine League championships plus the European Cup with players from within a 30-mile radius of Glasgow, was one of the finest feats in football.

WHAT THE PLAYERS SAY...

I learned a lot from playing with Bobby, and considered him one of the greatest midfield players in British football. He could read a game better than anybody, and his passes could slice open the tightest defence.   **– BILLY BREMNER**

Bobby has to take a lot of the credit for getting the Leeds show on the road back in the days when Don Revie had just taken over. He gave us discipline and direction in midfield, and was prominent in our Second Division promotion team.

– JACK CHARLTON

He was not only one of the most skilful midfield players around in the 1960s but also one of the most competitive. He had a will to win that rubbed off on the rest of the Leeds United players.

– IAN CALLAGHAN

Collins, a fiercely competitive midfield player, showed his resilience by coming back from an horrific injury.

Bobby Charlton

Born: Ashington, 11 October 1937.

Honours: Sir Bobby, knighted for his services to football, set what were two club records with Manchester United during his distinguished career: 198 goals in 606 League matches. His extraordinary honours haul after surviving the 1958 Munich air disaster included winner's medals in the World Cup (1966), European Cup (1968), League championship '57 '65 '67), and FA Cup (1963).

He holds the scoring record for England with 49 goals in 106 internationals. He was voted both FWA Footballer of the Year and European Footballer of the Year for 1966. Bobby was dynamic for England as a young, blond left-winger, played as a goalscoring inside-forward and then dropped back into midfield for his greatest days as a balding schemer with a lethal long-range shot.

He was briefly player-manager of Preston, and lifted his goals tally to 206 before retiring to go into the travel and coaching-schools business. Sir Bobby is now a director at Old Trafford.

His elder brother, Jack, won 35 England caps at centre-half and they both played in the 1966 World Cup-winning team. Two years later Bobby captained United to European Cup glory at Wembley when his two goals helped secure a dramatic 4-1 extra-time victory over Benfica.

Bobby Charlton salutes the crowd after making his 606th and last League appearance for Manchester United in 1973.

Bobby Charlton survived the Munich air disaster to captain Manchester United to European Cup victory over Benfica in 1968.

This was my year

If I am asked to name the outstanding moment of the season in which I won the Footballer of the Year award I can only say it was the whole World Cup campaign culminating in England lifting the trophy at Wembley in that memorable final against West Germany.

Manchester United were doing fine, but the World Cup win has become part of sporting history and, to this day, remains a main topic of conversation wherever I travel around the world.

Geoff Hurst, like me, is remembered for being a member of Sir Alf Ramsey's triumphant team, and his three goals. It is every footballer's dream to play for his country. It is a bigger dream to play in the World Cup. One dreams about winning the trophy, but it only happens to a few.

I did not set out on my career at Manchester United in 1953 dreaming of such heights. It just came to be in 1966 that England had a good team – the right players coming together at the right time – and we won. Geoff's shot that came down off the crossbar was a goal if anyone is interested in my opinion, but it did not matter anyway in a 4-2 victory. The referee and the Russian linesman did not have any say on the other three goals.

As a survivor of the Munich air crash and a Busby Babe, 1966 was memorable for me.

In my career I won two League championship medals and an FA Cup winner's medal. I collected 106 England caps, Manchester United reached the semi-finals of the European Cup in 1966, and then went on to win the trophy two years later on that wonderful night at Wembley against Benfica.

We had been League champions in 1965 and were to win again in 1967. I have had memorable moments galore, scoring twice on my debut against Charlton in 1956 and scoring on my international debut two years later against Scotland. But the 1966 World Cup is an extra special memory.

CARLING

My Dream Team

GORDON BANKS

DANNY McGRAIN   JOHN CHARLES   BOBBY MOORE   RAY WILSON

DANNY BLANCHFLOWER   DUNCAN EDWARDS   JOHNNY HAYNES   JIM BAXTER

GEORGE BEST   DENIS LAW

Boyhood heroes Stanley Matthews and Tom Finney would have been automatic choices if I had decided on a team with wingers but, as with Sir Alf Ramsey's all-conquering side of 1966, my selection can be another set of Wingless Wonders.

With the exception of right-back, the names of my team roll automatically off my tongue and I am happy with my 11.

Billy Wright could have come in at the back. He was England's centre-half and skipper when I made my international debut in 1958, and was a fine, commanding player. But I have to look beyond Bill and all the England centre-halves to the one and only John Charles.

He was a magnificent player for Wales, Leeds and Juventus, and is perhaps not such a familiar name to English supporters because his peak years were spent in Italy where he was idolised as The Gentle Giant. I am more than happy with Big John Charles and the immaculate Bobby Moore playing at the centre of my defence.

Many Scots came to mind when I was thinking of my team. Jinking Jimmy Johnstone, for instance, could have got a call. And Bobby Lennox. Lots of goals there. John White, so tragically killed by lightning while at the peak of his career with the exceptional Tottenham team of the early 1960s, was a great Scottish player, as was the lionheart Dave Mackay.

Ryan Giggs was one of the modern players that I considered. I reckon he will come into the frame in a year or two. Take my tip – he will become an automatic first choice for any future Dream Team, but at the moment he is crowded out by a queue of stars from the past who can be considered in the light of their entire career. Ryan has still got a long way to go.

Once I had decided to play without a pair of recognised wingers, I settled for a 4-4-2 formation.

Gordon Banks will always be my No. 1 goalkeeper. Joining him and Bobby Moore from the 1966 World Cup defence would be Ray Wilson, the best left-back I have ever seen. Right-back was the position that gave me the one little problem, but Danny McGrain was a class act and would be an excellent partner for Ray.

Duncan Edwards would come forward and score goals for me. Johnny Haynes, a marvellous England captain and inspirational player, could find the net as well as laying on perfect, long-range passes. The magical Jim Baxter would float through for goals and can conduct affairs from midfield. With Danny Blanchflower adding his creativity, the side would ooze confidence and class.

I was privileged to play with Denis Law and George Best at their peak and I have no hesitation in nominating them for the two front berths. They are certain to be united!

WHAT THE PLAYERS SAY...

When you looked up and saw Bobby Charlton coming out on to the pitch with you, you grew taller and more confident. In all my travels around the world I never found a place where he was not instantly recognised. He was our greatest footballing ambassador. – **GORDON BANKS**

It was not only his performances on the pitch but also his demeanour that made him loved and respected throughout the world of football. I always found him the perfect gentleman and he was a magnificent player.

– **FRANZ BECKENBAUER**

Bobby Charlton was not only a wonderful footballer but also a wonderful sportsman. I played against him several times and always considered it a privilege to be on the same pitch as him. He was great for England and great for football.

– **EUSEBIO**

Charlton made his England debut in 1958 and went on score a record 49 goals in 106 matches, his greatest moment coming in the 1966 World Cup final victory.

Jack Charlton

Born: Ashington, 8 May 1935.

Honours: Big Jack 'the Giraffe' played a club record 629 League matches for Leeds between 1952 and 1973 before becoming a successful club manager and then a walking, talking legend as manager of the Republic of Ireland football team.

He stood like a tower in the middle of the Leeds defence, playing a crucial role in their triumphs that included two League championships, one FA Cup success and two European Fairs Cup victories.

The older brother of Bobby Charlton, he followed him into the England team and they were both key members of the 1966 World Cup-winning team.

He was 31 before he won his first cap, and was an uncompromising centre-half alongside the cultured Bobby Moore over a span of 35 international matches.

Management brought him even greater success, and he was in charge at Middlesbrough and then Sheffield Wednesday before quitting football to concentrate on hunting, shooting and fishing, and a career in television.

But he was soon back as manager of Newcastle for a less-than-happy stay at St James's Park. Then, in 1986, he started his astonishing nine-year love affair with Ireland as he turned the Republic from whipping boys into one of the most respected teams in Europe, leading them to the 1990 and 1994 World Cup finals.

This was my year

To be honest, all my seasons at Leeds merge into one and it is difficult to separate them. We were always in the running for one or more prizes in those incredible years under Don Revie when we were not the best-loved team in the land but certainly one of the most effective. What I do know is that I collected my Footballer of the Year award the season after my brother had picked up the trophy. I don't suppose that will happen again.

Something I do vividly recall from the 1966-7 season is what was for me a painful defeat of England by Scotland at Wembley. They beat us 3-2 and I spent much of the game hobbling in attack with a broken toe. We played most of the match with only eight fit men and the Jocks had the cheek to claim they were the world champions after their win!

It was our first defeat in a run of 20 matches including the 1966 World Cup final victory. I had the satisfaction of banging in one of our goals.

Leeds were on the way to the European Fairs Cup final by the time I collected the Footballer of the Year award. We beat Kilmarnock in the semi-finals, and had to wait until the start of the following season before meeting Dynamo Zagreb in the final.

They beat us 2-0 on aggregate, but we made up for it the following season by beating the Hungarian side Ferencvaros in another delayed final . . . and I seem to remember that it was a big feller wearing the No. 5 Leeds shirt who scored the deciding goal!

Later in the season we won the League championship with what was then a record 67 points, with Bill Shankly's outstanding Liverpool team six points adrift in second place. Nobody could say we had not deserved it after twice finishing runners-up, with Manchester United pipping us on goal average in 1965 and Liverpool beating us by six points in 1966.

Jack Charlton, a tower of strength in the Leeds defence, shows his aerial power by out-jumping Tottenham's Martin Chivers.

My Dream Team

GORDON BANKS

GEORGE COHEN   JOHN CHARLES   BOBBY MOORE   RAY WILSON

JIMMY JOHNSTONE   BOBBY CHARLTON   BRYAN ROBSON   TOM FINNEY

GEORGE BEST   DENIS LAW

The first names on my team sheet are John Charles and Bobby Moore, my skipper in the England 1966 World Cup-winning side. Bobby would captain my side in a 4-4-2 formation.

I used to drum into my team-mates at Leeds that big John Charles, the Gentle Giant, was the outstanding player of our era. He scored 46 goals in a season for Leeds. He could play up front, at the back or in midfield. I played with him when he returned to Leeds from Juventus, where he was voted the Italian Footballer of the Year. To me he was, and still is today, just awesome. He was past his best when he came back to Elland Road but was still a class above most other players.

A lot of old pros tell me that Neil Franklin was the finest of all footballing centre-halves, but Big John not only had excellent skills but was also physically imposing. I recall seeing Franklin play at Newcastle when I was a lad, and he seemed quite small to me.

There is only one goalkeeper to merit my attention – Gordon Banks. He had a wonderful pair of hands, instinctive positional sense and made difficult saves look easy.

For full-backs I go with the pair who played alongside me for England in 1966, George Cohen and Ray Wilson, but I could equally have gone with my Leeds defensive partners, Paul Reaney and Terry Cooper. I recall that Terry was rated good enough to be named in the best world team in 1970 after his World Cup performances in Mexico.

You have to look at full-backs from an attacking viewpoint as well as purely defensive and Cohen and Wilson were as good as there have been. Scotland's Danny McGrain was a fine player but no better than George Cohen.

I want two wingers in my team and I plump for Jimmy Johnstone on the right although I could have picked Stanley Matthews. Jimmy played in a difficult era for wingers when the game was switching to the 4-3-3 and 4-4-2 wingless systems, but he jinked his way through games and beat people and crossed the ball. Finney has always been a big favourite of mine, and is an automatic choice.

My kid brother Bobby was a naturally-gifted player. He and Bryan Robson could do equally well on the left or the right. Bobby was well-balanced and had a tremendous shot with either foot. The strange thing about him is that he never knew when he was having a bad game. The worse he played, the more he tried. I remember once, when Ray Wilson was injured in an England game, Bobby dropped back into the left-back spot and did a thoroughly competent job. He actually tackled people! 'Our kid' would figure in any team of all-time greats that I picked.

The pairing of George Best and Denis Law excites me. I liked Denis immensely as a player. If I had been looking for a big lad to play an old-fashioned centre-forward role, I would have gone for Nat Lofthouse, but Best and Law will do for me.

WHAT THE PLAYERS SAY...

Big Jack was not the prettiest sight on a football field and did not have the grace of his brother Bobby. But he was a magnificent competitor and an intimidating barrier in the middle of the Leeds and England defences.

– FRANK McLINTOCK

Jack could be a real moaner at times, but it was always because he cared. He was a great man to have on your side when the going got tough and he gave Leeds United wonderful service.

– NORMAN HUNTER

The motivating powers that Jack had as a player served him well as a manager, and he had the respect of all his players because he had been there, done that. I have never known a manager in football as idolised as Jack was in Ireland.

– MAURICE SETTERS

Big Jack, who won 35 caps for England despite winning his first at the age of 31, gets the better of Tottenham's Alan Gilzean.

George Best

Born: Belfast, 22 May 1946.

Honours: George had ten sensational years with Manchester United, when his stunning skills on the pitch and his controversial behaviour off it meant he was continually in the headlines. He scored 137 goals in 361 League matches for United and won two League championship medals and a European Cup winner's medal. He was voted not only the FWA Footballer of the Year for 1968 but also the European Footballer of the Year.

He retired in 1973 following a series of altercations at Old Trafford, where he suddenly missed the guiding hand of his mentor Sir Matt Busby. But the pull of the game he graced with such style was too great and he returned to play for a string of clubs, including Stockport County, Cork Celtic, Los Angeles Aztecs, Fulham, Hibernian, Golden Bay and San José Earthquakes.

He made his debut for Northern Ireland in the same 1964 match as goalkeeper Pat Jennings. But while Pat went on to win 119 caps, George collected only 37. Since hanging up his boots, he has remained regularly in the public eye as a broadcaster and with a popular road show alongside another of the great entertainers, Rodney Marsh.

And, of course, George being George, he has continued to be surrounded by acres of controversy, much of it fuelled by the demon drink.

Best, who won just 37 caps for Northern Ireland, shows off the skills that grouped him with players such as Pele and Puskas.

The Irish genius, always in the spotlight on and off the pitch, hit 137 goals in 361 League games in ten years at Old Trafford.

This was my year

The month of May 1968 was, to say the least, pretty special for me. I collected my Footballer of the Year award two days before the FA Cup final, helped Manchester United beat Real Madrid in the European Cup semi-final the following week and, on 29 May, played in the European Cup final against Benfica at Wembley. That was the match of a lifetime, and our victory after extra time meant so much to everybody because we knew that it was the one thing that the boss, Matt Busby, wanted above all else.

What I recall most of all from the match was my extra-time goal. I had made up my mind that if I got the chance I would do something really spectacular, like take the ball round the goalkeeper and then flick it up and head it into the net. Passing the ball to myself and then scoring, that was my dream. But when it came to it the little imp that was always inside me battling to get out, stayed under control and I made do with a

fairly ordinary goal. Even now, all these years later, the showman in me is disappointed that I did not attempt something unique. But it was enough that we won the match for Matt Busby on what was an incredibly emotional night.

It was during that season of 1967-8 that I played what was probably my finest game for Northern Ireland.

We beat a very good Scotland side 1-0 at Windsor Park and everybody was telling me afterwards that it was the greatest individual display they had ever seen. I think that must have played a big part in getting me the vote of the football writers in a year when there were a lot of outstanding candidates.

Later in the year I went one better by getting elected European Footballer of the Year, following my Manchester United team-mates Denis Law and Bobby Charlton as a winner of the award. Yes, 1968 was quite a year.

My Dream Team

PAT JENNINGS

DANNY McGRAIN   **BILLY McNEILL**   **BOBBY MOORE**   **RAY WILSON**

PAT CRERAND   **BOBBY CHARLTON**

KENNY DALGLISH   **DENIS LAW**   **JIMMY GREAVES**   **RYAN GIGGS**

There is a strong influence on my team from the great United side of the 1960s when we were champions of Europe. And Sir Matt Busby would be the manager. He would have the respect of all the players, and would not try to restrain any of them with coaching mumbo-jumbo. Sir Matt used to encourage us to play it off the cuff. He knew what we could do, and let us get on with it.

Paddy Crerand is a key man in midfield. He was never given the credit he deserved for making that 1960s United team tick. He used to make up for a lack of speed with his instinctive positional sense, and his passing was just tremendous – 50-yard balls right into your path. Bobby Charlton will be playing behind the front three, unleashing those bombing long-range shots of his. Bobby and I were never the closest of team-mates, but I always had the greatest respect for his ability. It was the midfield linking of Crerand and Charlton that made that United team something special.

The one and only Denis Law will be up front in partnership with another outstanding Scot in Kenny Dalglish and the little goal-scoring genius Jimmy Greaves. No defence would feel safe with these three operating together. Denis, so fast and lethal anywhere near goal, was desperately unlucky with injuries and I admired the way he hid his personal disappointment at missing out on the European Cup final because of a knee problem.

Playing in attack with Law, Dalglish and Greavsie I have a modern Old Trafford idol in Ryan Giggs, one of the few players in the game today who would have got a place in Matt Busby's side. I like the way he takes on defenders, controls the ball and unsettles opponents with his pace and skill. He has got over all that rubbish about being the 'second George Best' and is now recognised as a brilliant player in his own right.

I select Pat Jennings as my goalkeeper simply because I never saw him have a bad game. There were a few times when United were playing Spurs that I managed to get the ball past him, and that used to give me a lot of satisfaction because I knew I was scoring against a master of a goalkeeper. Pat and I made our debuts together for Northern Ireland in 1964, and his displays for club and country were always out of the top drawer.

Billy McNeill, an immovable rock in defence for Scotland and Celtic's superb 1967 European Cup-winning team, will be my commanding centre-half alongside the greatest of all defenders, Bobby Moore. I had the pleasure of playing with Bobby at the end of our careers at Fulham when he said to me, 'We are now at that stage when we have to let our heads do the work our legs used to do.'

Bobby would captain the side, and my full-backs would be Danny McGrain and Ray Wilson who were both composed defenders with the ability to attack. It would be a team that would entertain, which is what football should be about.

Best celebrates one of the finest moments of his career after helping Manchester United win the 1968 European Cup.

Tony Book

Born: Bath, 9 September 1934.

Honours: Tony Book had a storybook entry into League football, not making his debut until he was 29. He had spent most of his career as a part-timer with his local club Bath City, combining football with his job as a bricklayer.

His coach at Bath was Malcolm Allison, who took him to Home Park when he became manager of Plymouth Argyle in 1964. Two years later, when appointed coach at Manchester City, Allison brought his right-back and captain with him to Maine Road.

Book was City skipper as they challenged the supremacy of neighbours Manchester United, winning the League championship, the FA Cup, League Cup and European Cup Winners' Cup in the space of three years. Book made 244 League appearances for City, and continued to serve them until 1996.

He had four years as manager, and was a long-serving member of the coaching staff. The loud, flamboyant Allison and the quiet, modest Book made a contrasting couple, but they brought the best out of each other, and Big Mal described the £17,500 fee that City paid for Book as 'the transfer bargain of the century'. Book's personality was reflected in his play. He went about his work in a quiet, unobtrusive way but was rarely beaten in man-to-man situations. He had a biting tackle and neat distribution.

Former bricklayer Book used his wall-building experiences in the Manchester City defence, where he played 244 League matches.

This was my year

The amazing thing is that I did not play until the January because of an Achilles tendon injury the year I shared the award with Dave Mackay. Although it was the only tie in the 50-year history of the FWA, Dave and I both collected a trophy. It was part of a fairy-tale story for me.

I was 32 years old when Malcolm Allison took me from Plymouth to Manchester City. In fact, the season before my award I played every game as City won the League championship, but any hope of my getting considered for the award that year disappeared because of the brilliance of George Best as Manchester United so memorably won the European Cup.

I returned to the side in time for an FA Cup tie against Newcastle in January 1969 and City went through to the final where we beat Leicester 1-0. That took us into the European Cup Winners' Cup, which we won the following season by defeating Gornik Zabrze 2-1 in the final in Vienna. It was an unbelievable time for me when you think that I had been playing non-League football just a few seasons earlier.

I played around 300 games for City before I hung up my boots at the age of 40. I carried on my association with the club for years after that on the coaching side and as manager. The memory of season 1968-9 and being voted Footballer of the Year stands out as my proudest memory.

I have heard the story of how two votes arrived second post, too late to be included in the poll that resulted in a tie.

Dennis Signy has told me the secret of who got the votes will stay with him to the grave. I am glad that Dave Mackay and I don't know if there could have been an outright winner if the postman had delivered them earlier.

I was privileged to share the award with a great player like Dave, who will feature prominently in my Dream Team.

My Dream Team

GORDON BANKS

JIMMY ARMFIELD   JOHN CHARLES   BOBBY MOORE   RAY WILSON

TOM FINNEY   DUNCAN EDWARDS   DAVE MACKAY   GEORGE BEST

JIMMY GREAVES   KENNY DALGLISH

John Charles was a colossus in my book and fully merits inclusion at the heart of the defence in my 4-4-2 formation, even though he could play with equal ability up front. Tom Finney is another with the capacity to play in more than one position, and is up there with Charles as a legend of the game.

Gordon Banks is the No. 1 choice between the sticks for his all-round goalkeeping ability. His agility was phenomenal, as we are continually reminded with the TV replays of his save from Pele in the 1970 World Cup.

Jimmy Armfield was a classy right-back who captained England with distinction and, as an old full-back myself, I admired both Jimmy and Ray Wilson, particularly the way they dealt with the tricky and flying wingers they used to encounter week after week.

I toyed with the idea of playing Alan Hansen between them, but decided in the end to go for a combination of John Charles and the unmatchable Bobby Moore. Just imagine Bobby operating behind the trio of Armfield, Charles and Wilson, picking up the pieces, taking the ball out and delivering immaculate, long passes. It would have been a piece of cake for him.

Duncan Edwards and Dave Mackay, patrolling in central midfield, would be a blend of power and energy that would bring dynamic life to the engine room of the team. Finney, as I have said, could play on the wing or up front and would be one of the first names on any manager's team sheet. Then there is George Best. Well, I played against him and have seen his ability at close range. They say Denis Law was deadly in the box and so-and-so could do this or that better than anybody in a particular role, but Best on his day could do everything. He could terrorise defences, show pace, score goals. You name it, he could do it.

Denis Law, another key man in that outstanding United team of the 1960s and 1970s that we at City were always chasing (and sometimes overtaking) was, in fact, in my thoughts for selection. He came into my mind along with Colin 'Nijinsky' Bell, who had an extra pair of lungs, Bobby Charlton and Jim Baxter. Slim Jim could make a ball talk.

Kenny Dalglish would lead the attack. Kenny, ever bright and alert, knew how to hurt defences and where the goal was – even when facing the wrong way. There has never been anybody to touch him for shielding a ball.

Playing alongside him in a deadly partnership I will have Jimmy Greaves, who could poach goals out of nowhere. He was deadly in front of goal, had pace and, one to one with a goalkeeper, you could back him 99 times out of 100.

Tony Book made up for lost time after his late arrival at Manchester City at the age of 29, helping them win four major trophies in three years.

Dave Mackay

Born: Edinburgh, 14 November 1934.

Honours: Dave Mackay played the game with a competitive spirit that made him famed and feared throughout the game. His puffed-out chest was his trademark, and his tackles were among the hardest ever witnessed on a football field.

He represented Scotland at schoolboy, Under-23 and full international level (22 full caps in all). With Hearts he won Scottish League Cup, Scottish Cup and Scottish League Championship medals.

Then, after joining Tottenham for £30,000 in March 1959, he won three FA Cup winner's medals (the last as captain in 1967), a League championship medal and a European Cup Winners' Cup medal, although missing the final because of injury.

Later, with Derby County, he won a Second Division championship medal, before moving to Swindon Town as player manager for two seasons.

As a manager – taking over at the Baseball Ground from his old boss Brian Clough – he steered Derby to the First Division title in 1974-5. He also managed Swindon Town, Nottingham Forest, Walsall, Doncaster Rovers and Birmingham City, and had a successful coaching career in the Middle East.

His greatest victory was over adversity. He twice made comebacks after breaking a leg. Not for nothing was he known as the Miracle Man of football.

Dave Mackay holds aloft the Second Division trophy after leading Derby County to promotion in convincing fashion in 1969.

The hard-tackling Scot, who made 22 international appearances, later managed Derby's championship winning team.

This was my year

To appreciate my winning of the Footballer of the Year award with Derby, you need to know how my Tottenham career finished. Spurs were beaten 3-1 by Manchester City in my last game for the club and when I say beaten I mean beaten. Frannie Lee, Mike Summerbee and company won on merit that day and set me thinking that I could not do the job I thought I could do in the old First Division. There were no excuses from me or Spurs for the way City won.

I think I had played well that season and am sure that no one at White Hart Lane was thinking of getting rid of me, but I went to the manager Bill Nicholson and told him I thought it was time to move on.

That was how I came to move to Derby County in 1968, to link up with Brian Clough in the Second Division and finish the season collecting a Footballer of the Year statuette in the only tie in the history of the competition alongside Tony

Book. It is a fact that I decided to go down a division to make life easier for myself and, in truth, it was very, very easy for me compared with the role I had in my swashbuckling days at Tottenham.

Cloughie asked me to play a cleaning-up job at the back of the Derby defence, and I found it something of a doddle playing alongside the then very promising centre-half Roy McFarland.

It was like a dream come true to collect the trophy as County won the Second Division title with seven points to spare over runners-up Crystal Palace, and this when there were only two points for a win. I was the golden oldie playing at the back in Cloughie's young side. They were memorable days for me.

I reckon Bill Nicholson must have looked at the way I slotted in at the back and thought to himself, 'I should have done that with him at Spurs.' That would have been interesting!

My Dream Team

	GORDON BANKS		
DANNY McGRAIN	JOHN CHARLES	BOBBY MOORE	RAY WILSON
	ROY KEANE	JIM BAXTER	
GEORGE BEST	ALAN SHEARER	DENIS LAW	TOM FINNEY

My Dream Team includes two modern-day players I have never played against in Roy Keane and Alan Shearer. They feature in a 4-2-4 formation, with two wingers.

Jimmy Johnstone got near my team, although when I played against him I rarely got near him and could not catch him. He was so quick off the mark. I also admired wee Willy Henderson. But both have to make way for the one and only George Best on the right and the versatile Tom Finney out on the left.

It hurts me that there is no place for two former Tottenham favourites – the late John White and the goal-scoring genius Jimmy Greaves – but you can only play 11 at one time.

I have seen three outstanding goalkeepers in my time – no Scottish ones I regret to say – but I give the verdict to Gordon Banks over Peter Shilton and Pat Jennings.

Full-backs are the least heralded players in the footballing world, but I had no hesitation in selecting Danny McGrain and Ray Wilson as the ideal combination.

When I was with Tottenham we travelled to Turin for a match against a Juventus side fielding John Charles at centre-forward. He was world class in that position, just as he was at centre-half. He was the main instigator of their 1-0 victory. The Gentle Giant made a big impression and fully justifies his place in my Dream Team.

Bobby Moore, unflappable Bobby, would skipper the side. He was a great reader of the game and always seemed to have so much time to get his work done.

Roy Keane is a marvel. He plays everywhere – at the back, in midfield – and as he gets older he gets better and has calmed down. As for Jim Baxter, he was a fantastic entertainer and had lashings of skill.

Alan Shearer would have the time of his life playing alongside Denis Law, who was a marvellous player, a marvellous goalscorer and a marvellous character. Imagine these two feeding on the crosses of George Best and Tom Finney, who just got my vote ahead of the old master Stanley Matthews.

I remember Spurs beating Preston 6-2 and Finney playing a one-two and going past me like a rocket. I couldn't catch him so I clipped his heels and he went down and hit his head. He had to go off in a daze and I was worried off my game about what I had done to such a great player for whom I had so much respect.

I could have picked half a dozen teams with a similar blend of skill and power, but I am happy with my final selection. I am not sure the opposition would be.

WHAT THE PLAYERS SAY...

I often used to offer up a silent prayer that Dave was on my side and not against me. He was the heart of the great Tottenham team of the early 1960s. We all remember him for his power and competitive spirit, but he was also a highly skilled player. **– JIMMY GREAVES**

Ron Burgess was a great player in the No 6 Tottenham shirt and I never thought I would see better, but then along came Mackay and he was every bit as good. And that's really saying something. He would be worth £10 million by today's values. **– BILL NICHOLSON**

When I stole Dave Mackay from Spurs I had a specific job in mind for him – to give the lead to our youngsters. And they could not have had a more inspiring leader. He gave us stability, strength and character. He was priceless. **– BRIAN CLOUGH**

You could almost hear the bagpipes playing when Dave went into action. He was not a particularly big man but the minute he pulled on a football jersey he would almost visibly grow and that chest of his would expand with pride. **– GEORGE GRAHAM**

Dave Mackay captained Tottenham's 1967 FA Cup winning side before taking over as the motivator in Brian Clough's successful young Derby County side.

A football feast poisoned by hooligans

FOOTBALL in England during the 1970s was two-faced, bringing the best of times and the worst of times. Liverpool and Nottingham Forest walked tall on the European stage, but the game was scarred by the curse of hooliganism which brought continual outbreaks of violence and shame to club terraces.

The decade started with the first £200,000 British transfer deal when Martin Peters moved to Tottenham for cash plus Jimmy Greaves. It finished with Trevor Francis becoming the first £1 million British footballer when he joined Brian Clough's Nottingham Forest from Birmingham City in 1979.

The decade kicked off in a blaze of glory, the flames fanned by arguably the greatest World Cup winning team of them all, Brazil. The faces (and feet) of their flair players became famous across the world as millions of television viewers watched their progress through to the 1970 final and an emphatic 4-1 victory over Italy. Has there been a more potent or poetic attacking force than Jairzinho, Tostao, Pele and Rivelino?

England went into the international wilderness, failing to qualify for the 1974 or 1978 World Cup finals after making a mess of their defence of the title in Mexico in 1970. They went out 3-2 after extra time to West Germany in the quarter-final after throwing away a two-goal lead. The media inquest concluded England had self-destructed. Goalkeeper Peter Bonetti, a late deputy for the suddenly unwell Gordon Banks, was blamed for two of the goals with little allowance being given for his lack of match fitness; he had hardly played competitively since the FA Cup final replay in April. Alf Ramsey was berated for substituting Bobby Charlton and Martin Peters with Norman Hunter and Colin Bell. The manager later revealed he had been saving Charlton for the semi-final.

Sir Alf survived another three years as manager before elimination from the World Cup qualifying tournament by Poland brought about his dismissal. Don Revie took over following a brief spell as caretaker manager by Joe Mercer. Revie, so successful at Leeds, struggled to adjust to the international stage and sensationally walked out on the job in 1977 to take over as the richly rewarded soccer supremo of the United Arab Emirates. 'Deserter Don' screamed the headlines. What upset so many people was the furtive manner in which he chose to make the break after 29 matches, including only 14 wins. He sneaked off for his job interview while the England team were touring South America, and then sold his story to one newspaper. That turned the rest of Fleet Street on him like a pack of wolves.

It was the second biggest story of the decade, beaten in the sensation department by the arrest in Colombia of England skipper Bobby Moore on a trumped-up jewel theft charge on his way to the 1970 World Cup finals. He was released on the eve of the tournament and proceeded to show that there was no better defender in the world.

This was the decade of Johan Cruyff and the Dutch masters from Ajax, of Franz Beckenbauer, Gerd Muller and the Bayern Munich machine, and of Mario Kempes and Argentina. While England struggled to make an impact at international level, the major clubs flourished. Arsenal repeated Tottenham's League and FA Cup double, while Liverpool won everything in sight. Bob Paisley, taking over the Liverpool helm from Bill Shankly, proved that an English team could rule in Europe, a lesson that was learned by Nottingham Forest, who won two successive European Cup finals.

Kevin Keegan went to Hamburg and proved British was best by twice being voted European Footballer of the Year. It was the age of flared trousers and permed hair and a football feast poisoned by the yobs who polluted the terraces.–**Norman Giller**

The Liverpool manager Bob Paisley hoists the European Cup during a six-year spell of English domination of the competition.

CARLING

Who won what

1969-70
League champions: Everton
FA Cup final: Chelsea 2, Leeds United 1 (aet and 2-2 draw)
League Cup final: Manchester City 2, West Bromwich Albion 1
First Division marksman: Jeff Astle (West Brom), 25
Footballer of the Year: Billy Bremner (Leeds United)
Scottish champions: Celtic
Scottish Cup final: Aberdeen 3, Celtic 1
Scottish Player of the Year: Pat Stanton (Hibernian)
European Cup final: Feyenoord 2, Celtic 1 (aet)
Cup Winners' Cup final: Manchester City 2, Gornik Zabrze 1
Fairs Cup final: Anderlecht 3, Arsenal 4 (3-1, 0-3)
European Footballer of the Year: Gerd Muller (Bayern Munich)
World Cup final: Brazil 4, Italy 1

1970-1
League champions: Arsenal
FA Cup final: Arsenal 2, Liverpool 1 (after extra time)
League Cup final: Tottenham 2, Aston Villa 0
First Division marksman: Tony Brown (West Brom), 28
Footballer of the Year: Frank McLintock (Arsenal)
Scottish champions: Celtic
Scottish Cup final: Celtic 2, Rangers 1 (after 1-1 draw)
Scottish Player of the Year: Martin Buchan (Aberdeen)
European Cup final: Ajax 2, Panathinaikos 0
Cup Winners' Cup final: Chelsea 2, Real Madrid 1 (after 1-1 draw)
Fairs Cup final: Juventus 3, Leeds United 3 (2-2, 1-1. Leeds won on the away-goals rule)
European Footballer of the Year: Johan Cruyff (Ajax)

1971-2
League champions: Derby County
FA Cup final: Leeds United 1, Arsenal 0
League Cup final: Stoke City 2, Chelsea 1
First Division marksman: Francis Lee (Man City), 33
Footballer of the Year: Gordon Banks (Stoke City)
Scottish champions: Celtic
Scottish Cup final: Celtic 6, Hibernian 1
Scottish Player of the Year: Dave Smith (Rangers)
European Cup final: Ajax 2, Inter Milan 0
Cup Winners' Cup final: Rangers 3, Dynamo Moscow 2
UEFA Cup: Tottenham 3, Wolves 2 (1-1, 2-1)
European Footballer of the Year: Franz Beckenbauer (Bayern Munich)
European Championship final: W Germany 3, USSR 0

1972-3
League champions: Liverpool
FA Cup final: Sunderland 1, Leeds United 0
League Cup final: Tottenham 1, Norwich City 0
First Division marksman: Bryan Robson (West Ham), 28
Footballer of the Year: Pat Jennings (Tottenham)
Scottish champions: Celtic
Scottish Cup final: Rangers 3, Celtic 2
Scottish Player of the Year: George Connelly (Celtic)
European Cup final: Ajax 1, Juventus 0
Cup Winners' Cup final: AC Milan 1, Leeds United 0
UEFA Cup final: Liverpool 3, Borussia Moenchengladbach 2 (3-0, 0-2)
European Footballer of the Year: Johan Cruyff (Barcelona)

1973-4
League champions: Leeds United
FA Cup final: Liverpool 3, Newcastle United 0
League Cup final: Wolves 2, Manchester City 1
First Division marksman: Mike Channon (So'ton), 21
Footballer of the Year: Ian Callaghan (Liverpool)
Scottish champions: Celtic
Scottish Cup final: Celtic 3, Dundee United 0
Scottish Player of the Year: Scotland World Cup squad
European Cup final: Bayern Munich 4, Atletico Madrid 0 (after a 1-1 draw)
Cup Winners' Cup final: FC Magdeburg 2, AC Milan 0
UEFA Cup final: Feyenoord 4, Tottenham 2 (2-2, 2-0)
European Footballer of the Year: Johan Cruyff (Barcelona)
World Cup final: West Gernany 2, Holland 1

1974-5
League champions: Derby County
FA Cup final: West Ham United 2, Fulham 0
League Cup final: Aston Villa 1, Norwich City 0
First Division marksman: Malcolm Macdonald (Newcastle), 21
Footballer of the Year: Alan Mullery (Fulham)
Scottish champions: Rangers
Scottish Cup final: Celtic 3, Airdrieonians 1
Scottish Player of the Year: Sandy Jardine (Rangers)
European Cup final: Bayern Munich 2, Leeds United 0
Cup Winners' Cup final: Dynamo Kiev 3, Ferencvaros 0
UEFA Cup final: Borussia Moenchengladbach 5, Twente Enschede 1 (0-0, 5-1)
European Footballer of the Year: Oleg Blokhin (Dynamo Kiev)

1975-6
League champions: Liverpool
FA Cup final: Southampton 1, Manchester United 0
League Cup final: Manchester City 2, Newcastle 1
First Division marksman: Ted MacDougall (Norwich), 23
Footballer of the Year: Kevin Keegan (Liverpool)
Scottish champions: Rangers
Scottish Cup final: Rangers 3, Heart of Midlothian 1
Scottish Player of the Year: John Greig (Rangers)
European Cup final: Bayern Munich 1, St Etienne 0
Cup Winners' Cup final: Anderlecht 4, West Ham 2
UEFA Cup final: Liverpool 4, Bruges 3 (3-2, 1-1)
European Footballer of the Year: Franz Beckenbauer (Bayern Munich)
European Championship final: Czechoslovakia 2, West Germany 2 (Czechs won on penalties)

1976-7
League champions: Liverpool
FA Cup final: Manchester United 2, Liverpool 1
League Cup final: Aston Villa 3, Everton 2 (after extra time, following 0-0 and 1-1 draws)
First Division marksmen: Andy Gray (Aston Villa) and Malcolm Macdonald (Arsenal), 25
Footballer of the Year: Emlyn Hughes (Liverpool)

Scottish champions: Celtic
Scottish Cup final: Celtic 1, Rangers 0
Scottish Player of the Year: Danny McGrain (Celtic)
European Cup final: Liverpool 3, Borussia Moenchengladbach 1
Cup Winners' Cup final: Hamburg 2, Anderlecht 0
UEFA Cup final: Juventus 2, Athletic Bilbao 2 (1-0, 1-2, Juventus won on away goals)
European Footballer of the Year: Allan Simonsen (Borussia Moenchengladbach)

1977-8
League champions: Nottingham Forest
FA Cup final: Ipswich Town 1, Arsenal 0
League Cup final: Nottingham Forest 1, Liverpool 0 (after 0-0 draw)
First Division marksman: Bob Latchford (Everton), 30
Footballer of the Year: Kenny Burns (Nottm Forest)
Scottish champions: Rangers
Scottish Cup final: Rangers 2, Aberdeen 1
Scottish Player of the Year: Derek Johnstone (Rangers)
European Cup final: Liverpool 1, FC Bruges 0
Cup Winners' Cup final: Anderlecht 4 Austria/WAC 0
UEFA Cup final: PSV Eindhoven 3, Bastia 0 (0-0 3-0)
European Footballer of the Year: Kevin Keegan (Hamburg)
World Cup final: Argentina 3, Holland 1 (after extra time)

1978-9
League champions: Liverpool
FA Cup final: Arsenal 3, Manchester United 2
League Cup final: Nottingham Forest 3, Southampton 2
First Division marksman: Frank Worthington (Bolton), 24
Footballer of the Year: Kenny Dalglish (Liverpool)
Scottish champions: Celtic
Scottish Cup final: Rangers 3, Hibernian 2 (after two 0-0 draws)
Scottish Player of the Year: Andy Ritchie (Morton)
European Cup final: Nottingham Forest 1, Malmo 0
Cup Winners' Cup final: Barcelona 4, Fortuna Dusseldorf 3 (after extra time)
UEFA Cup final: Borussia Moenchengladbach 2, Red Star Belgrade 1 (1-1, 1-0)
European Footballer of the Year: Kevin Keegan (Hamburg)

Pele in action during his last appearance for Brazil against Yugoslavia in 1971 close to the end of a career in which he scored more than 1,000 goals.

Billy Bremner

Born: Stirling, 9 December 1942.

Honours: Battling Billy was a driving, competitive player who motivated the men around him with his total commitment and determination. He liked to attack from a midfield base, and he snatched many crucial goals by being alert and brave in the penalty area. He had winning midfield partnerships with two outstanding pass-masters at Leeds, Bobby Collins and then Johnny Giles.

Billy scored 92 goals in 586 League appearances for Leeds before winding down his 18-year career with Hull City and then Doncaster Rovers. He made his debut on the right wing for Leeds at the age of 17 in 1960. Alongside him was player-manager Don Revie, with whom Billy had an almost father-son relationship. He became an extension of Revie on the pitch when he was appointed captain of the title-hunting Leeds team of the 1960s and 1970s. He won two League championship medals, one FA Cup winner's medal, and was in two European Fairs Cup-winning sides. He also captained Scotland, with whom he won 54 caps.

His competitive spirit used to spill over early in his career, and he had serious disciplinary problems before the responsibility of captaincy brought him under control. Standing at just over 5ft 5in, he was like a sawn-off shotgun and always made his presence felt on the pitch. He has managed at Leeds and Doncaster.

Bremner, right, whose disciplinary problems were greatly helped by the responsibilities of captaincy, played 586 League games for Leeds.

This was my year

Even now, more than 25 years on, it hurts to look back at the 1969-70 season. Leeds were asked to play eight games in just 14 days in an amazing climax. We were involved in going for the treble of League championship, FA Cup and European Cup – and, in the end, finished with nothing.

We were the better team in both games against Chelsea in the FA Cup final but, although I scored with six minutes to go in the replay at Old Trafford, they recovered to win the trophy.

If we had beaten Chelsea it would have been a big lift going to play Celtic in the European Cup semi-final, even though we were a goal down from the first leg at Elland Road. I scored at Hampden Park to make it 1-1, but it was Celtic who went through to the final. After the two cup exits, we then had the heartbreak of having to concede the championship to Everton at the last hurdle.

Those were the days when everyone wanted to beat Leeds. The manager Don Revie said to us every season, 'You have got to raise your game 20 per cent again.'

Winning the Footballer of the Year trophy helped mask my disappointment with the results. I am told that I collected a record 95 per cent of the votes, which is very gratifying.

The Football Writers' Association award is *the* one to win. I can remember when the PFA brought in their Player of the Year award in the mid-1970s. We used to sit in the dressing room and ask each other who we should put down for various positions or for the main award or the Young Player trophy. In the end you put down a name to complete the form.

As players we only saw other footballers twice a season. The football writers have an overall view of a season, see the top players on a regular basis and give their choice full consideration. That is why the trophy rates so highly in the game.

My Dream Team

GORDON BANKS

DANNY McGRAIN   JOHN CHARLES   DUNCAN EDWARDS   RAY WILSON

JOHNNY GILES   BOBBY CHARLTON

GEORGE BEST   TOMMY LAWTON   KENNY DAGLISH   TOM FINNEY

I was once asked to select a best-ever Scottish team and that posed problems galore for me. So, picking a British Dream Team has been a near impossible task.

I want wingers in my side and that means, after all the juggling, that I have had to leave out the incomparable Stanley Matthews for George Best and Tom Finney. Let me just run through a few more greats who have not made the team sheet: Peter Doherty, Bobby Moore, Raich Carter, Hughie Gallacher, Danny Blanchflower, Denis Law, Jimmy Greaves, Dave Mackay, Graeme Souness and Alex Young. As I say, it's an impossible task!

Jimmy Cowan, of Scotland, was my goalkeeper choice for my home country team but I go with Gordon Banks because I have never seen anyone better in goal. Wee Danny McGrain, a smashing little player, gets my vote over George Young for the problem right-back position because I like defenders who can play with skill rather than just aggression. Ray Wilson is the left-back choice because I didn't see many going by him.

John Charles and Duncan Edwards form my central defensive pairing. Don Revie and Jack Charlton brainwashed me about Charles. The Gaffer said he was one of the greatest of all time.

All the seasoned pros insist that Duncan Edwards was destined to be a legend. Even as a boy of 15, he was a man in physique and outlook. He had earned a regular England place at 18 when, at that time, you didn't make the

international grade until you were into your twenties. I think the combination of Charles and Edwards at the back would be phenomenal.

Bobby Moore, who has to step aside for that pair, was a fantastic player, better at international level than he was playing for his clubs. He managed to raise his game playing for England.

Bobby Charlton was one of the greatest footballers I have ever seen and was outstanding both for his club and country and could figure up front. He gave me more trouble than anyone I faced. He could go either way at you, was quick over a short distance and had a tremendous shot. A truly world-class player.

I played with Johnny Giles in the middle for years. He not only had great skill but was also as hard as nails. Johnny gets the edge over Graeme Souness.

The choice of strikers proved a problem. The Law man was dynamic. Greavsie could pick goals up just when you thought he had been tamed. Alan Shearer is marvellous and I have only read about Hughie Gallacher. Alex Young was smooth and silky, but from all I am told Tommy Lawton was the greatest and I have to put him up front alongside Kenny Dalglish.

WHAT THE PLAYERS SAY...

In an era when football was extremely competitive, Billy was just the man to have on your side. He would never admit defeat and could shame you into producing extra effort because of the way he used to pour himself into a game.

– JOHN GILES

I had my differences with Billy because he was such a feisty little so-and-so, but what a team player. He was the sort of 100-per-cent player who all managers pray for because he could make a team tick with his non-stop energy.

– JACK CHARLTON

You knew you were in for a war when Billy was in the opposing team, whether he was wearing the white shirt of Leeds or the blue of Scotland. He was ready to battle for every ball.

– ALAN MULLERY

Billy Bremner, the Leeds captain, is held aloft by team-mate Gordon McQueen after securing the second of his two League championship winner's medals in 1974.

Frank McLintock

Born: Glasgow, 28 December 1939.

Honours: Frank was the motivating force behind Arsenal's League and FA Cup double in 1971, when his captaincy inspired a fiercely competitive spirit. He had been a four-time loser at Wembley and considered himself jinxed until the Double year, when he proved he was every inch a winner.

He won nine caps with Scotland, and he played 313 League games for Arsenal after joining them from Leicester City for £80,000 in 1964. He was a buccaneering right-half at Leicester where he played in two losing FA Cup final teams.

In his early days at Arsenal under Billy Wright he played an attacking midfield role before coach Don Howe switched him to centre-half.

He was a constructive centre-half in the Queens Park Rangers team managed by Dave Sexton that finished runners-up in the First Division in 1975-6, and he later returned to Leicester as manager. Following a spell out of the game, he was drawn back in 1984 as manager of Brentford.

Awarded the MBE in 1972, he has had coaching spells at QPR and Millwall, where he was assistant manager, but has preferred to build up a business career that includes acting as representative for players and running a chain of cash-converter shops. He is also in demand as a radio and TV pundit.

Skipper McLintock shows off the FA Cup and League championship trophies after inspiring the Gunners to their 1971 Double.

McLintock was a loser four times in Wembley finals before leading Arsenal to their 2-1 FA Cup victory over Liverpool in 1971.

This was my year

Captaining Arsenal to the League championship and FA Cup double in 1971, and collecting my Footballer of the Year trophy two days before we played Liverpool at Wembley, climaxed an outstanding season for me. Winning the statuette was as important to me as winning the Cup and I have been to every Footballer of the Year dinner since. I regard it as an honour just to be part of such an illustrious band of winners.

There were outstanding players in that Arsenal side who might have won the award. Being captain brought me to people's attention and, if I say so myself, I was a good organiser both on and off the pitch.

I nearly lost Dennis Signy the job of notifying the winner of his selection. He rang me at a Midlands hotel on a Friday night to say the announcement would be made the following day and that it was hush-hush until then and that I was not to tell a soul. I guess I must have told team-mates in my excitement, because one of the newspapers got hold of the story.

I had been to four cup finals before the 1971 match against Liverpool and I had always been on the losing side. I thought in my mind that I was something of a jinx, although I always said publicly that I would go back to Wembley.

The game against Liverpool was played in something like 90 degrees heat and, when we went one down to a Steve Heighway goal I thought, 'Here we go again'. A fluke goal off Eddie Kelly's knee provided the equaliser – with George Graham claiming that he had got a touch, which he still claims to this day is true. Then Charlie George got the wonder-goal winner that crops up regularly on TV clips.

It was the perfect end to an unforgettable season. The Footballer of the Year award was, for me, the icing on the cake and there was nobody prouder than me to collect the trophy.

My Dream Team

GORDON BANKS

DANNY McGRAIN   **JOHN CHARLES**   **BOBBY MOORE**   **RAY WILSON**

STANLEY MATTHEWS **BOBBY CHARLTON** **DUNCAN EDWARDS** **GEORGE BEST**

KENNY DALGLISH   **JIMMY GREAVES**

I had real trouble picking a Dream Team and want to emphasise that I could select several different formations that would be every bit as good. Take the goalkeeper. There is a fingertip between Gordon Banks and Pat Jennings, and I go for Gordon because I played in front of him at Leicester and marvelled at his consistency.

My right-back Danny McGrain had everything. He bombed forward and had pace and a good delivery. Ray Wilson, too, was so quick and hard to beat. They would be perfect full-back partners.

Bobby Moore would be my captain and I can't believe that I have left out Dave Mackay, one of my heroes over the years, and an inspirational player. Jim Baxter and Denis Law, two more Scots, are other names I juggled with and regrettably left out.

I would play Bobby alongside the Welsh giant John Charles. Everyone who was in the game when Big John was at his peak talks in awe of his power and skill, and you will find many old pros who swear he was not only the greatest of all British centre-halves but also just as dominating at centre-forward. A combination of the cultured Moore and the immovable Charles would be unbeatable.

Everyone says that Duncan Edwards would have been one of the greats of the game, and the fact that he managed 18 caps for England as a youngster underlines the point and the tragedy of his untimely death at the age of just 22. Next to Banks and Jennings the choice that gave me the

McLintock, who played 313 League games for Arsenal following his move from Leicester in 1964, shows his aerial power.

biggest headache was between Stanley Matthews and Tom Finney, arguably the two greatest English forwards of all time. I saw Finney, a true gentleman, at the end of his career and was full of admiration for him and his style. People I have spoken to over the years argue in favour of Finney over Matthews, but I will stick with the maestro who is a living legend.

With Matthews and George Best in the same side, the only problem would be getting the ball off them! Jimmy Greaves, without question, was a goalscorer extraordinaire, and I have paired him with the one and only Kenny Dalglish, who was a master at setting up goals for others as well as taking them himself.

The mind boggles when you consider how much my team would be worth in today's transfer market. You would have to price each one of them at around £15 million, so this Dream Team can be said to be worth in the region of £165 million.

People today talk of superstars. The footballers in my team are supersonic.

Gordon Banks, in action for Stoke, shows the agility that earned him the accolade of being the world's greatest goalkeeper.

Gordon Banks

Born: Sheffield, 30 December 1937.

Honours: Gordon set what was then an England record of 73 caps between 1963 and 1972, reaching his peak as the last line of defence in the 1966 World Cup-winning team. Four years later in the 1970 finals in Mexico he underlined his claim to being the world's greatest goalkeeper when he made an incredible save against Pele.

A former coalbagger, he started his career with Third Division Chesterfield before joining Leicester City after National Service with the Army. He collected FA Cup runner's-up medals with Leicester in 1961 and 1963, and was in their 1964 League Cup winning team. Leicester were grooming a young understudy called Peter Shilton and decided they could afford to let England's No.1 goalkeeper move on to Stoke for £52,000 just a year after his World Cup triumph.

Gordon, who won 37 of his caps with Leicester and another 36 with Stoke, was still England's first-choice goalkeeper when a car crash in the autumn of 1972 robbed him of the sight of his right eye. He never played League football again, but during two seasons in the United States was voted Most Valuable Goalkeeper. Gordon kept 35 clean sheets during his 73 England games, and let in only 57 goals. Between 1964 and 1967 he played in 23 consecutive international matches without defeat.

This was my year

I was proud to be the first goalkeeper to win the Footballer of the Year award since my boyhood idol Bert Trautmann in 1956. What, I know, did a lot to help me get the vote was a save I made against my England team-mate Geoff Hurst during a League Cup semi-final marathon.

In the first match at Stoke, Geoff had scored from the penalty spot for West Ham. He had taken a long run-up to the ball and powered it right-footed into the net to my right and at about shoulder height. This penalty was still in my mind when I faced Geoff again from the penalty spot at West Ham in the second leg.

The match was into its final minutes and we were locked together on aggregate when I conceded a penalty after pulling down Harry Redknapp. I was determined to make up for my mistake.

I noticed that Geoff was taking exactly the same length and angled run-up to the ball as in the first match at Stoke, so I decided I would dive to my right in the hope that the ball would be driven to the same spot as before. My calculations could not have been better. I got to the ball with my outstretched right hand and it was moving with such force that it bounced up against the bar and high away into the crowd for a corner.

It was one of the most important and vital saves I had ever made, although it is my save against Pele in Mexico two years earlier that people always want to talk about.

West Ham took us to two exhausting replays before we finally made it to Wembley where we beat Dave Sexton's Chelsea to become the first Stoke City team to win a trophy after 108 years of trying.

The Potteries went potty, and I have never known supporters go so crazy as when we took the cup back to Stoke. They paraded us around the city as if *we* were trophies!

My Dream Team

PAT JENNINGS

JIMMY ARMFIELD   **JOHN CHARLES**   **BOBBY MOORE**   **RAY WILSON**

DUNCAN EDWARDS   **BOBBY CHARLTON**   **GEORGE BEST**

TOM FINNEY   **ALAN SHEARER**   **JIMMY GREAVES**

I have played the selecting game many times, and rarely come up with the same formation because so many great players keep coming to mind. Even so, I always have Pat Jennings in goal. Pat was the perfect goalkeeper: safe hands, razor sharp reflexes, an acute understanding of angles and positioning, brave without being foolish and a master of intelligent distribution. Above all he had a marvellous temperament. No matter how great the pressure, he was always calm and in control.

At right-back, I am torn between George Cohen and Jimmy Armfield. George was the more powerful player but lacked some of Jimmy's finesse going forward. My vote just goes to Armfield, particularly as I warmly remember him playing for Blackpool when I made my First Division debut for Leicester. Typical of this thoroughbred gentleman, he went out of his way to wish me luck before the kick-off.

There is no race for the left-back place. Ray Wilson is the only runner in my mind. Even if I was picking a world team, I would have Ray in the No. 3 shirt. He was a full-back who had beautiful balance and quick recovery powers. I admired Ray for his talent and liked him for his humour. Even in moments of crisis he always had something witty to say that would ease the tension. It's difficult to imagine him in his profession as an undertaker.

Bobby Moore is the obvious choice as my left-side central defender, although Dave Mackay came to mind because of the shuddering power of his tackles. But Bobby was the master of defensive football and was always constructive and creative when clearing the ball.

It's not so easy picking a centre-half. I considered outstanding players such as Maurice Norman, Brian Labone, Roy McFarland, Mike England and Jack Charlton, who was such a great competitor. But in the end I have plumped for John Charles because he was superior to Jack when it came to distributing the ball. I doubt if Britain has had a better footballing centre-half although I am told Neil Franklin had style to go with his strength.

For my formation I have gone for the 4-3-3 line-up that worked so smoothly for England in the 1966 World Cup. I have looked for balance as well as quality in midfield, with Duncan Edwards winning the ball on the right and then releasing it to his fellow Busby Babe Bobby Charlton, who had no peer as a midfield general. Bringing his box of tricks to a withdrawn winger's position on the left will be George Best, who bemused defences with his ball control and changes of pace and direction.

My front three strikers will be Tom Finney, a king of the game when I was a lad, the modern master Alan Shearer and the greatest of all goal poachers, Jimmy Greaves. Each has a vastly different style, but I am convinced they would mould together as a winning unit.

One more selection – Alf Ramsey as manager. There was nobody better.

England's last line of defence shows why he conceded only 57 goals in his 73 international appearances and two World Cups.

The safest hands in football earned Jennings a reputation as Mr Consistency . . . and five winners medals for Spurs and Arsenal.

Jennings proved a bargain for Arsenal after his £40,000 transfer from Tottenham in 1977, helping them to reach three FA Cup finals.

Pat Jennings

Born: Newry, Co. Down, 12 June 1945.

Honours: Pat, who had the biggest, safest hands in football, had a double career in north London where he was idolised first at Tottenham and then with their sworn rivals Arsenal.

His goalkeeping potential was first spotted while playing with his local club Newry Town, and he signed for Watford in 1963.

Within a year he moved to Tottenham where, during 13 seasons at White Hart Lane and 472 League appearances, he was a key player in triumphs in the FA Cup (1967), Football League Cup (1971 and 1973) and the UEFA Cup (1972).

His transfer to Arsenal in August 1977 for £40,000 was greeted by Tottenham fans with amazement bordering on disbelief. He played 237 League games for Arsenal, and helped them reach three successive FA Cup finals, finishing on the winning side in 1979.

Pat made his debut for Northern Ireland while with Watford in 1964, in the same match that George Best made his international bow. He was Mr Consistency, and played a then world record 119 matches.

He retired after playing his last game for Northern Ireland in the 1986 World Cup finals at the age of 41. He was awarded both an MBE and OBE, and continued his links with football when he returned to Tottenham as a goalkeeping coach.

This was my year

I was chosen as the Player of the Year by Tottenham supporters for five successive seasons from 1972, and I was tipped along the way to take over from Gordon Banks as the world's No. 1 goalkeeper.

Looking back after 757 League appearances for Watford, Spurs and Arsenal, and appearing in more than 1,000 first-class games, I have a host of memories but find it hard to reflect specifically on individual matches, even seasons. Don't forget that I made my record-breaking 119th appearance for Northern Ireland on my 41st birthday.

The FWA announcement of my award as Footballer of the Year in 1972-3 cited my 'many years of consistency at club and international level'.

The highlight of my season came on the morning of the Grand National when I saved two penalties at Anfield against Liverpool, who later went on to win the championship. When I collected my statuette I said: 'How could I avoid the award playing behind our defence?'

That year Spurs won the League Cup with a Wembley victory against Norwich and became the first team to have their name on the trophy for a second time.

But for me and the side it was another statistic in a remarkable cup record, the ninth senior final and the ninth win, the sixth under manager Bill Nicholson. Following the League Cup triumph in 1971 and the UEFA Cup in 1972 – we beat Wolves 3-2 on aggregate – it brought Spurs a remarkable hat-trick.

Add to that Northern Ireland's 1-0 win against England at Wembley with a Terry Neill goal and you can see how it was a satisfactory period for me. I had a good game at Wembley, giving it the 'one handers' as I pulled off saves. Plucking the ball out of the air one handed was a legacy of my days in Gaelic football.

My Dream Team

GORDON BANKS

DANNY McGRAIN   MIKE ENGLAND   DAVE MACKAY   RAY WILSON

GEORGE BEST   GLENN HODDLE   BOBBY CHARLTON   LIAM BRADY

DENIS LAW   JIMMY GREAVES

WHAT THE PLAYERS SAY...

Pat was a goalkeeper's goalkeeper, respected by every other 'keeper. He performed without fuss, and was always in command. I would describe him as the complete goalkeeping master. His behaviour was impeccable, and he was a great ambassador for our profession. **– BOB WILSON**

I considered myself lucky to have played with the two greatest goalkeepers of my generation, Gordon Banks with England and Pat with Tottenham. There was not a fingertip between them. It was reassuring to look back and see big Pat guarding the goal. He had great physical presence.

– ALAN MULLERY

Pat was a real poker face who never let on to forwards what he was thinking. He could make impossible saves look simple and was never unnecessarily spectacular. He was a super goalkeeper. **– JOE KINNEAR**

● ●

I have always resisted picking a Dream Team. It's just a nightmare for me. To be honest, I don't see how you can separate Mike England and David O'Leary, for instance, or put Liam Brady in front of Dave Mackay, or vice versa. It has always been against my principles to choose between the great players I have played with and against, and to all those legendary footballers I have left out I want to apologise and forcibly make the point that this team has been selected in consultation with the persuasive Dennis Signy.

I can remember Terry Venables having to plead for forgiveness when he chose Ted Ditchburn, his boyhood idol, ahead of me for an all-time great Spurs team. Television commentator Brian Moore called the decision 'disgraceful'. Former Spurs manager Bill Nicholson said he found it impossible to draw a line between us. I understand that. It is exactly the reason I have always refused to indulge in picking fantasy teams.

I was asked recently to name players from my career spanning 23 years who would be worth £15 million in today's domestic market. So, with that valuation in mind, the first names on my team sheet are George Best, Dave Mackay, Jimmy Greaves and Bobby Charlton.

Mackay would skipper the team. He was a born leader and the best all-round player I ever saw.

Best, who made his Northern Ireland debut at the same time as me against Wales at Swansea in 1964, had all-round talent and could play anywhere. He used to take the gloves off me during international training and make some great saves. He did everything a yard quicker than anyone else and could score goals from box to box.

I would have to include Greaves – there is still nobody like him for putting the ball into the net. Charlton had fantastic shooting power in both feet and superb ball-carrying ability on the run. He was a nightmare for any goalkeeper, especially from a range of 30-35 yards.

Gordon Banks was simply outstanding. But, in choosing him, I leave out three exceptional goalkeepers in Peter Shilton, Ray Clemence and Neville Southall. Ron Greenwood had the problem when he was England manager. He could not decide between Shilton and Clemence. I know how he felt.

I don't think there was anyone to touch Mike England in his prime, but David O'Leary was a defender who could play in any class and I hate leaving him out. Cyril Knowles, my former Spurs team-mate, was another left-

back who merits consideration. Who else have I left out? Kevin Keegan, who did the business at home and abroad . . . Kenny Dalglish . . . Martin Chivers . . . Johnny Giles . . . Jim Baxter . . . the names just go on and on.

Jennings made his Northern Ireland debut in the same match as George Best, but outlasted the flamboyant Manchester United winger by winning 119 caps before retiring at the age of 41.

Ian Callaghan

Born: Liverpool, 10 April 1942.

Honours: 'Cally' won just about every honour in the game at Liverpool, including five League championship medals, and winner's medals in the FA Cup (two), European Cup (two), UEFA Cup and Super Cup. He was awarded an OBE for his services to the game.

He played a club record 640 League matches for Liverpool between 1960 and 1978 before holding his passing-out parade at Swansea City, where his former Anfield team-mate John Toshack was manager. He started his career as an orthodox winger and later established himself as one of the most influential midfield players in the League.

Ian made his full England debut under Alf Ramsey in June 1966 and played in one World Cup finals match the following month. But he was then relegated to the international wilderness for 11 years before being recalled by Ron Greenwood for two appearances.

He virtually had two careers at Anfield. As a fleet-footed winger he could beat full-backs with speed and deft ball control before crossing accurately with either foot. Then, as wingers went out of fashion, he brought a new dimension to his game as a midfield marshal who could dictate the pace and pattern of a game with a procession of superbly placed passes.

Ian was a master of the game and a gentleman of the first order.

Callaghan won almost every honour in the game, including five League championships, two FA Cups and two European Cups.

This was my year

The 1973-4 season was probably the most outstanding of my career, culminating with me being voted Liverpool's first ever Footballer of the Year. I was 31 when the season started – 32 when I collected my statuette – and had enjoyed an unbelievable career at Anfield under my mentor, the legendary Bill Shankly. He saw me and signed me as a 16-year-old and looked after me as a father figure over the years.

I won three or four awards that season and I was nominated for the PFA Player of the Year. All in all it was the best year in my 14 with Liverpool.

One feature that caught the attention of the football writers was my never having been booked in the professional game. In fact, it was not until years later that I received my only booking, against Nottingham Forest. I shoulder-charged Peter Withe, all 6ft 4ins of him, and received a yellow card. I suppose I caught him in his ribs!

We reached the FA Cup final in 1974, going on to beat Newcastle 3-0 with two goals from Kevin Keegan and one from Steve Heighway. Bill Shankly accompanied me to the London hotel to collect my Footballer of the Year award two days before. He was strict about the build-up to Wembley and acted as my minder for the evening.

We did not attend for the meal, but Shanks escorted me in, heard me accept the award and whisked me back to the same team hotel at Hendon where I had prepared for the 1966 World Cup as a winger in Alf Ramsey's squad.

I remember that Freddie Trueman, the Test cricketer, was guest speaker but I don't remember much else as I was so nervous. When I looked along the top table and saw some of the greats who had preceded me as Footballer of the Year I nearly froze. Shanks said to me: 'You get out of this game what you put in – so enjoy the moment.'

It was great for me being the first player from Liverpool to get the accolade.

My Dream Team

GORDON BANKS

GEORGE COHEN   **RAY WILSON**

DUNCAN EDWARDS   **BOBBY MOORE**   **DAVE MACKAY**

STANLEY MATTHEWS   GEORGE BEST   KENNY DALGLISH   BOBBY CHARLTON   TOM FINNEY

WHAT THE PLAYERS SAY...

Cally's attitude and ability was an inspiration to everyone at Anfield. It was a joy to play with him and his controlled passing played a big part in Liverpool's success in the 1970s.

– KEVIN KEEGAN

When Liverpool won the European Cup for the first time it was Cally who helped make the team tick. He was a substitute for the FA Cup final but made all the difference when recalled for the European Cup final in Rome four days later. **– EMLYN HUGHES**

Ian was a wonderful ambassador for our game with his demeanour on and off the pitch. He was a dedicated professional, and adapted superbly when his role of winger became somewhat redundant.

– RON GREENWOOD

The first two names in my Dream Team were Gordon Banks and Bobby Moore, from England's World Cup-winning side of 1966. Bobby would be my skipper, as he was Sir Alf's. He earned the admiration and respect of everyone in the game with his skill, composure and dignified bearing. He was an ideal example of a professional player. A lovely man. I would play him in an old style centre-half role in a 2-3-5 formation.

I nominate two more 1966 international team-mates at full-back, although I found it tough picking a right-back. I settled for the reliable George Cohen. Left-back was easier. I played against Ray Wilson and know how good he was. They served their clubs and country well and reached their peak during our World Cup triumph.

John Charles came into my reckoning for the centre-half spot, and also to play up front. But I did not personally see enough of him to appreciate just how good he was as he had his greatest days in the Italian league with Juventus.

I had no hesitation in choosing Duncan Edwards and Dave Mackay as outstanding wing-halves. Their power would mean we would have little problem regaining the ball in the unlikely situation of us losing possession.

George Best, who I would use as an inside forward alongside Stanley Matthews, was without doubt the best player I have ever seen, while his Manchester United team-mate Bobby Charlton was the most explosive. Kenny Dalglish selects himself

as one of the greatest strikers. He was always so comfortable on the ball and aware exactly where the goal was, even when he had his back to the target. I was tempted to pick many of my old Liverpool team-mates, but in the end I went for what I consider a perfectly balanced team.

Picking Tom Finney goes without saying. If you had Bill Shankly as your manager you grew up being told tales of how he was the greatest. All the players at Anfield under Shanks were brought up on Finney stories. I only saw him play at the end of his career, but he was as at home on the right as on the left and scored goals galore from centre-

forward. Finney is in my team on merit – it is me picking him, not dear old Shanks.

It also goes without saying that I would have Shanks as the manager. He could motivate a lamp-post into becoming mobile!

Ian Callaghan's controlled passing was a key factor for Liverpool when they first won the European Cup in Rome in 1977.

FOOTBALLER OF THE YEAR
1975

Alan Mullery

Born: Notting Hill, London, 23 November 1941.

Honours: A tenacious tackler, Alan patrolled in midfield where he was a master at winning the ball then using it accurately and intelligently. He played 199 League games for Fulham in his first spell at Craven Cottage, and then another 164 matches following his return from Tottenham.

He was capped 35 times by England (1965-72), once as captain. He had two spells at Fulham, sandwiching 312 League games for Spurs during which he scored 25 goals.

An FA Cup winner with Tottenham against Chelsea in 1967, Alan helped steer them to a UEFA Cup triumph. He also captained runners-up Fulham against West Ham in the 1975 final two days after collecting his Footballer of the Year award. Following his retirement he managed Charlton Athletic (twice), Brighton and Queens Park Rangers before going into insurance and a career as a broadcaster. In 1996 he was persuaded to return to the game briefly as director of football at Barnet.

In the 1968 European Championship semi-final against Yugoslavia, he had the unfortunate distinction of being the first player to be sent off while wearing an England shirt. He would much rather prefer being remembered as the man who kept Pele in check during the 1970 World Cup finals, and for his inspiring performances as a captain with both Fulham and Spurs.

This was my year

At the end of the FA Cup final in 1975, after Fulham had been beaten 2-0 by West Ham, I thanked the players for helping the two old men of the team, Bobby Moore and me, to get to Wembley.

Winning the Footballer of the Year trophy two days earlier climaxed a fairy-tale for me. I had left Spurs in 1972 to return to my first-love at Craven Cottage and a couple of years later the manager Alec Stock asked me how I got on with Moore.

'I slept with him for four years with England,' I replied.

'I didn't know he was like that,' said Alec – and promptly sent me off in a minicab with the club secretary and the transfer forms to persuade Bobby to join us.

'Tell him it's a fun club,' said Alec. Bobby duly signed – and we were four goals down against Middlesbrough in his first match. As the fourth goal went in, Bobby looked at me and said: 'I think I might have made a mistake.' Playing for Alec Stock and Fulham in the Second Division was fun, just as Alec had promised. It took us 14 games to get to Wembley, including four against Nottingham Forest.

Alec had persuaded me to sign for him rather than Bert Head at Crystal Palace with the offer of a four-year deal and taking over from him at the end of the contract. He said he would become general manager. A persuasive man Alec.

Palace were offering me £15,000 as a signing-on fee; I signed for Fulham for my Spurs wages and £5,000 over the four years. At the end of my contract, though, Alec did not want to give up – and then lost his job to Bobby Campbell.

After playing for England and at the top level in Europe with Spurs, it was something of an irony to win the most coveted trophy in football as a Second Division player with Fulham. As Greavsie says, it's a funny old game.

Mullery, capped 35 times for England, was a tenacious tackler in midfield who could use the ball accurately and intelligently.

My Dream Team

GORDON BANKS

ROGER BYRNE   PAUL McGRATH   BOBBY MOORE   RAY WILSON

BOBBY CHARLTON   DUNCAN EDWARDS

GEORGE BEST   JIMMY GREAVES   DENIS LAW   TOM FINNEY

My Dream Team is a 4-2-4 selection. The choice between Gordon Banks and Pat Jennings in goal was really difficult because there was nothing to choose between them. I go with Gordon because I cannot remember him ever having a bad game, and I was a witness on the pitch when he made that fantastic save against Pele in the 1970 World Cup finals.

I was marking Pele, and he screamed 'G-o-a-l!' as he connected with his header. To this day I don't know how Gordon managed to get across the goal and tip the ball up and away. It was simply sensational.

I saw Roger Byrne playing at Highbury the Saturday before he died in the Munich air disaster. I know he is out of position at right-back, but he was so talented that he would have adjusted. He had pace and a splendid delivery of the ball, and would have been the ideal partner for my left-back Ray Wilson. He was a magnificent player, and you very rarely saw anybody going past him.

Bobby Moore would be my inspirational captain. He was the complete defender, and so commanding and composed that he always seemed to have time to get his tackle in or make a clearance while everybody else around him was in a state of panic. You never ever saw him waste a ball out of defence. It was always cleared to a team-mate.

Paul McGrath continues to amaze me to this day as the ultimate ball playing centre-half, and would have been the perfect foil for Bobby at the heart of the defence. Bobby Charlton, of course, had great presence on the ball and Duncan Edwards would, I am sure, have beaten Moore's 108 caps for England if he had not died at Munich. He was a giant and was destined to become one of the all-time greats.

What can you say about George Best? The man was just a genius who took teams to pieces.

Tom Finney was a fantastic all-round player who perhaps never got the credit he deserved in an era of great players. I played against him in his last game, and he had a presence about him that was almost regal. He was not the slightest bit arrogant, yet you were in awe of him because of all that he had achieved in the game.

Jimmy Greaves and Denis Law are my marksmen. Greavsie the king of the goal poachers. The Lawman an electric player with amazing reflexes. You wouldn't sleep the night before if you were playing against them with Best and Finney alongside.

What a team! I would walk a million miles to see them play.

Mullery, in action at Wembley as skipper of the Fulham team in the 1975 FA Cup final against West Ham, shields the ball from Trevor Brooking. But he failed to prevent his Second Division side losing 2-0.

Kevin Keegan

Born: Armthorpe, Yorkshire, 14 February 1951.

Honours: The only British player to be twice elected European Footballer of the Year, Kevin captained England 29 times in 63 appearances. He joined Liverpool from Third Division Scunthorpe in 1971 and was an influential member of the team that won the FA Cup (1974), the Football League championship (1973, 1976, 1977), the UEFA Cup (1973, 1976) and, the pinnacle of his Anfield career, the European Cup (1977).

He left Liverpool for SV Hamburg in the summer of 1977 and helped them to the Bundesliga title in 1979 and the final of the European Cup in 1980. It was while with Hamburg that he was voted European Footballer of the Year two years in succession. Missed by all the major clubs when a youngster, he made up for a lack of flair with a high work-rate allied to a sharp footballing brain. He also had a good scoring instinct as he proved with 21 goals for England.

He returned to England in 1980 for two seasons with Southampton before moving to Newcastle United for two successful years as a player at St James's Park. After eight years out of the game, he made a hero's return to Newcastle as manager and had nearly five years of headline-hitting championship challenges before sensationally quitting midway through the 1996-7 season.

Kevin Keegan, who spent a highly successful six-year spell at Anfield, played a leading role in Bill Shankly's Red Revolution.

What Keegan lacked in flair he more than made up for in athleticism, a trait that won him almost every honour possible at Liverpool.

This was my year

The 1975-6 season stands out in my memory. Liverpool repeated their 1973 double by capturing the League championship and the UEFA Cup. I was then given the highest honour of all when Don Revie made me England captain for the first time against Wales in March, 1976. A few weeks later I was elected Footballer of the Year.

In my acceptance speech I told the football writers: 'I am not the best player in the country by a mile, but I'm working on it. And I'm not the most popular because I have done some stupid things. But I'm learning from my mistakes. I will do all I can to live up to the standards set by the illustrious players who have won this award before me.'

The night before, I had helped Liverpool to a 3-2 victory over Bruges in the first leg of the UEFA Cup final at Anfield. We then turned our attention to the League championship. Dave Sexton's Queens Park Rangers made a bold bid to win the title for the first time. They beat Leeds 2-0 on the last Saturday of the season to go one point ahead of us at the top of the table. We had one more match to play, at Wolverhampton on the Tuesday after the FA Cup final.

Wolves needed a win to avoid relegation, while a low-scoring draw or victory for us would give Liverpool the League championship for a record ninth time.

Steve Kindon put Wolves into the lead and their defence soaked up a lot of pressure before I squeezed an equaliser in the 76th minute. Wolves, fighting for their First Division life, had to throw everything into attack and left gaps that were exploited by John Toshack and Ray Kennedy.

We then wrapped up our unfinished business in the UEFA Cup. I completed what was for me an unforgettable season when I snatched an equaliser to give us a 4-3 aggregate victory. Bob Paisley's silverware collection had started in style.

My Dream Team

GORDON BANKS

DANNY McGRAIN DAVE WATSON BOBBY MOORE RAY WILSON

BILLY BREMNER   BOBBY CHARLTON

PETER BEARDSLEY

JIMMY JOHNSTONE   GEOFF HURST   GEORGE BEST

One thing's for certain, I would have Bill Shankly managing my Dream Team. He was the Great Persuader and could bring the best out of any team with simple, easily understood instructions. He never made the mistake of complicating what is in essence a simple game.

That's the easy part over! When it comes to picking a team I have restricted my selections to footballers I played with or against, so current players of the calibre of Alan Shearer, Paul Gascoigne and Ryan Giggs were not considered.

Gordon Banks gets my vote as goalkeeper, a fingertip ahead of Peter Shilton, Pat Jennings and Ray Clemence. I remember the great Gerd Muller saying of Gordon: 'He is the one goalkeeper who makes me feel unsettled. He has incredible concentration and such fine positional sense that he gives you little glimpse of the goal.'

I played against Gordon in what was to prove his final top-level match for Stoke at Anfield. The next day he lost the sight of an eye in a car crash, and English football was robbed of one of its truly world-class players.

Scotland's Danny McGrain would be my right-back. He and I used to cancel each other out when we played in England-Scotland matches. There was not a weakness in his game. His partner at left-back would be the cultured Ray Wilson, who was quick enough to catch pigeons.

I choose my centre-backs on the basis of having one player to win the ball and the other to

Keegan shows the opportunism, against Borussia Moenchengladbach, that earned him two successive European Player of the Year awards.

use it. Dave Watson was remarkably consistent when we used to play together for England, and was just about unbeatable in the air. Alongside him will be The Master, Bobby Moore, who will also captain the team. Bobby was always a thought ahead of his opponents, and made up for his lack of speed with his uncanny positional sense. He was always immaculate with his passes out of defence that continually prompted counter attacks.

My old antagonist Billy Bremner will patrol on the right side of midfield, winning the ball and then

WHAT THE PLAYERS SAY...

Kevin had an electric change of pace that continually used to catch defenders out. He always knew where to be to make the most of any situation, and was a marvellous, unselfish team player. He was a great motivator both as a player and as a manager. **– PETER BEARDSLEY**

Kevin and I had an almost telepathic understanding when playing together at Liverpool, and he was responsible for making many of my goals for me. He had bags of energy, and used to run his markers into the ground. **– JOHN TOSHACK**

There have been more talented players than Kevin, but few to match his all-round ability. Whether ferreting in midfield or making space in the penalty area, he was a class act and a joy to play with. **– TREVOR BROOKING**

feeding it to Bobby Charlton for the decisive passes. Billy and I were once sent off together for fighting in a Charity Shield match at Wembley, but we never held it against each other. It was all just a heat-of-the-moment thing, and we both regretted it afterwards. We were both totally committed to winning, and you cannot knock that.

I shall have my old Newcastle buddy Peter Beardsley playing just behind the front three in a 4-2-1-3 formation. He is a gifted touch player, who can make an attack tick with his clever probing.

Geoff Hurst, a great shielder of the ball and a positive finisher, will strike down the middle where he will feed off the stunningly skilled service of Jimmy Johnstone and George Best.

Best would be the first name on the team sheet. There can be no argument that he was the greatest British footballer of my generation, possibly of all time. The publicity he attracted off the pitch can never overshadow the fact that he was a genius in football boots.

1977

Hughes, who moved to Anfield in 1967 for £65,000, proved a bargain after playing 474 League games for Liverpool.

Hughes, who played 474 League games in an 11-year spell at Anfield, celebrates their League championship victory in 1976.

Emlyn Hughes

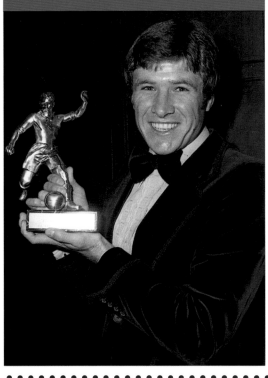

Born: Barrow, 28 August 1947.

Honours: Emlyn's father was a Great Britain rugby league international and passed his competitive qualities on to his son. There were more highly skilled players, but few with his drive and determination. A born leader, he gave Liverpool magnificent service wherever he played. He was solid at full-back, adventurous at left-half, and disciplined in the centre of the defence where his tigerish tackling made up for a lack of authority in the air. He had a thundering, if somewhat unpredictable shot, and was affectionately known as Crazy Horse by the Anfield fans.

Emlyn played 474 League games for Liverpool between 1967 and 1978 after joining them from Blackpool for £65,000. He captained Liverpool to three League championships in four years, to UEFA Cup and FA Cup triumphs, and to the first two of their European Cup victories. He then moved on to Wolves, and in his first season skippered them to a League Cup win. This completed his collection, because the League Cup was the one trophy he had failed to get his hands on at Anfield.

He played 62 England internationals, 23 of them as captain. He was awarded an OBE, and in 1981 started a career in management as player-manager of Rotherham before later becoming a popular television personality.

This was my year

I was named Footballer of the Year in 1977, the season that Liverpool won just about everything: The League championship, to go towards the record 18 they have won, and the European Cup for the first time with a 3-1 win against Borussia Moenchengladbach in a memorable final in Rome. We got to Wembley in the FA Cup final, too, only to go down 2-1 to our deadly rivals Manchester United. But the European Cup triumph four days later was the perfect consolation, and we went on to win the Super Cup.

To be fair, I got the votes because I was the chap who lifted the trophies, not because I was a better player than Kevin Keegan or whoever . . . and because the football writers were running out of Liverpool players to give it to!

Every one of that Liverpool squad, in my view, was a Footballer of the Year that season as we went for glory on three fronts. Kevin had won the award the previous season and I was followed a couple of years later by Kenny Dalglish and Terry McDermott.

It was just about impossible at that time not to pick a Liverpool winner of the award and, much as I treasure my statuette, I realise how lucky I was to get the votes with so many worthy candidates around. It was a year not to be forgotten by anyone at Anfield. We did it all.

The stand-out memories are of going for the treble, playing in Europe, collecting vital points in the League and playing so many important cup ties. Every game in the last third of that season was a like a cup final as we travelled at home and abroad taking on and beating all-comers.

It was all like a dream come true for me, and despite all the things I have achieved and enjoyed since I still pick as the highlight of my career that season in which Liverpool led the way and I was named the Footballer of the Year. Great, great days.

My Dream Team

GORDON BANKS

DANNY McGRAIN   **JOHN CHARLES**   **BOBBY MOORE**   **TOMMY GEMMELL**

MARTIN PETERS   **GRAEME SOUNESS**   **BOBBY CHARLTON**   **GEORGE BEST**

JIMMY GREAVES   **KENNY DALGLISH**

The first name on my 4-4-2 formation team sheet would be the inspirational skipper of the side, Bobby Moore, followed by the greatest player I ever saw, George Best. George was undoubtedly the best. He had everything, and that also goes for Bobby Charlton and Kenny Dalglish. The prospect of Kenny working up front with Jimmy Greaves, the finest goalscorer I have seen, is just mouthwatering.

But I have to pick Bobby Moore at the head of the class. Even Pele acknowledged his magnificence. Bobby was probably England's most intelligent defender of all time. We tend to build players to superstar status in this country and then try to knock them off their pedestal.

People used to say Bobby had no pace and he couldn't do this or that. No pace? Let me assure you that he was five yards quicker in his head than any other player I have known. He was a leader at club and international level and would certainly be at the helm of my team.

One short sentence sums up why I select Gordon Banks between the sticks. He is the world's best-ever goalkeeper.

My problem is nominating two full-backs. I don't think Britain has been blessed with great backs over the years. Let's face it, I played some 40 games of my 62 appearances for England at left-back and I was essentially right-footed! I have finally gone for a Scottish pairing from Celtic in Danny McGrain and Tommy Gemmell. John Charles was in Italy for much of his career and I base his selection on what I have seen of him on TV clips and his deserved reputation among his contemporaries as a gentle giant and a versatile player who did as well up front as at the heart of defence.

I am sorry I cannot find a place in the side for Geoff Hurst, England's hat-trick hero in 1966. The pairing of Geoff and Martin Peters, a superb partnership in my mind, would have been ideal. But Geoff has to stay on the substitutes' bench. If it is any consolation to him he would be sitting alongside another great goalscorer in Denis Law because, after much deliberation, I put Jimmy Greaves ahead of the field as a striker. He was the tops.

Graeme Souness is there as a ball-winner in midfield but also because he had the attribute of always wanting to play a forward ball to get attacks going. He only played it square when there was no option. Graeme was a winner. And I think that sums up my Dream Team. It's a winner.

The industrious Emlyn Hughes never knew when he was beaten, and his competitive edge helped him earn 62 caps for England, 23 of them as captain.

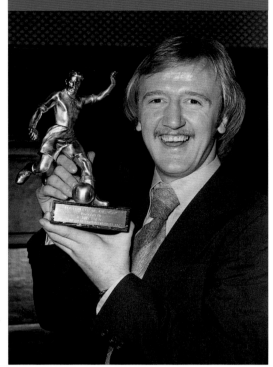

Kenny Burns

Born: Glasgow, 23 September 1953.

Honours: Kenny was the first player Brian Clough and Peter Taylor purchased when they took Nottingham Forest up into the First Division in 1977. It was a deal that astonished many people because he had a reputation as something of a wild man on and off the pitch. But Clough and Taylor had a specific role in mind for him, and he answered the challenge of his new job as a sweeper with tremendous enthusiasm, mixing strength and a ruthless competitive nature with his considerable skill.

His disciplined, dominating displays at the centre of defence were a crucial factor in Forest's successful run that brought them the League championship and two European Cup triumphs.

Kenny played 137 League games for Forest after joining them from Birmingham City in July 1977 for £145,000. He later played for Leeds and had spells with Derby, Notts County and Barnsley in a career that spanned 14 years from 1971. He was a striker at Birmingham, but his game blossomed following his switch to the back of the Forest defence where he was a revelation alongside first Larry Lloyd and then David Needham. He was capped 20 times by Scotland and was a member of the 1978 World Cup squad.

Kenny became landlord of a pub in Derbyshire following his retirement from football.

Burns was a vital factor in Brian Clough's rebuilding of Forest into a European force and made 137 League appearances for them.

This was my year

The instruction that manager Brian Clough gave us at Nottingham Forest was to play the game a certain way - very simply. We followed that line in 1977-8 to win the championship for the club for the first time ever and to clinch the League Cup with a 1-0 win over Liverpool in a replay after drawing the first game 0-0.

That led to two European Cup finals and two winner's medals. We beat Malmo 1-0 in Munich and then Hamburg 1-0 in Madrid a year later.

You will notice one thing about all these games – Forest kept a clean sheet. We adapted to Clough's 4-4-2 formation and were in many respects like the Liverpool side of that time. They probably had more quality man for man, but we more than matched them with our battling spirit.

There are many memories of that championship season when I won the Footballer of the Year award, none more vivid than a stunning save that Peter Shilton made from Mike Ferguson at Coventry. One major factor in our success was that Clough and his right-hand man Peter Taylor convinced John Robertson that he was a world-class player. Robbo had been a bit of a rebel and a fun figure, but he knuckled down under Clough's motivation and was an inspiration to the team.

I can remember Cloughie's reaction when Dennis Signy phoned him with the news that I had won the award. We were playing at Liverpool on the Thursday evening of the dinner and Cloughie asked what time it started. He said that we would all fly down after the game. Considering that the match ended at Anfield at 9.10p.m. and the function had been going for over an hour, that wasn't on. Cloughie tried in vain to get Liverpool to bring the match forward but, in the end, I travelled from Nottingham with the then Forest chairman Brian Appleby and missed the game. Billy Connolly was the guest speaker on what was a memorable Scottish-flavoured night for me.

My Dream Team

PAT JENNINGS

VIV ANDERSON   ALAN HANSEN   NORMAN HUNTER   TERRY COOPER

JIMMY JOHNSTONE   GLENN HODDLE   JIM BAXTER   LIAM BRADY

KENNY DALGLISH   DENIS LAW

I've had more experience than most of picking dream teams. There are always discussions in my pub in Derby on this topic and we argue for hours on end as to the merits of various players. Everyone has their own opinion, but this time mine goes into print for posterity. There is nobody who can shout 'time gentlemen, please' on me!

I have a strong Scottish thread running through my team, with five Scots supported by two Irishmen and four Englishmen.

It will not surprise anyone to find that I have a bit of steel at the back along with the class. This was how we played it in those glory days in Europe with Forest. We mixed good football with a strong competitive spirit.

I select Pat Jennings just ahead of my old team-mate Peter Shilton and England's old hero Gordon Banks. Jennings was not only a fine, imposing goalkeeper but also a great ambassador for the game.

Viv Anderson and Terry Cooper are both attacking full-backs who would be able to dig in with the tackles when necessary. Alan Hansen will be all style in the centre of defence alongside Norman Hunter, who as we all remember could bite legs!

Norman was unlucky to be in the shadow of Bobby Moore for much of his career, but he was a much better player than just a clogger. He could use the ball intelligently with that left foot of his.

Good luck to anybody trying to go past him! My regret is that I am unable to find a place for my former Forest and Scotland team-mate John Robertson. But putting Robbo in would have meant leaving out either the incomparable Jim Baxter or the immaculate Liam Brady. John will be my substitute, ready to bring his left-sided skill into the attack at a moment's notice.

Glenn Hoddle and Liam Brady will share the scheming duties, with Jim Baxter having a free role to go where he thinks he can cause most damage . . . as he did so often against England in international matches. Playing a withdrawn winger's role on the right in my 4-4-2 formation will be jinking Jimmy Johnstone, who was such a key member of Jock Stein's great Celtic team of the 1960s.

The crowning glory for my team is provided by two kings of Scottish football: Kenny Dalglish and Denis Law. I cannot think of a more potent combination, and no defence would be be able to contain them for long.

I will have Brian Clough and Peter Taylor as my joint managers, just as when Forest were dominating in Europe. And the instruction will be the same as Cloughie used to give: 'Just keep it simple.'

One thing's for sure, my selection will cause a lot of arguments in my pub. Time gentlemen, please!

WHAT THE PLAYERS SAY...

A lot of people thought we were barmy when we signed Kenny. They predicted that he would give us nothing but trouble. As it turned out, he was the perfect professional and was a vital cog in our team. There have been few better players in a competitive sense. He gave us the sort of strength and stability that Dave Mackay had given us at Derby. **– BRIAN CLOUGH**

Kenny took to defending like a duck to water, and because he was a converted striker knew what his opponents were trying to do. His positional play was superb. **– PETER SHILTON**

Any forward trying to go past Kenny felt his presence! He was hard, and had a good footballing brain. He was unquestionably a key man for Forest. **– TREVOR FRANCIS**

Burns, a disciplined and uncompromising defender, cradles the League championship trophy after guiding Forest to glory in 1978.

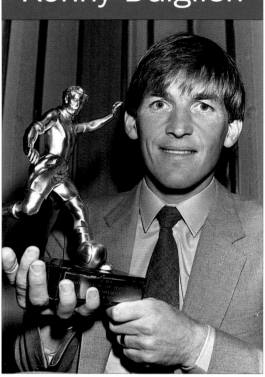

Kenny Dalglish

Born: Glasgow, 4 March 1951.

Honours: One of football's most honoured players, Kenny has been equally successful as a manager. He joined Celtic in 1970, helping them win nine major titles before moving to Liverpool in 1977 as successor to Kevin Keegan for a then British record fee of £440,000. He was an influential member of the Liverpool team which won the European Cup (1978, '81, '84), the FA Cup (1986), the League title six times (1979, '80, '82, '83, '84, '86) and the League Cup for four consecutive years (1981, '82, '83, '84).

He followed 112 League goals at Celtic with 118 for Liverpool and is the only player to have scored 100 goals in both the English and Scottish leagues. Kenny won a record 102 Scottish caps, and equalled Denis Law's 30-goal international record. In 1985 he became Liverpool player-manager, and in his first season led them to the League and Cup double. He repeated the League championship success in 1988 and 1990. He made his last League appearance in May 1989 and early in 1991 shocked the football world by quitting.

Kenny returned in October that year as manager of Blackburn Rovers, helping them win promotion from the Second Division in 1992 and capturing the championship three years later. Following another spell out of the game, he returned to manage Newcastle – again treading in the footsteps of Kevin Keegan.

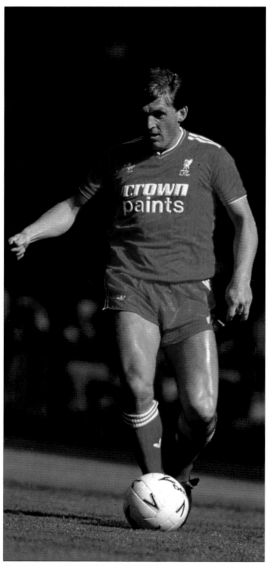

Dalglish, who scored 100 goals in both the English and Scottish leagues, won 14 major trophies in his playing days at Liverpool.

This was my year

It was my privilege to win the Footballer of the Year award twice, and I was in the best of company because those who achieved this before me were legendary names in the game: Stanley Matthews, Tom Finney and Danny Blanchflower. I was delighted to be the first Scot to do it.

The first award was particularly satisfying because it showed that I had established myself in the English League after taking over Kevin Keegan's No. 7 shirt at Anfield. That was the season in which we made up for going out of the European Cup against Nottingham Forest by racing away with the League championship with what was then a record 68 points.

When accepting the award I made the point that I was receiving it on behalf of an outstanding Liverpool team. I had managed to score 21 of our 84 goals in the League, while our magnificent defence conceded only 16 goals in 42 matches – an all-time First Division record. I never tire of

saying that football is a team game, and this was never more evident than at Anfield where we all played for each other.

My second award came at the end of a 1982-3 season when we completed a double of League championship and League Cup. This time I told the audience when receiving the statuette that Ian Rush deserved to be alongside me because between us we had scored 42 First Division goals. I had earlier won the PFA Player of the Year award, with Ian taking the Young Player of the Year title. Our partnership certainly flourished that season!

I particularly remember the 1983 League Cup final because it was Bob Paisley's last visit to Wembley as manager, and we made him climb the famous steps to collect the trophy after we had beaten Manchester United 2-1.

A year later we completed a hat-trick of League championship victories in what were golden years for Liverpool and their unbelievable supporters.

My Dream Team

RONNIE SIMPSON

DANNY McGRAIN ALAN HANSEN MARK LAWRENSON WILLIE DONACHIE

JIMMY JOHNSTONE GRAEME SOUNESS TERRY McDERMOTT RAY KENNEDY

IAN RUSH DENIS LAW

WHAT THE PLAYERS SAY...

For shielding the ball, scoring from impossible angles and creating chances for others, there was nobody to touch Kenny. He had the 'impossible' job of following Kevin Keegan into the No. 7 Liverpool shirt and became an even greater hero.

– PHIL THOMPSON

I owed Kenny at least half my goals at Liverpool. He was a master at making space in the penalty area and then laying the ball off. His finishing was clinical and he always seemed to have so much time to do things on and off the ball. **– IAN RUSH**

Kenny was the complete forward. He could score exceptional goals or make them for a team-mate with devastating change of pace and a perfectly weighted pass. He was a master of the footballing arts. **– JOE ROYLE**

I T will not come as a shock to anybody that I have selected a team with a big Liverpool and Scottish bias. I restricted my selections to those I played with, and I know one or two will cause a surprise.

For instance, I have found a Scottish goalkeeper who ranks with the best despite all the nonsense talked about our goalies. When I made my Celtic debut in 1969 Ronnie Simpson was coming to the end of his remarkable career.

He won FA Cup winner's medals with Newcastle in 1952 and 1955 and then, more than ten years later, stood at the back of the famous Celtic side that became the first British team to lift the European Cup in 1967.

At the heart of my defence I have two players who were outstanding partners for Liverpool. Alan Hansen and Mark Lawrenson were footballing defenders who never panicked under pressure and always played the ball out of defence with thought and accuracy.

Danny McGrain was without argument one of the finest right-backs of any era, and accompanying him at left-back I have Willie Donachie, who I played with at international level when he impressed me with his competitive attitude and positional sense.

Jimmy Johnstone, another hero from Celtic's 1967 European Cup winning team, will play as a

A master of scoring from impossible angles, Dalglish hit 118 League goals in a Liverpool playing career that spanned 12 years.

withdrawn winger who can cause mayhem down the right with his jinking runs.

Bossing the midfield will be three men who were the heart of the great Liverpool team of the 1980s: Graeme Souness, Terry McDermott and Ray Kennedy. Souness will be the leader, bringing the best out of the players around him with his inspirational style. McDermott will be the organiser, and will come through from deep positions to steal goals. Kennedy's educated left foot will make him the master of the left side of midfield.

My front two are proven goal kings, Ian Rush and Denis Law. I had some of the greatest

moments of my playing career alongside Ian, who was unselfish and prepared to run himself into the ground to make and take goals for the team. We fed off each other for a long time at Liverpool and always had mutual respect.

I played with Denis near the end of his international career when he was recalled for the 1974 World Cup campaign. It was a thrill for a young player like me to operate with one of the finest finishers of all time. One of my proudest achievements was to equal his Scottish international record of 30 goals. He and Ian would establish a formidable partnership that no defence would fancy facing, particularly with Jimmy Johnstone performing his tricks on the right wing. While the defenders are trying to take care of these three, Ray Kennedy will be creeping up on the left to hammer in shots with his left foot.

It is a beautifully balanced side that I would certainly consider an honour to manage.

Tragedies that darkened a decade

Three appalling disasters plunged the 1980s into the blackest decade in the history of British football. The game was sent reeling by the Bradford City fire of 1985 that cost 56 lives at the Valley Parade ground, followed just three weeks later by the horror of Heysel Stadium. Thirty-nine spectators died from crushing and suffocation during the European Cup final between Juventus and Liverpool in Brussels on 29 May.

The heartbreak of Heysel generated an international debate on hooliganism and scarred the reputation of English football supporters. Subsequent investigations into the tragedy laid the blame on the fans, and the repercussions were felt throughout the English game. All League clubs were banned by UEFA from taking part in European competitions, leaving English football to stagnate. By the time the ban was lifted in 1990 English teams were trailing their European rivals tactically.

And just as the nightmare was coming to an end a third devastating tragedy struck. Ninety-five spectators were killed and 170 injured on overcrowded terraces during the Liverpool-Nottingham Forest FA Cup semi-final at Hillsborough on 15 April 1989. It was a catastrophe witnessed by millions on television, and led to a whirlwind of change.

The 1980s had got off to a flying start on the playing field, with Forest, Aston Villa and Liverpool leading the way in Europe. It was Liverpool who dominated on the domestic stage, winning the League championship six times during the decade including a hat-trick between 1982 and 1984. Bob Paisley handed over the manager's baton to Joe Fagan before Kenny Dalglish took over to keep alight the red flame first ignited by Bill Shankly.

On the World Cup stage, Italy were winners in 1982 and Maradona-motivated Argentina in 1986. Paolo Rossi, restored to the national team after a ban for his involvement in a bribery scandal, shot Italy to victory in the World Cup final against West Germany. Diego Maradona, getting away with a 'hand of God' handball goal against England in the quarter-finals, skippered the Argentine team that beat West Germany in the 1986 final in Mexico. Gary Lineker was top marksman with six goals.

The English soccer scene became truly international during the 1980s. Argentines Osvaldo Ardiles and Ricardo Villa and Dutchmen Arnold Muhren and Franz Thijssen lead a flood of overseas players who were to rejuvenate what had become a stereotyped English game. Wimbledon brought some romance (if a little ruggedly) to the home front by battling their way from the Fourth Division to the First and shocking Liverpool to defeat in the 1988 FA Cup final.

In the European Championship, West Germany in 1980, with Karl-Heinz Rummenigge in full flow, became the first team to win a second title. France, inspired by Michel Platini, won the championship with flair in 1984, and Holland were the 1988 victors thanks to the goalscoring of Marco van Basten and the style of Ruud Gullit.

Seven-figure British transfers became commonplace in the 1980s, with Bryan Robson setting a new record in 1981 in a £1.5 million move from West Bromwich Albion to Manchester United. By the end of the decade United had broken the British record again by paying Middlesbrough £2.3 million for central defender Gary Pallister. Mark Hughes (£2.3 million to Barcelona), Gary Lineker (£2.75 million to Barcelona), Ian Rush (£2.8 million to Juventus) and Chris Waddle (£4.25 million to Marseille) were among the big-money exports. But all four would eventually return to an English game that was getting its act together after a decade that will be remembered for all the wrong reasons.

–Norman Giller

The Heysel Stadium disaster marred the 1985 Champions Cup final and kept English teams out of European competition for five seasons.

Injured fans were carried on advertising boards during the 1989 Hillsborough tragedy, which led to huge changes in stadia design.

Who won what

1979-80

League champions: Liverpool
FA Cup final: West Ham United 1, Arsenal 0
League Cup final: Wolves 1, Nottingham Forest 0
First Division marksman: Phil Boyer (So'ton), 23
Footballer of the Year: Terry McDermott (Liverpool)
Scottish champions: Aberdeen
Scottish Cup final: Celtic 1, Rangers 0
Scottish Player of the Year: Gordon Strachan (Aberdeen)
European Cup final: Nottm Forest 1, SV Hamburg 0
Cup Winners' Cup final: Valencia 0, Arsenal 0 (Valencia won 5-4 on penalties)
UEFA Cup final: Eintracht Frankfurt 3, Borussia Moenchengladbach 3 (Eintracht on away goals)
European Footballer of the Year: Karl-Heinz Rummenigge (Bayern Munich)
European Championship final: West Germany 2, Belgium 1

1980-1

League champions: Aston Villa
FA Cup final: Tottenham 3, Man City 2 (after l-1 draw)
League Cup final: Liverpool 2, West Ham 1 (after 1-1 draw)
First Division marksmen: Steve Archibald (Spurs), Peter Withe (Aston Villa), 20
Footballer of the Year: Frans Thijssen (Ipswich Town)
Scottish champions: Celtic
Scottish Cup final: Rangers 4, Dundee Utd 1 (after a 0-0 draw)
Scottish Player of the Year: Alan Rough (P Thistle)
European Cup final: Liverpool 1, Real Madrid 0
Cup Winners' Cup final: Dynamo Tbilisi 2, Carl Zeiss Jena 1
UEFA Cup final: Ipswich 5, AZ 67 Alkmaar 4 (3-0, 2-4)
European Footballer of the Year: Karl-Heinz Rummenigge (Bayem Munich)

1981-2

League champions: Liverpool
FA Cup final: Tottenham 1, QPR 0 (after 1-1 draw)
League Cup final: Liverpool 3, Tottenham 1 (aet)
First Division marksman: Kevin Keegan (So'ton), 26
Footballer of the Year: Steve Perryman (Tottenham)
Scottish champions: Celtic
Scottish Cup final: Aberdeen 4, Rangers 1 (aet)
Scottish Player of the Year: Paul Sturrock (Dundee Utd)
European Cup final: Aston Villa 1, Bayern Munich 0
Cup Winners' Cup final: Barcelona 2, Standard Liege 1
UEFA Cup final: IFK Gothenburg 4, Hamburg 0 (1-0, 3-0)
European Footballer of the Year: Paolo Rossi (Juventus)
World Cup final: Italy 3, West Germany 1

1982-3

League champions: Liverpool
FA Cup final: Man Utd 4, Brighton 0 (after 2-2 draw)
League Cup final: Liverpool 2, Manchester United 1 (aet)
First Division marksman: Luther Blissett (Watford), 27
Footballer of the Year: Kenny Dalglish (Liverpool)
Scottish champions: Dundee United
Scottish Cup final: Aberdeen 1, Rangers 0 (aet)
Scottish Player of the Year: Charlie Nicholas (Celtic)

European Cup final: SV Hamburg 1, Juventus 0
Cup Winners' Cup final: Aberdeen 2, Real Madrid I (aet)
UEFA Cup final: Anderlecht 2, Benfica 1 (1-0, 1-1)
European Footballer of the Year: Michel Platini (Juventus)

1983-4

League champions: Liverpool
FA Cup final: Everton 2. Watford 0
League Cup final: Liverpool 1, Everton 0 (after 0-0 draw)
First Division marksman: Ian Rush (Liverpool), 32
Footballer of the Year: Ian Rush (Liverpool)
Scottish champions: Aberdeen
Scottish Cup final: Aberdeen 2, Celtic I (aet)
Scottish Player of the Year: Willie Miller (Aberdeen)
European Cup final: Liverpool 1, AS Roma 1 (Liverpool won 4-2 on penalties)
Cup Winners' Cup final: Juventus 2, Porto 1
UEFA Cup final: Spurs 2, Anderlecht 2 (1-1, 1-1; Spurs won 4-3 on penalties)
European Footballer of the Year: Michel Platini (Juventus)
European Championship final: France 2, Spain 0

1984-5

League champions: Everton
FA Cup final: Manchester United 1, Everton 0 (aet)
League Cup final: Norwich City 1, Sunderland 0
First Division marksman: Kerry Dixon (Chelsea), 24
Footballer of the Year: Neville Southall (Everton)
Scottish champions: Aberdeen
Scottish Cup final: Celtic 2, Dundee United 1
Scottish Player of the Year: Hamish McAlpine (Dundee United)
European Cup final: Juventus 1, Liverpool 0
Cup Winners' Cup final: Everton 3, Rapid Vienna 1
UEFA Cup final: Real Madrid 3, Videoton 1 (3-0, 0-1)
European Footballer of the Year: Michel Platini (Juventus)

1985-6

League champions: Liverpool
FA Cup final: Liverpool 3, Everton 1
League Cup final: Oxford United 3, QPR 0
First Division marksman: Gary Lineker (Everton), 30
Footballer of the Year: Gary Lineker (Everton)
Scottish champions: Celtic
Scottish Cup final: Aberdeen 3, Hearts 0
Scottish Player of the Year: Sandy Jardine (Hearts)
European Cup final: Steaua Bucharest 0, Barcelona 0 (Steaua won 2-0 on penalties)
Cup Winners' Cup final: Dynarno Kiev 3, Atletico Madrid 0
UEFA Cup final: Real Madrid 5, Cologne 3 (5-1, 0-2)
European Footballer of the Year: Igor Belanov (Dynamo Kiev)
World Cup final: Argentina 3, West Germany 2

1986-7

League champions: Everton
FA Cup final: Coventry City 3, Tottenham Hotspur 2
League Cup final: Arsenal 2, Liverpool 1
First Division marksman: Clive Allen (Tottenharn), 33
Footballer of the Year: Clive Allen (Tottenham)
Scottish champions: Rangers
Scottish Cup final: St Mirren 1, Dundee Utd 0 (aet)

Scottish Player of the Year: Brian McClair (Celtic)
European Cup final: FC Porto 2, Bayern Munich 1
Cup Winners' Cup final: Ajax 1, Lokomotiv Leipzig 0
UEFA Cup final: IFK Gothenburg 2, Dundee Utd I (1-0, 1-1)
European Footballer of the Year: Ruud Gullit (AC Milan)

1987-8

League champions: Liverpool
FA Cup final: Wimbledon 1, Liverpool 0
League Cup final: Luton Town 3, Arsenal 2
First Division marksman: John Aldridge (Liverpool), 29
Footballer of the Year: John Barnes (Liverpool)
Scottish champions: Celtic
Scottish Cup final: Celtic 2, Dundee United 1
Scottish Player of the Year: Paul McStay (Celtic)
European Cup final: PSV Eindhoven 0, Benfica 0 (PSV won 6-5 on penalties)
Cup Winners' Cup final: Mechelen 1, Ajax 0
UEFA Cup final: Bayer Leverkusen 3, Espanol 3 (0-3, 3-0, Bayer won 3-2 on penalties)
European Footballer of the Year: Marco van Basten (AC Milan)
European Championship final: Holland 2, Russia 0

1988-9

League champions: Arsenal
FA Cup final: Liverpool 3, Everton 2 (aet)
League Cup final: Nottingham Forest 3, Luton Town 1
First Division marksman: Alan Smith (Arsenal), 23
Footballer of the Year: Steve Nicol (Liverpool)
Scottish champions: Rangers
Scottish Cup final: Celtic 1, Rangers 0
Scottish Player of the Year: Richard Gough (Rangers)
European Cup final: AC Milan 4, Steaua Bucharest 0
Cup Winners' Cup final: Barcelona 2, Sampdoria 0
UEFA Cup final: Napoli 5, Stuttgart 4 (2-1, 3-3)
European Footballer of the Year: Marco van Basten (AC Milan)

Ruud Gullit, the 1987 European Footballer of the Year, helped to transform AC Milan into one of the world's greatest club sides.

Terry McDermott

Born: Kirby, Liverpool, 8 December 1951.

Honours: Terry was a dynamic midfield player, who scored 54 goals in 232 League games for Liverpool between two spells with Newcastle United. He escaped the Mersey net of both Liverpool and Everton and started his career with Bury before joining Newcastle in 1973.

Terry played for Newcastle against Liverpool in the 1974 FA Cup final and in the same year moved to Anfield in a £160,000 deal.

He has four League championship and three European Cup winner's medals as consolation for being on the losing side in FA Cup finals with Newcastle and Liverpool. In his peak season of 1979-80 he became the first player to be voted both the Football Writers' and the Professional Footballers' Association Player of the Year.

Terry made his England debut in Ron Greenwood's first match as manager in 1978, and went on to win 25 caps. He was not a prolific scorer, but when he did find the net, coming through from his midfield base, it was usually with a spectacular shot delivered with his right foot. His distribution was accurate and imaginative. He returned to football as Kevin Keegan's loyal right-hand man during his eventful spell as manager of Newcastle United, and he then became number two at St James' Park to another old Anfield club-mate, Kenny Dalglish.

McDermott, a dynamic midfield player who was always conscious of the team's needs, made 232 League games for Liverpool.

This was his year

The highlight of a memorable season for Terry was one of the finest goals he ever scored. It came in the sixth round of the FA Cup at Tottenham. He picked up a loose ball, flicked it in the air with his right foot and as it came down volleyed it into the top left-hand corner of the net from a tight angle.

The goal lifted Liverpool to a 1-0 victory, and it was replayed so many times on television that it probably went a long way to clinching for him both the PFA and Football Writers' Player of the Year awards.

On the day that Terry was due to collect the Football Writers' award at a glittering ceremony in London, he sent a midday message to say that he would not be attending. It was reported that this keen follower of the horses was at the races and urgent broadcasts were relayed at the course. There was a panic because more than 700 football dignitaries were gathered to welcome their guest of honour. Then a late message arrived to say that he had to withdraw because of a family illness. This was very sad. He became the only player in the 50-year history of the award who failed for reasons other than a football engagement to turn up to collect it.

It was his genial manager Bob Paisley who stepped forward to receive the award on his behalf. He said that Terry had earned the award with his unselfish team play. 'He would be the first to share the credit for this award with his team-mates,' said Paisley. 'We have always believed at Anfield that the team is more important than the individual, and there are few better team players than Terry. His 11 goals for us in the League this season were vital in helping us to regain the championship. The fact he has been recognised as the top man by both the players and the football writers says everything about his season. He has been magnificent.'

His Dream Team

RAY CLEMENCE

PHIL NEAL   TOMMY SMITH   RAY KENNEDY   JOEY JONES

JIMMY CASE   IAN CALLAGHAN   EMLYN HUGHES   TERRY McDERMOTT

KEVIN KEEGAN   STEVE HEIGHWAY

It was Terry's magnificent goal that set us on the way to victory in the first European Cup final in Rome in 1977. The way he found space and then finished with a scorching shot epitomised the way he combined power and intelligence as one of the great midfield players. **– KEVIN KEEGAN**

Terry was always ready to put the needs of the team above his own and gave every side he played for drive and direction. His contribution to the successful Liverpool team of the 1970s and 1980s was invaluable. **– KENNY DALGLISH**

Terry was a master at finding space from a deep position, and then using the ball with accuracy either for a measured pass or a powerful shot. He perfected the modern midfielder's game. **– MALCOLM MACDONALD**

● ●

Terry McDermott declined to select a team, so we have come up with a side that will live for ever in his memory: the Liverpool team that lifted the European Cup for the first time in Rome on 25 May 1977.

Just four days earlier League champions Liverpool had stumbled in their bid for an ambitious treble when they lost in the FA Cup final against Manchester United. For the European Cup final against Borussia Moenchengladbach, manager Bob Paisley decided on a change of tactics and formation. He recalled veteran Ian Callaghan to the midfield and switched from 4-3-3 at Wembley to a 4-4-2 formation. Kevin Keegan was given the responsibility of a central striking role in what would be his last match for Liverpool.

It was a magical goal by McDermott after 27 minutes that put Liverpool on the way to a memorable 3-1 victory. Callaghan began the move after winning the ball close to the half-way line. He provided a quick pass to Heighway on the right and then made an overlapping support run on the outside of the long-striding Irishman. This left the scampering German defenders pondering who to mark. They were so concerned with the poser set by Callaghan, who was moving with such menace down the touchline, and Heighway, with the ball, that they failed to spot Terry McDermott's 50-yard sprint from midfield.

Heighway, now cutting diagonally towards goal, knew McDermott would be powering into position

McDermott was the first player to win the Football Writers' and the Professional Footballers' Association awards.

because it was evident that this was a rehearsed movement. He released a perfectly weighted pass between two defenders; McDermott and the ball arrived together in the penalty area with only goalkeeper Kneib aware of the sudden danger. The German international did his best to cover his goal as he came forward to narrow the angle but he was beaten comprehensively by McDermott's shot on the run that arrowed into the left-hand corner of the net. It was a goal fit to hang in an art gallery.

Borussia equalised early in the second half, but then a rare headed goal by Tommy Smith put

Liverpool back in command. The victory was wrapped up by an electric run by Keegan who panicked his marker Berti Vogts into a desperate tackle that brought Liverpool an 83rd-minute penalty. Liverpool's penalty taker was dead-eye shot Phil Neal, a spot-kick specialist who powered the ball into the net to complete the greatest night in Liverpool's history.

Terry McDermott played a key role in the victory, and was singled out for praise by manager Bob Paisley. 'It was Terry's goal that gave us the spark we needed,' he said. 'We were feeling down in the dumps after our defeat by Manchester United at Wembley, and this was just the pick-up we needed. His run through the middle to collect the ball was typical of the way he plays the game. Terry Mac is a great team player whose best work is not always given the recognition it deserves.'

Three years later McDermott got the recognition with his then unique double of the PFA and FWA awards.

Frans Thijssen

Born: Heuman, Holland, 23 January 1952.

Honours: Frans was the second Dutch international to join Ipswich Town from Twente Enschede. Ipswich paid £200,000 for him in January 1979, six months after signing Arnold Muhren. Frans began his career with NEC Nijmegen and moved to FC Twente for £75,000 in 1974. His consistent displays in midfield for Ipswich earned him a recall to his national side in the 1980 European Championship, and he was also voted Ipswich's Player of the Year in the 1979-80 season.

He played 123 League matches for Ipswich and helped them win the UEFA Cup in 1981, scoring a goal in each leg of the final against his old Dutch rivals Alkmaar. In 1982 he moved to Vancouver Whitecaps before a short spell back in English football in 1983-4 with Nottingham Forest. He then returned to Holland for the final shots of his career with Fortuna Sittard, FC Groningen and Vitesse Arnhem, where he settled into a job as team coach before moving to FC Malmo.

Thijssen won over the Ipswich supporters with his workmanlike performances that were not as polished as those of his Dutch team-mate Muhren, but often more effective. It was their harnessing in midfield that gave Ipswich a combination of flair and fire, and they were the key to turning Bobby Robson's Ipswich into one of the strongest teams in Europe.

Frans Thijssen followed Arnold Muhren to Ipswich Town from Holland to form a double Dutch act.

This was my year

It was one of my better decisions to follow my Twente Enschede team-mate Arnold Muhren to Ipswich. I recall that it was Arnold who recommended me to manager Bobby Robson and he flew to Holland to try to persuade me to team up with Arnold at Portman Road.

Bobby had reluctantly just sold Brian Talbot to Arsenal and he saw me as his replacement. Twente did not want to let me go, but the offer came when they had no money coming in because of the bad winter and so they accepted the £200,000 bid.

Bobby, who was kind enough to call it one of the great bargain buys, told me that he was convinced that Ipswich could win major trophies with Arnold and I operating together in wide midfield positions. He was proved right in 1980-1 when Ipswich were in the running for the treble of League championship, FA Cup and the UEFA Cup. It was a fairytale season for me because not only

did I score a goal in each leg of the UEFA Cup final against my old Dutch rivals Alkmaar but I had the great honour of being elected Footballer of the Year.

This meant an enormous amount to me, and I can honestly say that it was one of the proudest moments of my career. I had always been a keen follower of English football, and I was aware of the standing of the award. I saw it as a reward for the Ipswich team as much as for me.

We played magnificent football throughout the season, and with a little luck might have beaten Aston Villa to the title. Manchester City put us out in the semi-final of the FA Cup, but we hung on to win the UEFA Cup. What was particularly satisfying for me is that I managed to have a winning end to a season which early on looked like being wrecked by hamstring problems. It meant I was not always able to train properly, but all those competitive matches kept me fit!

My Dream Team

GORDON BANKS

VIV ANDERSON   TERRY BUTCHER   BOBBY MOORE   KENNY SANSOM

KEVIN KEEGAN   GLENN HODDLE   BRYAN ROBSON   BOBBY CHARLTON

ALAN SHEARER   GEORGE BEST

IT has been my intention to select a team that combines the best of English football with the physical side of the game. Bryan Robson will bring muscle as well as method to the midfield, and my old Ipswich team-mate Terry Butcher will be the heart of the defence with his combative style of play.

I was tempted to select several of my former team-mates, but finally settled for just Terry and Viv Anderson, with whom I played at Nottingham Forest during a brief return to England. I cannot think of a more commanding central defensive partnership than Butcher and the unmatchable Bobby Moore.

Terry would be the master in the air and Bobby would tidy up everything on the floor before triggering counter attacks with those penetrating passes of his that served England so well in the 1966 World Cup. They will have the sure and safe Gordon Banks collecting anything that gets past them. Viv will team up with Kenny Sansom at full-back, and both can come forward as modern wing-backs.

With Glenn Hoddle and Bobby Charlton providing the passes and Kevin Keegan making his thrusting runs from a deep position, I am confident my midfield is as strong and skilful as it can be. As an old midfield player myself, I like to see players in that vital engine room of the team who can use the ball with intelligence. The combination of Kevin Keegan, Glenn Hoddle, Bryan Robson and

Bobby Charlton guarantees that my team will ooze with class.

I have been immensely impressed by the performances of Alan Shearer, and I have paired him with the one and only George Best at the front of the attack. I considered playing Gary Lineker alongside Shearer, but just could not leave out the wonderfully talented Best. Gary will have to make do with the substitute's shirt. What a player to have waiting to come on from your bench!

My captain will be that great British ambassador Bobby Charlton, who will no doubt frighten the life out of the goalkeepers with those long-range rocket shots of his. My manager will be Bobby Robson, who has had such an eventful time since leaving Ipswich where I had so many memorable times under his management.

I would, of course, have been tempted to select my countryman Arnold Muhren, who made such a great impression in English football while with Ipswich and then Manchester United. But my understanding is that I should select only British players, and I would say that my team presents the best of British and is a balanced mix of the old and the new.

Thijssen, who made 123 League appearances for Ipswich Town, scored a vital goal in each leg of the 1981 UEFA Cup final.

Steve Perryman

Born: Ealing, London, 21 December 1957.

Honours: When Tottenham manager Bill Nicholson introduced Steve as a fresh-faced 17-year-old in 1969 he described him as 'a diamond of a prospect'. More than 700 League and Cup games later he had certainly lived up to his promise. Tottenham have rarely had a more dedicated player.

Steve won one England cap (awarded by Ron Greenwood in a 1-1 draw with Iceland in 1982 at the age of 30 and when accustomed to the tag of England's best uncapped player). He played a club record 655 games for Tottenham (1969-85) before winding down with Oxford United and Brentford.

His strength as a marauding midfield player was his dynamic energy, and he used to cover every inch of the field in support of his team-mates. He captained Tottenham to victories in the FA Cup finals of 1981 and 1982, and provided the bite to go with the brilliance of Ossie Ardiles. His tackling was hard but fair, and his passing accurate if somewhat unimaginative. Other players took the eye, but invariably it was Steve who triggered winning movements.

He had spells as manager at Brentford and Watford before returning to White Hart Lane as assistant manager and then caretaker manager prior to the arrival of Gerry Francis. In 1996 he moved to Japan to work with his old Tottenham team-mate Ardiles.

Steve Perryman, a marauding midfielder, played more than 700 matches for Spurs during an illustrious 17-year career at the club.

Always the reluctant hero, Steve Perryman skippered Tottenham to successive FA Cup final triumphs in 1981 and 1982.

This was my year

I will always remember the reaction of Ron Atkinson when it was announced that I was the Footballer of the Year. Ron wrote a piece for a free newspaper (probably for £100, just joking Ron), when he stated that I should not have won the award. 'It should go to a player with flair,' he wrote. I understood that thinking but my feeling has always been that for every Hoddle and Ardiles you need one of me.

There was so much happening the year I won the award. Spurs had captured the FA Cup the previous season, beating Manchester City 3-2 after a 1-1 draw at Wembley. As captain, I was bang in the middle of things and this season was even more hectic. We were going for four trophies and were top of the League at one stage. In the event we won the Cup again with a 1-0 replay win over Queens Park Rangers.

But we fell short in the championship, lost to Liverpool in the League Cup and lost in the semi-finals of the European Cup Winners' Cup. The Footballer of the Year award was an unexpected bonus.

There was a certain irony when Dennis Signy contacted me to say I was the choice of the Football Writers' Association because, years before, I had a Sunday morning trial for Brentford. There were dozens of us young hopefuls at Griffin Park that morning and I was one of many who received a tap on the shoulder and was told: 'Sorry, son, we don't need to see any more.'

A few weeks later Dennis, then general manager of Brentford, turned up at my home in west London with Bill Gray, the team manager, to ask me to sign. It seems they had heard of the reputation of the youngster who had been turned away and wanted to make amends. I can remember my brother telling them they were too late ... I had signed for Spurs. To this day Dennis insists he told me he would make me a star!

My Dream Team

PAT JENNINGS

DANNY McGRAIN   ROY McFARLAND   ALAN HANSEN   CYRIL KNOWLES

MARTIN PETERS   GLENN HODDLE   GRAEME SOUNESS   OSSIE ARDILES   GEORGE BEST

KENNY DALGLISH

WHAT THE PLAYERS SAY...

Perryman's energetic style won him the respect of his fellow professionals but only one international appearance for England.

I have selected my Dream Team in a 4-5-1 formation, with the emphasis on attack. I agonised over whether to play my old team-mate Alan Gilzean alongside Kenny Dalglish up front. In the end it boiled down to Gilzean or Ossie Ardiles to play a supporting role. I opted for Ossie, with whom I am now working in Japan for the Shimizu-S-Pulse club that won their League Cup in our first season in 1996. Kenny Dalglish will be

comfortable on his own at the front because he would know there was a lot of support going to come from all the talented players behind him. My reasoning is that with Martin Peters, Glenn Hoddle and George Best pouring through from midfield you are still going to get a lot of goals.

My choice as captain would be Graeme Souness, who is an inspirational leader in the mould of an old Spurs hero, Dave Mackay.

Pat Jennings was my selection in goal just ahead of Gordon Banks and Peter Shilton. He was the goalkeeper when I first made my break through into the Spurs team, and it used to fill me with confidence to look back and see him on our goal-line with his huge hands.

Danny McGrain and dear old Cyril Knowles would be full-backs with flair, and the combination of Roy McFarland and Alan Hansen in the middle of the defence would mean a tough time for any attackers trying to get through.

Souness would be the ball-winner in midfield, and he would then let Hoddle and Ardiles take over. They would unlock defences with their perfect passes, and Martin Peters would ghost into goal-scoring positions in that unique style of his.

I have put George Best down on the left side of midfield, but he would have a free role and could go wherever he thought he could do most damage. I can see him twisting and turning past tackles before releasing the ball to Dalglish, who

Steve knew his limitations and never tried to add frills to his game. He concentrated on playing for the team, and could always be relied on to give every ounce of effort. Other players would take the eye, but the real pros knew that it was Steve who was helping make the team tick. **– GLENN HODDLE**

I never ceased to be amazed at Steve's non-stop energy. He would run and run and chase and chase and never take a moment's rest. He was the heart of that Tottenham team that did so well coming into the 1980s. **– OSSIE ARDILES**

I was pleased to get the chance to give Steve the cap he so richly deserved. At any other time he might have won many more caps, but his peak years coincided with a period when England had many outstanding midfield players. **– RON GREENWOOD**

Steve had not made any great impact with me when I was at West Ham, but on joining him at Tottenham I began to appreciate his contribution to the team. He was an unselfish player who inspired the players around him with his competitive attitude.

– MARTIN PETERS

• •

was always deadly in front of goal. Hoddle and Ardiles would be in charge of deadball situations. I was always amazed at the different permutations they could come up with when we used to play together for Tottenham. They were continually a thought ahead of the opposition.

Glenn could strike a ball so sweetly, and he should have been rewarded with many more caps. It was laughable to hear him described as a luxury player. He could take any defence apart with just one beautifully-flighted pass.

This is a team that I would willingly pay to watch, and it would be a dream to manage them.

FOOTBALLER OF THE YEAR
1984

Ian Rush

Born: St Asaph, Flintshire, 20 October 1961.

Honours: One of the great goalscorers of modern times, Ian will always be associated with his glory years at Liverpool when he was a vital member of the team which won the European Cup in 1984, League championship 1982, '83, '84, '86, '90, League Cup 1981, '82, '83, '84, and the FA Cup in 1986, '89, '92. He missed the championship success of 1986 during an unsettled and unsatisfactory season in Italian football with Juventus.

Ian won schoolboy international honours with Wales before starting his professional career with Chester City, moving on to Anfield in 1980. In his two spells with Liverpool, he scored 139 goals in 224 League appearances and then another 90 goals in 245 League games. He joined Leeds on a free transfer in the summer of 1996, and started to respond to the motivating influence of manager George Graham after struggling during a season at Elland Road.

He has won more than 75 caps with Wales, and has overtaken Trevor Ford and Ivor Allchurch as their top international goal scorer, reaching the 30-goal milestone. He is a direct, no-fuss-and-frills striker, who has a dramatic change of pace and, while favouring his right foot, is also an accurate finisher with his left. He specialises in glided rather than power headers, and is an instinctive positional player.

Rush scored 229 goals in 469 League appearances for Liverpool, despite an unhappy one-year break in Italy with Juventus.

This was my year

There are 50 good reasons why the season in which I won the Footballer of the Year accolade stands out in my memory. I scored 49 goals that season, and I made it an unofficial half century in the most important match of all. We finished locked at 1-1 with Roma after extra time in the European Cup final on their home pitch at the Olympic Stadium. I was one of four Liverpool players who found the net in the penalty shoot-out to give us a 4-2 victory.

This completed an unforgettable hat-trick of cups. We had earlier won the League championship in a nail-biting finish with Southampton. I managed four goals against Coventry that helped to clinch the title in the second week in May, which proves it went down to the wire. We had already wrapped up the League Cup for a fourth time in a row by beating our Merseyside rivals Everton 1-0 in a replay.

Thirty-two of my goals came in the League as Liverpool won the First Division championship for the 15th time. This made us only the third club after Huddersfield and Arsenal to win the title three years in succession.

It was an unbelievable first season in charge for our manager Joe Fagan, who had the tough job of following Bob Paisley. The most striking thing about that year was our consistency. Everything went like clockwork, and Joe hardly had to make a team change. In fact he used only 15 players from our squad all season.

As I said when accepting my Footballer of the Year trophy, the secret of Liverpool's success was team-work. It was everybody playing for the team rather than themselves that made us such a formidable side. It was during that season that the Italian clubs started to make approaches for me. I finally gave in and moved to Juventus, but to be honest my heart was always at Anfield and I could not wait to get back.

My Dream Team

NEVILLE SOUTHALL

DANNY McGRAIN ALAN HANSEN PAUL McGRATH KENNY SANSOM

BRYAN ROBSON GRAEME SOUNESS

KEVIN KEEGAN RYAN GIGGS

JOHN CHARLES KENNY DALGLISH

I have dipped back into the past for just one player in my Dream Team: John Charles, the player whose path I followed to Juventus and Leeds and into the Wales team. You could not grow up in Welsh football without hearing the legend of Charles, a giant who was equally at home in the centre of defence or leading the attack. When I moved briefly to Juventus they still talked in awe of his performances in Italy, and old-timers at Leeds swear that he was the greatest player they ever saw.

So Charles is a must for my side, and I have decided to play him in attack alongside my old Anfield partner Kenny Dalglish. I am happy to acknowledge that Kenny made me a much better player with his unselfish running, clever decoy play and accurate touch-off passes.

One of my heroes when I was a youngster was Denis Law, and I wondered how I could get him into my team. I have finally settled for making him the substitute. What a player to be able to bring on!

Attacking down the right flank I have Kevin Keegan, who Kenny followed into the No. 7 shirt at Liverpool. I was just starting out on my career with Chester when Kevin made the move from Liverpool to Hamburg, but I saw enough of him to know that he used to make things happen with his non-stop running and clever changes of pace.

Out on the left I have one of the greatest players ever to come out of Wales in Ryan Giggs,

whose ball control and speed means he can take apart any defence when in full flow. Holding the midfield together will be two positive players in Bryan Robson and Graeme Souness. Bryan will need no encouragement to come forward to support the attack, while Graeme will be the ball winner. I will also make him the captain because he was always such an inspiring team-mate when we were together in the great days at Anfield.

I have settled for a full-back combination of Danny McGrain and Kenny Sansom because both were firm in the tackle and quick to come forward on attacking runs.

At the heart of my defence I have the calculating Jocky Hansen and the extremely competitive Paul McGrath, who is never easy to play against because of his refusal to admit defeat. They will be an ideal balance for each other.

I have played enough times with Neville Southall for Wales to appreciate that he is a class above most goalkeepers. He has great presence and always makes it difficult for forwards to find a space for their shots. His positioning is rarely wrong, and when he is caught out he quickly gets himself out of trouble with his brave diving and reflex saves. My team is built for attack and I cannot think there would be a defence in the world able to stand up to the twin thrusts of the giant John Charles and the quick and clever Kenny Dalglish.

WHAT THE PLAYERS SAY...

Ian always made himself easy to find by getting into space, and then when the ball was played to his feet you could bet on him finding the target. We had a terrific understanding and knew where to be to get the best out of each other.

– KENNY DALGLISH

There were times when Ian was really motoring that you thought that every time the ball was played to him he was going to stick it into the net. He was lucky to have Kenny Dalglish playing with him, but he was good enough to make the most of it.

– ALAN HANSEN

He never snatches at his goal chances, but takes deliberate aim and is a deadly finisher. Ian has been a world class player for Wales.

– NEVILLE SOUTHALL

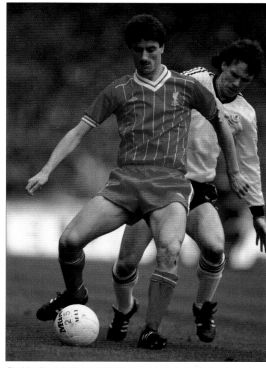

Rush's direct style brought him more than 75 Wales caps and 13 major trophies in one of Liverpool's most successful sides.

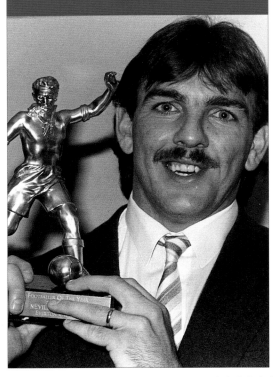

Neville Southall

Born: Llandudno, 16 September 1958.

Honours: Neville came late into League football at the age of 21 after being discovered with local Welsh club Winsford United in 1980 by Bury, who paid £6,000 for him. Within a year Howard Kendall had bought him for Everton in a £150,000 deal that looked a rocky investment when Neville let in five goals against Liverpool at Goodison.

He moved to Port Vale on loan, but following his return after nine League games he cemented himself into the Everton team for a club record run of more than 570 League matches.

Neville got his first taste of glory when collecting an FA Cup winner's medal in 1984, and was a defiant last line of defence the following season when Everton won the League championship, the European Cup Winners' Cup and were runners-up in the FA Cup.

He became the first Everton player elected FWA Footballer of the Year.

A back injury kept him out of the 1986 FA Cup final, and interrupted his run of Welsh international caps that climbed to a record 90.

Neville, powerfully built at 6ft 1in and 14 stone, has a great physical presence, and incredibly quick reflexes. And he was back at Wembley as a runner-up in the 1989 FA Cup Final against Liverpool, and six years later was a Wembley winner against Manchester United.

Neville Southall was the first Everton player to be voted FWA Footballer of the Year, and was the Goodison man for all seasons.

This was my year

One save stands out in my memory above all others from that unforgettable season when I was voted Footballer of the Year. It came during a match against Queens Park Rangers when we knew that a victory would clinch the championship.

It was, I recall, a Bank Holiday Monday and Goodison was packed with a 50,000-plus crowd willing us to win the title. The game was evenly balanced when the Rangers striker Mark Falco was put clean through. Even I thought a goal was a certainty, but somehow I managed to get myself into position to make as important a save as I had ever made. I don't know who was more surprised, Mark Falco or me!

We went on to win the match and the championship on our way to what was nearly a fantastic treble. Nine days later we completed the second leg when we beat Rapid Vienna 3-1 in Rotterdam to win the European Cup Winners' Cup. The next evening I collected my Footballer of the Year statuette, and I was proud to be told that I was the first Everton player to win it. That amazed me when you consider all the fabulous players who had worn the Everton colours before me.

Two days later I was in goal for Everton against Manchester United in the FA Cup final when a superb goal by Norman Whiteside finished our bid for the treble. It had been a great season by any standards, but it all turned sour and sad of course. We were stopped from challenging for the European Cup because of the ban on all Football League clubs following the Heysel Stadium tragedy.

That was an exceptional Everton team, and there is no knowing what we might have achieved under Howard Kendall's management. But at least we had the consolation of capturing the Cup Winners' Cup before the ban on English clubs. I am convinced that we were good enough to have made a winning challenge for the European Cup, but it was just not meant to be.

My Dream Team

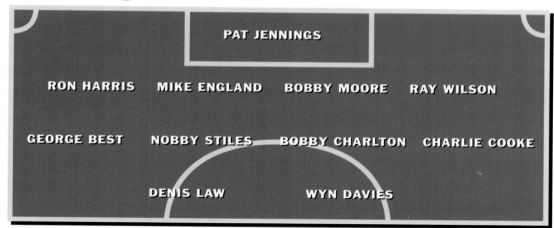

PAT JENNINGS

RON HARRIS   MIKE ENGLAND   BOBBY MOORE   RAY WILSON

GEORGE BEST   NOBBY STILES   BOBBY CHARLTON   CHARLIE COOKE

DENIS LAW   WYN DAVIES

The first name on my team sheet was the captain, Bobby Moore. He was an outstanding professional who led by example. I have never seen a better reader of the game and he always looked so calm and full of authority even when up against the best players in the world. He will play alongside one of the greatest centre-halves to come out of Wales in Mike England, who stood like a Welsh mountain in the middle of the Tottenham defence during the 1960s and 1970s.

Mike was a tower of strength in the air and could play the ball with both feet on the ground. He was remarkably well balanced for such a big man.

Flanking them will be a full-back pairing that will astonish a lot of people. Playing out of position at right-back I have Ron Harris, who was one of the best tacklers there has been. He was nicknamed Chopper because of the strength of his challenges for Chelsea and few players will fancy trying to pass him! On the left I have Ray Wilson, who was such an important part of England's 1966 World Cup winning team. He had a firm tackle plus skill and speed when coming forward.

The last line of defence will be the one and only Pat Jennings, who was admired by all of us in the Goalkeepers' Appreciation Society for his total control of the goal area. There was not a single weakness in his game, and he was completely unflappable. He could make difficult saves look easy by his perfect positioning, and all his work

was carried out without fuss. And those huge hands of his were a goalkeeper's dream!

My midfield will be made up of one ball winner, one playmaker and two ball-playing masters. Nobby Stiles will be the anchorman, winning the ball and then releasing it to his old Manchester United team-mate Bobby Charlton. Bobby will dictate the pace of the match and will unleash his powerful, swerving shots that made life so difficult for goalkeepers. Chelsea's dribbling entertainer Charlie Cooke will operate alongside him, always on the look-out for the chance to run at the defence and cause panic with his bewildering ball control. The unique George Best will have the freedom to go where he feels he can cause most damage. He was out on his own as a master of the footballing arts.

Another Manchester United hero, Denis Law, will play up front alongside that brave Welsh lion of a forward Wyn Davies, who used to trouble the tightest defences with his all-action style. I considered that exceptional finisher Ian Rush for this role, but finally decided that the pairing of Law and Davies

WHAT THE PLAYERS SAY...

would make for a better balance. My substitute will be Jimmy Johnstone, the Celtic wing wizard. If he comes on with Charlie Cooke and George Best, I just wonder how the opposition will ever get the ball off them!

Southall, whose safe hands earned him 90-plus Wales caps, has proved a bargain buy for Everton since his £150,000 transfer in 1981, making more than 570 League appearances for the

FOOTBALLER OF THE YEAR 1986

Gary Lineker

Born: Leicester, 30 November 1960.

Honours: Gary was given the middle name Winston because he shares Churchill's birthday, and had many 'finest hours' on the football field. He won 80 England caps (1984-92), and was captain 18 times. His haul of 48 goals is second on the all-time list only to Bobby Charlton, who scored 49 in 106 England games. He was top scorer in the 1986 World Cup finals in Mexico with six goals, including a hat-trick against Poland.

Gary played for Leicester City (194 League games, 95 goals), Everton (41 League games, 30 goals), Barcelona (99 League games, 44 goals) and Tottenham (105 League games, 67 goals) before winding down his career with Grampus Eight in Japan where a recurring toe injury forced his retirement in 1994.

He cost £800,000 when joining Everton from Leicester City, £2.75 million when moving to Barcelona a year later, and £1.5 million when joining up with his old Barcelona boss Terry Venables at Tottenham.

Club honours included an FA Cup runner's-up medal with Everton in 1986, a Spanish League championship medal with Barcelona and an FA Cup winner's medal with Tottenham in 1991. An attack of hepatitis when at his peak robbed him of pace and power, but he recovered to regain his England place for the 1990 World Cup finals. He is now a successful presenter on both BBC TV and Radio 5 Live.

Lineker scored 67 goals in 105 League appearances for Tottenham, where he won an FA Cup winner's medal in 1991.

This was my year

Winning the Footballer of the Year trophy twice and joining double winners Stanley Matthews, Tom Finney, Danny Blanchflower and Kenny Dalglish – John Barnes won it twice after me – was very fulfilling.

The first time, when I joined Everton from Leicester, came at the end of a memorable season in which I managed to score 38 goals as a member of the best club side I have ever played for. Peter Reid, Paul Bracewell, Trevor Steven and Kevin Sheedy was some midfield and we should have achieved the Double that year, but finally had to settle for runners-up to Liverpool.

Two days after receiving the Footballer of the Year trophy from the one and only Bobby Moore, I had the satisfaction of scoring the first goal in the FA Cup final at Wembley – but Liverpool came back to win 3-1 and pip us on both counts.

Looking back, it had been a hard job following Andy Gray into the Everton striker's role and I had some teething difficulties with a small section of the crowd. A goal against Manchester United in a 3-1 win at Christmas and two goals against Coventry and Sheffield Wednesday won over the fans and Graeme Sharp and I managed some 60 goals that season.

It was a difficult decision to leave, and I would not have gone to any club other than Barcelona.

I reckon my second award, when I came back from Spain to sign for Tottenham, was more of an achievement. Spurs were not as good a side as Everton had been and, with Terry Venables moving upstairs and putting Peter Shreeves in charge of the team, and Paul Gascoigne being out through injury, we were not challengers and finished 15th in the League and were knocked out of the FA Cup in a third-round replay by Aston Villa.

I still managed 33 goals, and a few for England, and guess I got something of a sympathy vote after coming back from hepatitis.

My Dream Team

PETER SHILTON

VIV ANDERSON   BOBBY MOORE   ALAN HANSEN   KENNY SANSOM

GLENN HODDLE   BRYAN ROBSON

GEORGE BEST   BOBBY CHARLTON

KENNY DALGLISH   IAN RUSH

You will see from my Dream Team selection that I agree to some extent with the football writers who voted for me . . . I have chosen six Footballers of the Year in a side that I feel has a good balance and a high skill factor.

I have stuck with players from my generation. People will no doubt be surprised to find that I have omitted Jimmy Greaves, but it is simply because I never had the good fortune to see him play. From all I have heard from old pros in the game, I am sure that if I had seen Jimmy guiding the ball into the net in his inimitable style I would have happily selected him alongside Kenny Dalglish.

Two of my choices, Bobby Charlton and George Best, were in the Manchester United side that beat Leicester City in the first game I ever saw, as a seven-year-old. Both scored that day and made a lasting impression. I won't have to justify their inclusions.

Peter Shilton was one of my boyhood heroes at Leicester and was an unbelievable goalkeeper. I roomed with him for years with England and chose him as a perfectionist goalie. It is amazing, having watched him as a boy, that he is still going strong and I have retired from the game.

I'm not very good at assessing defenders. Viv Anderson, who had the distinction of being the first black player to be chosen for England, may seem a surprise choice but he was very athletic and an enterprising player who got forward and made a

few goals for me. He was a fantastic character to have around a dressing-room and had strong motivating powers.

Kenny Sansom's 86 England caps speak volumes for him; he was technically very good and extremely quick. I saw Bobby Moore in the last few years of his career and go for him along with Alan Hansen, who was a great player at his best and who just gets the nod over the lightning quick Des Walker.

Alongside Bobby Charlton and George Best I opt for Glenn Hoddle, an awesome talent, and Bryan Robson who, if he had avoided injuries, would have qualified as one of the all-time greats. He had everything, good technique, a strong tackle and he could find the net. Paul Gascoigne came into my thoughts. He was at his best in the early 1990s, but he has had more than his share of problems.

Kenny Dalglish is another player who had everything. It is noticeable that Ian Rush's goal ratio at Liverpool was never the same when Kenny was not alongside him.

They are ideal partners to give my attack the perfect finish.

WHAT THE PLAYERS SAY...

Gary had electric pace and a natural instinct for knowing where to be at the right time to put the ball into the net. He was always a handful to mark, and if you let your concentration lapse for a split second he would punish you. **– ALAN HANSEN**

Gary's performances in the 1986 World Cup finals proved he was a striker comparable with the best in the world. He had the knack of being able to turn a half-chance into a goal, and defenders dare not take their eye off him. **– BRYAN ROBSON**

He was great to play with, and could be counted on to come up with the all-important goals when I was with him at Tottenham and in the England team in the 1990 World Cup when he was a real class act. **– PAUL GASCOIGNE**

I watched his career with interest from when he was just a slip of a lad at Leicester. He was the only England striker who could really be compared with Jimmy Greaves. I can give him no higher praise. **– PETER SHILTON**

Lineker, in action during Everton's 1986 FA Cup final defeat against Liverpool at Wembley, shows the sort of determination that brought him more than 200 League goals in England and Spain.

CARLING

Clive Allen

Clive Allen scored a record 49 goals for Tottenham in the 1986-7 season, overtaking the mark set by club legend Jimmy Greaves.

Born: Stepney, East London, 20 May 1961.

Honours: Clive has a thoroughbred footballing pedigree. He was born the month that his father Les helped Tottenham complete the first League and Cup double this century. His uncles and cousins are all part of a huge football dynasty.

He was capped five times by England during a have-boots-will-travel career that, between 1978 and 1996, took him to Queens Park Rangers (twice), Arsenal, Crystal Palace, Tottenham, Bordeaux, Manchester City, Chelsea, West Ham United, Millwall and, for the final shots of his career, Carlisle. Clive played for England at schools, youth, Under-21 and senior level, and started his career as an apprentice at QPR where his father was a popular centre-forward and, briefly, club manager.

His £1 million transfer to Arsenal from Rangers in 1981 set a record in that he never kicked a ball for the Gunners. He was used as the £1 million bait to bring Kenny Sansom from Palace to Highbury in a swap deal.

Clive won three of his caps while with Rangers, and the last two at Spurs. His international debut was as a substitute for Tony Woodcock against Brazil in 1984 when John Barnes scored that classic goal.

He officially retired from football in 1996, and has started a career as a television football pundit, and remains involved in professional sport as a kicker for the London Monarchs.

This was my year

I scored a hat-trick at Villa Park for Spurs on the opening day of the 1986-7 season – and that was the start of an adventure that led to me collecting the Footballer of the Year trophy the following May. In all competitions with Tottenham that season, I scored 49 goals. Thirty-three came in the League, and my 12 in the League Cup remains a record to this day.

David Pleat was the Tottenham manager, and we enjoyed a fabulous season even though we did not, in the end, win anything.

I followed my opening day hat-trick against Aston Villa with a home goal against Newcastle and added five more in three games against Chelsea, Leicester and Everton. There was a turning point to our season when David decided to play five men across the midfield with me on my own up front.

He introduced the system for a game at Oxford, and Spurs were quickly two goals down.

We rallied to win 4-2 and then went off on a run that saw only three defeats in the next 15 games. The system suited the players in the side at that time. Glenn Hoddle had a free role and my goal-scoring task was made easier by having Chris Waddle and Tony Galvin wide making opportunities for me. I was getting clear-cut chances galore. I particularly remember a classic 3-3 draw at Old Trafford and a 1-0 victory at Liverpool.

My confidence was high from the opening game, but Spurs had to settle for third place in the championship behind Everton and Liverpool. We reached the semi-finals of the League Cup where we went out to Arsenal in a replay, and we went all the way to Wembley for the FA Cup final, only to go down 3-2 to Coventry two days after I collected my Footballer of the Year award.

I look back on that season with personal pride. Some teams don't manage 49 goals in a season. I feel that my record will take some beating.

My Dream Team

PAT JENNINGS

DANNY McGRAIN **BOBBY MOORE** **DAVE MACKAY** **KENNY SANSOM**

GEORGE BEST **GRAEME SOUNESS** **GLENN HODDLE** **BOBBY CHARLTON**

KENNY DALGLISH **JIMMY GREAVES**

WHAT THE PLAYERS SAY...

Clive's consistency during that 1986-7 season had to be seen to be believed. You just felt that every time the ball fell to his feet he was going to find the net, and 49 times he did exactly that!
– DAVID PLEAT

My job was simply to get the ball into the middle to Clive and leave the rest to him. His finishing accuracy was just phenomenal. It was one of those seasons when everything he touched turn to gold . . . or should that be goals. **– CHRIS WADDLE**

I had known Clive since his pram days and I was delighted to see him hitting the back of the net with such regularity . . . even though it meant my Tottenham club scoring record was going for a burton!
– JIMMY GREAVES

My first choice for my Dream Team was the incomparable Bobby Moore. I want him as captain and playing at the heart of the defence alongside Dave Mackay. My dad has filled me with legendary tales about Mackay, who was such a driving force in Tottenham's Double team for which Dad scored 23 League goals in that memorable 1960-1 season. Dad said that Mackay was simply the greatest footballer he had ever played with or against. So how can I leave him out of my team? He will be at the back of the defence, a role he played with such style at Derby . . . although I am assured that his greatest performances were in midfield.

I have no doubt that Pat Jennings is the right man for the goalkeeping job, even taking into account outstanding England players such as Gordon Banks, Peter Shilton and Ray Clemence. Big Pat was at Arsenal when I was around the playing scene, but I watched him at Tottenham when I was a youngster and feel he had everything. He had such great physical presence, and was always in command of his area. His 119 caps for Northern Ireland is evidence of his extraordinary consistency.

My full-backs, Danny McGrain and Kenny Sansom, get the vote for their skill, speed and professionalism. They were sound in defence and both could make vital overlapping runs to boost the attack. Every one of the players in the back line can pass the ball with accuracy and imagination, and would be looking to put pressure on the opposition even from deep in their own half.

I have got a strong Scottish influence running through my team. Graeme Souness was a perfect midfield player, tenacious and with flair. Linking him in the middle of the park with Manchester United maestros George Best and Bobby Charlton would give the team an unbelievably high skill factor which would bring the best out of my fourth midfield man, the pass master Glenn Hoddle. I cannot believe any defensive system in the world would be able to keep out a team that has Charlton blitzing in long-range shots, Hoddle chipping the defenders silly and George Best just running them dizzy.

And just look at my pair of strikers: Kenny Dalglish and Jimmy Greaves. I can see Kenny shielding the ball in that unique style of his before turning to slip it into the path of Greavsie, who had nobody to touch him for finding the net. My dad was a great admirer of Jimmy, even though at times he had to live in his shadow both at Chelsea and Tottenham.

It is staggering that Jimmy did not win the Footballer of the Year award of which I am so proud.

Allen, capped five times by England, celebrates his goal in the 1987 FA Cup final. But despite his early strike against Coventry he had to settle for a runner's-up medal.

FOOTBALLER OF THE YEAR 1988

Barnes, who made 79 appearances for England, has won every domestic honour since joining Liverpool from Watford in 1987.

John Barnes

Born: Jamaica, 7 September 1963.

Honours: John will always be remembered for his first goal for England, a samba-rhythm dribble and controlled finish against Brazil at the Maracana Stadium in Rio in 1984; and the dignity he displayed during a period of ignorant racist taunts from so-called England supporters.

Capped 79 times from 1983 to 1996, he started his international career under Bobby Robson and finished it during the reign of Terry Venables.

He won the first 31 of his caps while at Watford, the club with which he launched his career after moving to England with his family when his father, an Army officer, got a London posting. It was at Watford that he came under the wing of Graham Taylor, who was to have an important influence on his career at club and country level.

John joined Liverpool for £900,000 on 19 June 1987. He has since won every domestic honour at Anfield and has skippered the club on his way to more than 300 first-team appearances. He has developed from a striking-from-the-wing role to that of midfield orchestrator, conducting the young team built by Roy Evans.

Away from the football field, John has been laying the foundations for a career as a television pundit with the ITV team (his mother is an experienced television presenter).

This was my year

I reckon that any three or four of the Liverpool side in 1987-8 could have won the Footballer of the Year award. Kenny Dalglish had taken over from Joe Fagan as manager in 1985 and, when I signed from Watford, I thought we were set for a transitional period that clubs go through when new signings arrive. But we all clicked right from the first kick.

What a side we had. It included Peter Beardsley, Ray Houghton and the prodigious goalscoring of John Aldridge. I won the PFA award as the Player of the Year as Liverpool moved towards the League championship and looked set for a Double with an FA Cup final date against Wimbledon. Six or seven of us were nominated for the PFA First Division team. The structure of the side was just right and my feeling is that we would have dominated in Europe if English clubs had been allowed to compete at that time.

It is well recorded that I wanted to go to Italy to play from my early days, but an injury wrecked that dream and I am fatalist enough to accept that it was not meant to be. The compensation, though, was staying and playing in that wonderful Liverpool side. Perhaps I earned the votes ahead of the others because I was more flamboyant than some of my team-mates and caught the eye more, but I honestly feel I collected the trophy for being part of a superb team performance.

Liverpool were runners-up in the League championship when I won again in 1990 and I remember being linked with those all-time greats Stanley Matthews and Tom Finney as the third of three wingers among the select band of players who have won the trophy for a second time.

I never had the pleasure of seeing Tom Finney play, but I was flattered when he commented that I was bringing wing skills back into the game. It was a great compliment from one of the masters, and this lad from Jamaica felt extremely proud.

My Dream Team

PETER SHILTON

PHIL NEAL   BOBBY MOORE   ALAN HANSEN   KENNY SANSOM

GLENN HODDLE   LIAM BRADY   BOBBY CHARLTON   GEORGE BEST

IAN RUSH   KENNY DALGLISH

I go with Peter Shilton rather than Gordon Banks for my Dream Team goalkeeper purely on the basis that I know him and have played with him. He was exceptional and really commanded the goal area.

Nobody was in any doubt about who was in charge when Peter was making his presence felt at the back of the England defence.

Phil Neal was an intelligent right-back, and there is nobody better to have taking penalties for you. At left-back Kenny Sansom would be all style and skill. It was a privilege to have him as my team-mate for years in the England side. Phil and Kenny were the full-backs when I made my debut for England, and I was always impressed by their performances together.

Bobby Moore, so cultured and never seeming to be ruffled, is an obvious choice. I would play him alongside my old Liverpool team-mate Alan Hansen, the best defensive player I have seen. I cannot believe there could be a better partnership in the middle of a defence. It could be argued they might be in trouble in the air, but Peter Shilton will be there to clear up any problems.

I was a fan of both Glenn Hoddle and Liam Brady, and they would provide the perfect balance for each other in midfield. Liam, with his Claw left foot, and Glenn with his deadly right, would unlock the tightest defence with inch-perfect passes.

Alongside them would be Bobby Charlton,

coming through from deep to unleash his bombshell shots from either foot. But it is the legendary George Best who I can see running the show from a midfield base. It could be argued that I have not got a ball winner in the middle, but with the skill factor this team has it would not need anybody to get the ball because they simply would not give it away!

I considered giving one of the striking roles to the redoubtable Alan Shearer, but in the end I voted for a partnership of Ian Rush and Kenny Dalglish. They went together like bacon and eggs for Liverpool and they always knew where to be to get the best out of each other. I like partnerships, such as Eric Cantona and Andy Cole, but I don't want my two up front just to be out-and-out goalscorers. Kenny could do so much to help others as well as contributing his quota of goals. He was a gifted player who could turn a half-chance into a goal.

My team is full of players capable of producing the unexpected and I cannot believe there is a defence that could have stood up to them.

WHAT THE PLAYERS SAY...

I felt fortunate to inherit John in the Liverpool squad when I became manager at Anfield. He was a key player in what was an outstanding team and has always represented Liverpool with distinction.

– KENNY DALGLISH

John always brought an extra dimension to the Liverpool team with his probing work on the left wing. If anything he has become even more of an influence on the team since his switch to midfield where his vision and accuracy with the ball are exceptional. **– ALAN HANSEN**

Nobody who was in the Maracana Stadium when John scored his wonder goal for England will ever forget it. He gave the whole team and the country a lift and he continued to give excellent service to England for more than ten years.

– BOBBY ROBSON

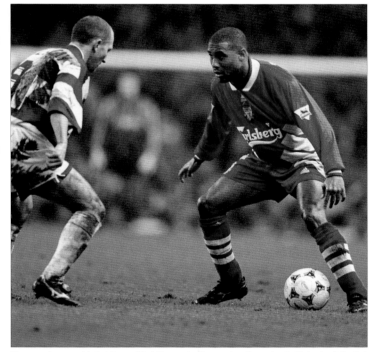

Barnes, whose probing style provided Liverpool with an extra dimension to their play following his move from Watford, was key to Kenny Dalglish's successful side of the late 1980s.

FOOTBALLER OF THE YEAR 1989

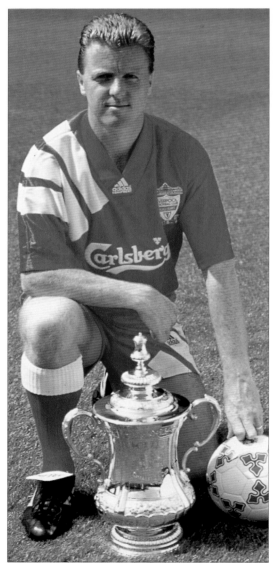

Nicol poses with the FA Cup following Liverpool's emotional win over Merseyside rivals Everton in the post-Hillsborough final.

Steve Nicol

Born: Irvine, Scotland, 11 December 1961.

Honours: Steve is acknowledged by his peers as a players' player whose best work is not always noticed by the crowd. He was capped 27 times by Scotland (1985-92) after joining Liverpool from Ayr United for £300,000 in October 1981. While with Ayr he played 89 Scottish League matches, and he had established himself in the Scottish Under-21 team before moving to Anfield.

He collected 11 League and Cup medals in his 13 seasons at Liverpool (four League championships, three FA Cups and one runner's-up, one League Cup, one European Cup and one runner's-up). In January 1995 he joined Notts County on a free transfer and played 32 matches in the Second Division before moving back into the Premiership with Sheffield Wednesday in November 1995.

Steve scored 36 goals in 343 League matches for Liverpool, and was equally effective in defence or midfield. His versatility was also appreciated by Scotland, and he proudly wore his country's shirt in several different roles. His 27 international appearances included three games in the 1990 World Cup finals.

All-rounder Steve represented Ayrshire at rugby and athletics before deciding on football as a career. He is a low handicap golfer and plays tennis and squash. Competitive and skilful, he is certain one day to pass on his knowledge as a coach or manager.

This was my year

The 1988-9 season when I collected the Footballer of the Year trophy just floated by. We finished runners-up in the League championship race and won the FA Cup, beating our Merseyside rivals Everton 3-2 after extra time in the final at Wembley.

Yet it came as a complete surprise to me to be chosen by the Football Writers' Association for the coveted award. After all, I was playing alongside such worthy contenders as Alan Hansen – one of the great players who has not won the award – Ronnie Whelan, Peter Beardsley, Ian Rush, Ray Houghton and John Barnes.

Any one of them would have been a worthy winner of the trophy, and I was honestly not expecting to be picked out. After all, I did not have an eye-catching role with Liverpool. I was used as a utility player, doing whatever job was considered the most useful for the team. The team comes before any individual at Anfield, and I was always happy to carry out any instructions I was given. Every game in 1988-9, well almost every game, was like a dream coming true. Everything seemed to work, everything seemed to click. It was as if there was no way we were going to lose a game and I seemed to know what I was doing all the time. It was incredible how confident we all felt, and it is confidence that breeds success. The mood we were all in, it was a sheer pleasure to play each game.

People talk about stress in football. I can assure you I felt no stress that season and I don't think any of the other lads did either. When you are around the top of the table and winning, it is not stressful.

The moment I realised just what I had achieved came when I looked at the list of all the previous winners of the Footballer of the Year award. You look at the roll of honour and think, 'Wow! I am with that elite band.' It is a great feeling.

My Dream Team

PETER SHILTON

DANNY McGRAIN   MARK LAWRENSON   ALAN HANSEN   STUART PEARCE

GEORGE BEST   GRAEME SOUNESS   RAY KENNEDY   JOHN BARNES

KENNY DALGLISH   IAN RUSH

I have to admit there is a bit of a Liverpool bias about my Dream Team, which would be captained by Graeme Souness. He taught me a great deal in his time at Anfield and if I don't have bad habits it is down to him. You would want Graeme behind you in the side . . . not coming at you.

Peter Shilton gets my vote as goalkeeper and it stems from a save I saw him make against Kenny Dalglish when I was a youngster in Scotland watching television. The game was Scotland versus England and, as usual, the English won 1-0 after the Scots had tanked them!

I will always remember that Shilton save from Dalglish, as I am sure he does. The shot went true to the top left-hand corner of the goal; Shilts soared like a bird taking off, put his right hand out and made the save look easy. That stuck in my memory and I have seen Peter produce many brilliant performances since.

That great Scottish full-back Danny McGrain gave me a tingle every time I saw him play. No one got past him. He surged forward, he had pace, he had ability.

I found choosing a left-back the most difficult task, but Stuart Pearce gets the vote because in his prime he was an inspirational figure who got forward and had a marvellous shot to go with his tackling and defending ability.

Mark Lawrenson and Alan Hansen would be my

Nicol, who collected 11 League and Cup medals in 13 seasons at Liverpool, was equally effective in midfield and defence.

pair of central defenders. They strolled through games, knocking the ball about. Both were excellent on the ground and in the air. I can't remember anyone giving them the runaround.

George Best needs no justification for inclusion, and I had no hesitation in picking Kenny Dalglish and Ian Rush as my two front strikers.

WHAT THE PLAYERS SAY...

For dedication and discipline, Steve at his peak was as good as they come. Give him a job to do and you could count on him to do it in style. He could shut out some of the finest forwards in the game and he always performed without fuss or frills. A great pro.

– GRAEME SOUNESS

Steve was our secret weapon. Other Liverpool players took the eye with their skill and flair, but when you analysed matches that we had won you would invariably find that it was Steve who had played a major role without getting the headlines.

– JOHN BARNES

I did not hesitate in bringing Steve back into the Premiership to Sheffield Wednesday from Notts County. He is a thinking footballer who reads the game really well and has a competitive streak that rubs off on the players around him.

– DAVID PLEAT

Ray Kennedy would ghost forward to score goals. He was a striker masquerading as a midfield player and did a magnificent job for both Arsenal and Liverpool.

John Barnes just walked past people in his prime and if you had put Joe Bloggs in the centre when he was on song, Joe Bloggs would have managed 25 goals a season. Not only that but John also did his share of tracking back and helping out in defence. John was Footballer of the Year the season before me and the season after, and I was honoured to be rated the man to take the trophy in between.

I can't believe as I study my selection that I have left out Scottish heroes like Denis Law, Ian St John and big Ron Yeats. I will just nominate them for the substitutes' bench and get out of the selection game before I think who else I have missed.

Grounds for hope amid the sleaze

The triple tragedy of the Bradford fire, Heysel and Hillsborough was a springboard for a football revolution in England. In the immediate post-war years there was standing room only at the Football League's packed grounds. Now there was to be no standing room at all. All-seater stadia gradually replaced the Victorian mausoleums that had become a blot on the football landscape, and with the new look came a new competition: the FA Carling Premiership.

By the mid-1990s the game at the top was awash with money. Millions were poured into the Premier League by the satellite television company BSkyB in return for wall-to-wall coverage dished up for their subscribers. But it brought mixed fortunes as the lower division clubs of the old Football League scratched a living, while the Premiership fat cats made money like never before.

Football had stopped being a sport, it was big business. Mega-rich owners like Jack Walker (Blackburn) virtually bought success, and tycoons such as Sir John Hall (Newcastle United) floated their clubs on the Stock Market, and shareholders had to be satisfied along with the supporters.

They said in 1947 when Tommy Lawton moved from Chelsea to Notts County for £20,000 that the game was going crazy. Fifty-one years later Alan Shearer, the Lawton of his time, was sold by Blackburn to Newcastle for a world record £15 million. Players earning £10,000 a week was commonplace, and several were on much more as clubs tried to attract the best talent. England was suddenly a gold mine for overseas stars, attracting the likes of Klinsmann, Bergkamp, Cantona, Gullit, Juninho, Zola, Ravanelli and Asprilla.

With the money came controversy, and stories of betting and bung scandals dominated the headlines. It all culminated in a court case featuring prominent players on bribery charges and the dismissal by Arsenal of their successful manager, George Graham, for allegedly taking what was euphemistically described as 'a bung'. In eight years at Highbury, Graham had won six trophies, including two League championships.

But Graham could not match the achievements of his fellow Scot Alex Ferguson at Old Trafford. Manchester United all but monopolised the Premiership, winning it four times in the first five years. They also captured the Cup Winners' Cup, two FA Cups and the League Cup. The only major prize that eluded Ferguson was the European Cup, which developed into a League competition to satisfy the great god of television.

On the international front, Bobby Robson's England made an impressive bid for the World Cup in 1990 when they were beaten in the semi-finals by West Germany on penalties. The tournament turned a tearful Geordie called Paul Gascoigne into a star, and he proved he had the talent but not always the temperament to cope with the fame.

Graham Taylor took over from Robson until hounded out by a baying press following England's failure to qualify for the 1994 World Cup finals. Terry Venables replaced him after a public bust-up with Alan Sugar at Tottenham, where he had been part owner. El Tel, who had won the Spanish League title at Barcelona, restored English pride with an inspiring challenge as host nation for the Euro 96 title. They were finally eliminated after another semi-final shoot-out against Germany.

Brazil, the 1994 World Cup winners in a tournament blackened by a drug scandal involving Diego Maradona, were the early favourites to retain the trophy in France in 1998. England, now under Glenn Hoddle, had their fingers crossed that they would qualify and so regain their place as a major power in world football.–**Norman Giller**

Bruce Grobbelaar was at the centre of an inquiry following allegations of deliberately throwing matches while at Liverpool.

Manchester United's refurbished Old Trafford stadium brought them a change of fortunes and a host of trophies during the 1990s.

Who won what

1989-90
League champions: Liverpool
FA Cup final: Manchester United 1, Crystal Palace 0 (after 3-3 draw)
League Cup final: Nottingham Forest 1, Oldham 0
First Division marksman: Gary Lineker (Tottenham) 24
Footballer of the Year: John Barnes (Liverpool)
Scottish champions: Rangers
Scottish Cup final: Aberdeen 0, Celtic 0 (Aberdeen won 9-8 on penalties)
Scottish Player of the Year: Alex McLeish (Aberdeen)
European Cup final: AC Milan 1, Benfica 0
Cup Winners' Cup final: Sampdoria 2, Anderlecht 0 (aet)
UEFA Cup final: Juventus 3, Fiorentina 1 (3-1, 0-0)
European Footballer of the Year: Lothar Matthaus (Inter Milan)

1990-1
League champions: Arsenal
FA Cup Final: Tottenham 2, Nottingham Forest 1
League Cup final: Sheffield Wednesday 1, Manchester United 0
First Division marksman: Alan Smith (Arsenal), 23 goals
Footballer of the Year: Gordon Strachan (Leeds United)
Scottish champions: Rangers
Scottish Cup final: Motherwell 4, Dundee United 3 (aet)
Scottish Player of the Year: Maurice Malpas (Dundee United)
European Cup final: Red Star Belgrade 0, Marseille 0 (Red Star won 5-3 on penalties)
Cup Winners' Cup final: Manchester United 2, Barcelona 1
UEFA Cup final: Inter Milan 2, Roma 1 (2-0, 0-1)
European Footballer of the Year: Jean-Pierre Papin (Marseille)

1991-2
League champions: Leeds United
FA Cup final: Liverpool 2, Sunderland 0
League Cup final: Manchester United 1, Nottingham Forest 0
First Division marksman: Ian Wright (Arsenal), 29 goals
Footballer of the Year: Jurgen Klinsmann (Tottenham)
Scottish champions: Rangers
Scottish Cup final: Rangers 2, Airdrie 1
Scottish Player of the Year: Ally McCoist (Rangers)
European Cup final: Barcelona 1, Sampdoria 0
Cup Winners' Cup final: Werder Bremen 2, Monaco 0
UEFA Cup final: Torino 2, Ajax 2 (2-2, 0-0. Ajax won on away goals)
European Footballer of the Year: Marco van Basten (AC Milan)
European Championship final: Holland 2, CIS 0

1992-3
FA Premier League: Manchester United
FA Cup final: Arsenal 2, Sheff Wednesday 1 (after 1-1 draw)
League Cup final: Arsenal 2, Sheffield Wednesday 1
Premiership marksman: Teddy Sheringham (Nottingham Forest and Tottenham) 22
Footballer of the Year: Chris Waddle (Sheffield Wednesday)
Scottish champions: Rangers
Scottish Cup final: Rangers 2, Aberdeen 1

Scottish Player of the Year: Andy Goram (Rangers)
European Cup final: Marseille 1, AC Milan 0 (Marseille subsequently stripped of title)
European Cup Winners' Cup final: Parma 3, Antwerp 1
UEFA Cup final: Juventus 6, Borussia Dortmund 1 (3-1, 3-0)
European Footballer of the Year: Roberto Baggio (Juventus)

1993-4
Carling Premiership champions: Manchester United
FA Cup final: Manchester United 4, Chelsea 0
League Cup final: Aston Villa 3, Manchester United 1
Premiership marksman: Andy Cole (Newcastle United), 34
Footballer of the Year: Alan Shearer (Blackburn Rovers)
Scottish champions: Rangers
Scottish Cup final: Dundee United 1, Rangers 0
Scottish Player of the Year: Mark Hateley (Rangers)
European Cup final: AC Milan 4, Barcelona 0
Cup Winners' Cup final: Arsenal 1, Parma 0
UEFA Cup final: Inter Milan 2, Salzburg 0 (1-0, 1-0)
European Footballer of the Year: Hristo Stoichkov (Barcelona)

1994-5
Carling Premiership champions: Blackburn Rovers
FA Cup final: Everton 1, Manchester United 0
League Cup final: Liverpool 2, Bolton Wanderers 1
Premiership marksman: Alan Shearer (Blackburn Rovers), 34
Footballer of the Year: Jurgen Klinsmann (Tottenham)
Scottish champions: Rangers
Scottish Cup final: Celtic 1, Airdrie 0
Scottish Player of the Year: Brian Laudrup (Rangers)
European Cup final: Ajax 1, AC Milan 0
European Cup Winners' Cup final: Real Zaragosa 2, Arsenal 1 (after extra time)

UEFA Cup final: Parma 2, Juventus 1 (1-0, 1-1)
European Footballer of the Year: George Weah (AC Milan)

1995-6
Carling Premiership champions: Manchester United
FA Cup final: Manchester United 1, Liverpool 0
League Cup final: Aston Villa 3, Leeds United 0
Premiership marksman: Alan Shearer (Blackburn Rovers), 31
Footballer of the Year: Eric Cantona (Manchester United)
Scottish champions: Rangers
Scottish Cup final: Rangers 5, Hearts 1
Scottish Player of the Year: Paul Gascoigne (Rangers)
European Cup final: Juventus 1, Ajax 1 (Juventus won 4-2 on penalties)
Cup Winners' Cup final: Paris St Germain 1, Rapid Vienna 0
UEFA Cup final: Bayern Munich 5, Bordeaux 1 (2-0, 3-1)
European Footballer of the Year: Matthias Sammer (Borussia Dortmund)

1996-7
Carling Premiership champions: Manchester United
FA Cup final: Chelsea 2, Middlesbrough 0
League Cup final: Leicester City 1, Middlesbrough 0 (after 1-1 draw)
Premiership marksman: Alan Shearer (Newcastle) 25
Footballer of the Year: Gianfranco Zola (Chelsea)
Scottish champions: Rangers
Scottish Cup final: Kilmarnock 1, Falkirk 0
Scottish Player of the Year: Brian Laudrup (Rangers)
European Cup final: Borussia Dortmund 3 Juventus 1
Cup Winners' Cup final: Barcelona 1 Paris St Germain 0
UEFA Cup final: Schalke 1, Inter Milan 1 (1-0, 0-1. Schalke won 4-1 on penalties)

Alan Shearer is the centre of attention at St James's Park during the completion of his £15 million world record move to Newcastle United from Blackburn in the summer of 1996. The England striker proved his worth by becoming the leading scorer during the European Championship.

FOOTBALLER OF THE YEAR

1991

Strachan, whose leadership has always inspired those around him, captained Leeds to the 1992 League championship.

Gordon Strachan

Born: Edinburgh, 9 February 1957.

Honours: Gordon set a unique record in becoming the first footballer to collect both the English and Scottish Footballer of the Year awards. He picked up the trophy from the Scottish football writers in 1980 at the end of a season with Aberdeen in which he won the first of his 50 Scotland caps. Three years later his battling midfield performances were an outstanding feature when Aberdeen captured the European Cup Winners' Cup under the management of Alex Ferguson, who sold him to Manchester United for £500,000 two years before following him to Old Trafford in 1986.

Gordon first made an impact with Dundee before joining Aberdeen, for whom he scored 55 goals in 183 League games. He notched 33 goals in 160 League appearances for Manchester United and helped them win the FA Cup in 1985. He signed for Leeds in 1989, and in 1992 captained them to the League championship. It was then on to Coventry City in 1994-5 for his final shots, and in 1996 he took over from his old Manchester United manager Ron Atkinson as team manager at Highfield Road.

Gordon's explosive energy was his trademark with every one of his teams, and his driving performances motivated his team-mates. While essentially a ball winner, he scored many vital goals as an auxiliary attacker.

This was my year

It was enormously satisfying to me when I was named Footballer of the Year because it proved a lot of people wrong. There were many who thought my career was on a downhill path when I left Manchester United to join Leeds in 1989. But instead of being a backward step I found that the move gave me new motivation, and the winning of the award was just the extra boost I needed after finishing runner up to my old Manchester United team-mate Mark Hughes in the Professional Footballers' Association vote.

I felt particularly proud of myself when it was pointed out to me that I was the first player ever to win the Footballer of the Year award in both Scotland and England. I felt ancient when I was reminded that it was way back in 1980 when I won the Scottish award while with Aberdeen.

We did not win any major prize at Elland Road the year I won the statuette, but I was confident manager Howard Wilkinson had laid the foundation for something very special. There was a strong team spirit, and the football we were playing was of an extremely high quality. It was only a run of injury problems that stopped us making more of an impact. We just could not get a settled defence because we lost no fewer than four left-backs with injuries during the season.

I told the audience at the presentation ceremony that I was sure that Leeds were on the verge of winning a major trophy. Sure enough, the following season we won the League championship and I was able to say that without any question my switch from Old Trafford to Elland Road had been a great move for me after a rewarding stay at Manchester United.

I thoroughly enjoyed my football at Leeds, and found that the younger players in the side responded to my captaincy, and this gave me the appetite for the team leadership that was later offered to me by Coventry City.

My Dream Team

PAT JENNINGS

DANNY McGRAIN   BOBBY MOORE   GARY PALLISTER   STUART PEARCE

BRYAN ROBSON   BOBBY CHARLTON

JIMMY JOHNSTONE   KENNY DALGLISH   ALAN SHEARER   GEORGE BEST

To make life easier I have chosen only players I have either seen, played with or against. This meant overlooking old giants of the game like John Charles, Stanley Matthews and Tom Finney.

The first thing I wanted was stability at the back, and while I could have gone for a Scottish goalkeeper in Alan Rough I decided to plump for Pat Jennings. He always seemed so commanding and unflappable for Arsenal, Tottenham and Northern Ireland, and had such a safe pair of hands. When you have a goalkeeper of his stature, it spreads confidence right through the team

The central defenders in front of Pat will be the interesting partnership of Bobby Moore and Gary Pallister. Both are excellent readers of the game, and their positional play will make it difficult for any forwards to break through. Bobby, Mr Cool, will tidy up and organise the players around him, and his constructive passes out of defence will encourage everybody to try to match his skilful approach to the game. Gary will handle the more physical side of things and, supported by Jennings, will take care of the balls in the air.

They will be flanked by full-backs Danny McGrain and Stuart Pearce, both are sound in defence and can contribute in attack. McGrain was a master at jockeying strikers down cul-de-sacs, while the shuddering power of Pearce's tackles would frighten the life out of the opposition.

Bossing the midfield will be my old Manchester

Gordon Strachan shows the terrier-like determination and non-stop running for Leeds that brought him 50 Scotland caps.

United team-mate Bryan Robson, an out-and-out winner who brought drive to the engine room of any team for which he played.

My chief playmaker is a Manchester United hero from an earlier era, Bobby Charlton. He would be certain to provide an accurate delivery, and will also worry the goalkeeper with his crashing shots. Robson and Charlton operating alongside each other will be the perfect tandem team, enabling us to play a positive 4-2-4 formation.

I have chosen another Old Trafford idol, George Best, on the left wing but I will leave it to him

WHAT THE PLAYERS SAY...

Gordon's enthusiasm was infectious and he was interested only in winning. He brought biting determination to every team for which he played and never gave less than a hundred per cent.

– RON ATKINSON

He is only a small man but he grows the minute he crosses the touchline and comes on to the pitch. I reckon he trod on every blade of grass at Old Trafford during his time with Manchester United. He just never stopped running and it was a great experience to play alongside him.

– BRYAN ROBSON

Gordon was not just an all-action player he was also skilful and played with intelligence as well as total effort. He was outstanding in our championship year and was a captain who led by example.

– HOWARD WILKINSON

• •

where he positions himself on the pitch. He would be told to go where he thinks he can cause most damage with his unique skill and his instinct for knowing when to take on one or more defenders.

Giving extra width to the attack I have Jimmy Johnstone out on the right. His dribbling runs would cause havoc in the tightest of defences, and Kenny Dalglish and Alan Shearer would be waiting in the middle to put the finishing touch to his creative work. Dalglish is the master of holding and shielding the ball, and would be the ideal foil for the raw power and energetic leadership of Shearer.

My team is built with attacking play in mind, but in the unlikely situation of us losing possession I know the defence will be more than capable of resisting any counter attacks. One thing is for sure, I would not fancy being the opposing goalkeeper with Pearce, Charlton and Shearer coming into shooting range!

Chris Waddle

Born: Felling, Tyne & Wear, 14 December 1960.
Honours: Chris is a throwback to the old-fashioned dribbler, and crowds love his mazy runs and now-you-see-me-now-you-don't trickery. He played for England in the 1986 and 1990 World Cup finals, and would prefer not to be reminded that he followed Stuart Pearce in putting his spot-kick off target in the semi-final shoot-out against West Germany. He is one of the great entertainers.

He won the first of his 62 caps under fellow Geordie Bobby Robson in 1985 and his last under Graham Taylor against Turkey in 1991. He joined Newcastle United from his local club Tow Law Town in 1980 and scored 46 goals in 169 League games before moving on to Tottenham for £590,000 in July 1985.

Chris became a great favourite with the White Hart Lane supporters, but Marseille made a £4.25 million offer that manager Terry Venables could not refuse and he reluctantly broke up his revived partnership with former Newcastle club-mate Paul Gascoigne.

Sheffield Wednesday brought him back into the English game for £1 million in 1992 after he had scored 22 goals in 107 French League appearances. He scored 10 League goals in 109 Premiership matches for the Hillsborough club before moving 'down the road' to Bradford City for an entertaining extension to his career, followed by a nostalgic return 'home' to Sunderland and then on to Burnley as player-manager.

Waddle's jinking style made him almost impossible to tackle and made him popular with supporters in England and France.

This was my year

When I came back to England to play for Sheffield Wednesday after my time in France with Marseille people queried the £1 million fee. They asked, 'Is he still the same Waddle? Why has he returned? Has he come home to take the money and finish off what had been a top-drawer career?'

It was a fair point, as I was 32 at the time. When I was injured early on in the season, the mutterings increased. But I was able to answer the critics, and Wednesday enjoyed some classic games during the season, culminating in reaching the finals of the League Cup and the FA Cup.

That meant more Wembley appearances for the returning 'veteran'. There was great pleasure for me in the way Wednesday played that season even though, in the event, we finished runners-up to Arsenal in both competitions. We lost 2-1 in the League Cup game at Wembley and by the same score in an FA Cup final replay after I had scored one of my most memorable goals. Wednesday played some superb football that season and I relished my return to the English game. The great consolation for our defeats in the two finals was my collecting the Footballer of the Year award – a cherished statuette that holds pride of place in a cabinet at home. It was proof that I had shown people I could still do the business.

I look back and think I have everything but a winner's medal to show for that season.

I thought my chance for the award had gone when I did not figure in the PFA awards, and I assumed the football writers would vote for someone from the top or second team. I had earlier thought my chance had gone when I left Tottenham for Marseille.

Wednesday manager Trevor Francis got out the champagne when we heard I had won the prestigious FWA award. The bubbly had never tasted better.

My Dream Team

GORDON BANKS

ALAN HANSEN   BOBBY MOORE   DAVE MACKAY

BRYAN ROBSON   PAUL GASCOIGNE   GLENN HODDLE

BOBBY CHARLTON   GEORGE BEST

GARY LINEKER   KENNY DALGLISH

WHAT THE PLAYERS SAY...

Chris is a delight to the eye unless you are unlucky enough to be marking him. He has a Matthews-like ability to run rings round defenders. He has given every team he has played for a touch of flair and the unexpected. **– TERRY VENABLES**

Chris is a magic player, and I was really disappointed that we did not get to play together more at Tottenham. He has got more tricks than a barrel load of monkeys. **– PAUL GASCOIGNE**

I'll tell my grandchildren that I played with one of the great dribblers. His ball control is fantastic, and there is hardly a defender in the world you would back against Chris in a one-on-one situation. He could thread the ball through the eye of a needle. **– BRYAN ROBSON**

There are just three players at the back in my attack-minded Dream Team. The five players in midfield are all capable of scoring goals, while up front I have two goal masters.

All are chosen on the basis that they are comfortable and skilful on the ball and can pass. Most importantly, they are all talented players who could move into any system. I am sure coaches would throw up their hands and say that I have not paid enough attention to defence, but just think of the entertainment this team would provide.

There would not be a stadium big enough in the world to house the fans who would want to see them play.

Although I choose Captain Marvels Bobby Moore and Bryan Robson, the skipper's armband goes to Dave Mackay. I saw a little of him when he was at Derby, and Arthur Cox always said that Dave was a wonderful motivator. He is certainly the most aggressive player in my team, with a will to win, and would lead by example.

Robson was more like a stuntman, the injuries he collected in the service of England and his clubs.

Choosing a 'keeper was difficult. I had to look at Peter Shilton and Ray Clemence, and felt that Pat Jennings, who I saw late in his career, was first-class. Gordon Banks got my vote, though, as the most complete.

We keep producing the best goalkeepers in

Chris Waddle showed he had lost none of his skill after Sheffield Wednesday brought him back from Marseille in 1992 for £1m.

this country; they are not as fancy as the Continentals, they catch a ball rather than punch away, and are more reliable, a different breed. I played against Alan Hansen at Liverpool and felt he was a very cultured player. He was a big part of

the Anfield success story over the years and it would be a dream to see him playing alongside Bobby Moore.

Just look at my midfield: the Fantastic Five. There's Glenn Hoddle, who was a sheer pleasure to watch and play with. Gazza in his prime was a gifted, one-off complete player. Bryan Robson, Bobby Charlton and George Best were all legends at Old Trafford, and would grace my team with their skill and explosive power.

Gary Lineker gets in up front simply because of the amount of goals he scored at different times for England, and Kenny Dalglish gets my vote just ahead of another Manchester United goal maestro in Denis Law. I saw more of Kenny, who shielded the ball so well, was unselfish and could turn a half-chance into a goal.

The word 'great' is over used in sport, but with the team I have selected, 'great' hardly does the players justice. Let's say that these are great greats!

Alan Shearer

Born: Newcastle, 13 August 1970.

Honours: Britain's most expensive footballer of all time, Alan has forced himself into the land of footballing legend with his goals at club and country level. His hometown club Newcastle United paid Blackburn Rovers £15 million for him in 1996 after he had become the first post-war player to score 30 or more League goals in three consecutive seasons in the top division. In 1994-5 he helped shoot Blackburn to the Premier League title. His contribution was a Premiership record-equalling haul of 34 goals.

Alan scored 112 goals in 138 League matches for Blackburn after joining them from Southampton in the summer of 1992 for what was then a British record fee of £3.6 million. He was a trainee at The Dell, and scored 23 goals for the Saints in 118 League matches (including a hat-trick in his First Division debut against Arsenal at the age of 17).

It was while with Southampton that he made his England debut, scoring in his first match against France at Wembley in February 1992.

He was outstanding in the 1996 European Championship, convincing the then Newcastle manager Kevin Keegan he was worth the investment of £15 million. His first season at St James's Park was hindered by a recurring groin injury after he had been appointed England captain.

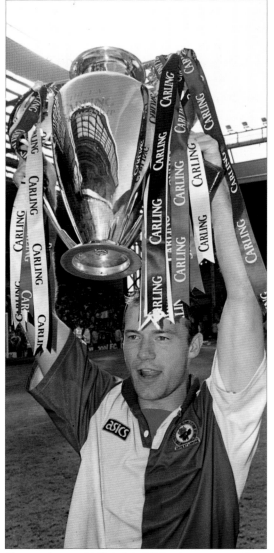

Shearer, who scored 112 goals in 138 League appearances for Blackburn, became the world's first £15million player.

This was my year

It was one of the proudest moments of my career when I collected the Footballer of the Year award at the end of the 1993-4 season, particularly when I looked down at the honours list showing previous winners. It read like a Who's Who of football, and it was overwhelming to find myself included in the company of legends of the game such as Stanley Matthews, Tom Finney, Bobby Moore and George Best.

In my acceptance speech I made the point that the award belonged as much to my Blackburn team-mates as to me. I was the one who was managing to bang the ball into the net, but you cannot play the game on your own. It is a team game, and I was grateful to everybody at the club for the part they had played in my success. Manager Kenny Dalglish and his right-hand man Ray Harford also deserved credit, because their tactics helped us make an impact. We challenged strongly for the championship and finished

runners-up to Manchester United. There were 34 reasons for me to feel pleased with my contribution to that season. That was the number of goals I scored in 35 matches for Blackburn. Yet I started the season battling to overcome an injury, and had to sit out the opening games.

It was frustrating watching from the sidelines, but the turning point came when I managed to score my first goal of the season in Blackburn's fifth match at, of all places, my hometown club Newcastle. It was disappointing not to win the championship, but for me the Footballer of the Year award was a tremendous consolation.

Our performances gave us confidence to go all out for the title the following season, and we had the satisfaction of winning it for club owner Jack Walker. I will always have warm memories of my stay at Ewood Park, and the night I received my Footballer of the Year award was one of the great highlights.

My Dream Team

PETER SHILTON

JIMMY ARMFIELD   JOHN CHARLES   BOBBY MOORE   STUART PEARCE

BILLY BREMNER   KEVIN KEEGAN

STANLEY MATTHEWS   JACKIE MILBURN   KENNY DALGLISH   GEORGE BEST

WHAT THE PLAYERS SAY...

There was never a single doubt in my mind that Alan was worth the money. He is the greatest striker of modern times, and all the old-timers say he is up there with the Tommy Lawtons and Nat Lofthouses. As well as being an outstanding player, he is also blessed with a strong character.

– KEVIN KEEGAN

I did not think I would see a centre-forward like Alan appear in the modern game. He has got two good feet, is powerful in the air and has outstanding positional sense. **– NAT LOFTHOUSE**

Alan is a natural, brilliant on the ground or in the air. He is always looking to make space, often with unselfish decoy runs to draw defenders out of position. His finishing power is just unbelievable.

– PETER BEARDSLEY

● ●

I have selected my team as much from my heart as my head. I know in my heart, for instance, that even though I did not see them play Stanley Matthews and George Best were the greatest wingers of all time. On the many videos I have seen of them in action, both had the talent to take on and beat just about any defender in man-to-man situations. It must have been fantastic to have been a centre-forward like Tommy Lawton or Nat Lofthouse playing with Matthews supplying passes. His crosses from the wing were so accurate that he made scoring so much easier for his team-mates. Best looked much faster than Matthews, and some of his ball juggling was just unbelievable.

Waiting in the middle to make the most of the creative work of Matthews and Best will be two players who mean a lot to me. Kenny Dalglish was one of my idols when I was first falling in love with the game, and I had the thrill of playing for him when he came to Blackburn as manager and then linked up again with him at St James's Park. He was a magnificent shielder of the ball, who could make room for himself in confined space.

Growing up like I did in Newcastle, you could not help but feed on the legend of 'Wor' Jackie Milburn. He was a footballing god on Tyneside, and I learnt enough about him to know that he is a must for a fantasy team like this. From the old black and white film I have seen of him, he was

Shearer has predatory skills and power that have made him England's main marksman.

incredibly quick and could finish with either foot or his head.

Bossing the midfield for me will be Billy Bremner, who was full of energy and a great ball winner. Playing alongside him will be another schoolboy hero of mine in Kevin Keegan, who would support the attack and come through from deep positions to score vital goals. I had the pleasure of playing for Kevin at Newcastle, and discovered in the short time that we were together that he knows the game inside out. I like his

attacking approach to the game, and you will see from my team that I agree with his philosophy.

I have heard enough from old timers in the game to appreciate that John Charles is a must for the middle of my defence, and I had no hesitation in selecting Bobby Moore as his partner. Bobby will wear the captain's armband because he proved with England that he was a marvellous skipper who led by example. Jimmy Armfield will be at right-back because I am told he had great poise and control under pressure. My left-back is a player I know well. Stuart Pearce will make any player think twice about trying to go past him, and his power shooting will give another dimension to our attack.

In goal I select Peter Shilton, whose 125 caps say everything about his consistency. His international career was over by the time I broke into the England team, but I saw enough of him to appreciate that he was a goalkeeper of exceptional ability.

Jurgen Klinsmann

Born: Geopingen, Germany, 30 June 1964.

Honours: 'Have Boots Will Travel' could have been the motto for Jurgen, who started his football journey with Stuttgart Kickers in 1982. He moved to FC Stuttgart and helped them reach the 1989 UEFA Cup final before travelling the soccer roundabout with Inter Milan, Real Madrid, Monaco and, most memorably for British fans, Tottenham. He then completed the circle by returning home to play for Bayern Munich before going back to Italy with Sampdoria. Along the way he was voted European Footballer of the Year following his outstanding displays for Germany in the 1988 European Championship. He played a prominent part in West Germany's World Cup triumph of 1990, and was a UEFA Cup winner with Inter in 1991.

He had just one headline-grabbing season with Tottenham after chairman Alan Sugar had negotiated his surprise transfer from Monaco for £2 million in the summer of 1994. He scored 20 goals in 41 Premiership matches and won even the hearts of non-Spurs fans with his vitality and goal-scoring skill. He netted in his first seven appearances and quickly became a White Hart Lane hero. It was with stunned disbelief that his army of fans discovered he was exercising a contractual opt-out clause that released him from Tottenham after just one unforgettable year in British football.

This was my year

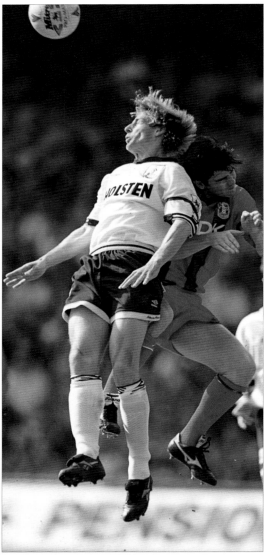

Klinsmann, who has leapt to great heights during a glittering career throughout Europe, transformed Tottenham's 1994-5 season.

The personal highlight for me of the memorable season that I spent in English football was when I went to Liverpool with the Tottenham team for a sixth round FA Cup match. The Anfield ground has a place in football legend and I wondered what sort of reception we would get from the famous Liverpool fans if we knocked them out of the Cup.

Well, we tested them to the limit with a 2-1 victory, and I was the man who managed to score a very late winner that must have been extremely disappointing for them. Imagine my surprise when the Liverpool fans gave me a standing ovation. It was an incredible show of sportsmanship. The memory of it will live with me for ever.

Football has a habit of bringing you down to earth, and our hopes of getting to Wembley were destroyed in the semi-final when Everton beat us 4-1. So teams from Liverpool provided me with my highest and lowest points while playing in England.

I had a wonderful rapport with the Tottenham supporters. It was sad that it was such a brief relationship but this is how things work out in football where nothing is ever permanent.

It was my 28 goals during the season that helped me clinch the Footballer of the Year award, and I was thrilled to become the second German after Bert Trautmann to be honoured with the selection. Bert made a special trip to see me collect the award, and we had a long talk about the way the game has changed.

When I accepted the trophy, I had mixed feelings because I knew that I would be shortly leaving a club that will always have a special place in my affections. I made a point of thanking Teddy Sheringham for his contribution. He and I had a great understanding, as the 38 goals we scored between us in the Premiership proves.

It was an extremely satisfying way to end my stay in England that I will always look back on with pride . . . and fond memories.

My Dream Team

PAT JENNINGS

ALF RAMSEY   JACK CHARLTON   BOBBY MOORE   ROGER BYRNE

KEVIN KEEGAN   BOBBY CHARLTON

STANLEY MATTHEWS   GEORGE BEST

GARY LINEKER   JIMMY GREAVES

My selections are based on what I know about the great players of British football and also on what I learned during many conversations with knowledgeable Tottenham supporters. You will see that I have four former Spurs favourites in my line-up in Pat Jennings, Alf Ramsey, Gary Lineker and Jimmy Greaves.

As a specialist goal scorer myself, I know all about the exploits of Lineker and Greaves. Gary was outstanding for England in the World Cup finals of 1986 and 1990. I remember very well his performance against West Germany in the semi-final in Italy when his excellent goal forced extra time. We got through by the skin of our teeth in the penalty shoot-out. As for my selection of Jimmy Greaves, you cannot spend any time at Tottenham without quickly learning of the legend of the man they call Greavsie. His 220 League goals for the club is a monument to his great skill as a finisher.

Lineker and Greaves, in my formation of six attacking players, will be very hard to contain. They will be supported by the energetic Kevin Keegan, who was nicknamed Mighty Mouse when twice winning the European Footballer of the Year award while with Hamburg. He was an exceptional player who always worked very hard for his team. There was nothing selfish about his game.

The one and only Sir Bobby Charlton, almost as famous in Germany as he is in England, will control the midfield as he did against West Germany in the 1966 World Cup final. I was just two years old and too young to know what was happening, but as I grew up I began to appreciate the part Sir Bobby played in those finals.

Playing as withdrawn wingers will be two footballers whose ball control has never been surpassed. Sir Stanley Matthews, one of the fathers of football, will captain the side. Those baffling tricks of his that I have seen on old black and white films will be worth travelling a long way to see. George Best will operate on the left, causing havoc in defence with his speed and skill.

My central defenders will be Jack Charlton and Bobby Moore, who served the 1966 World Cup winners so well. Charlton was commanding in the air, and Bobby Moore was the nearest to a British Franz Beckenbauer with his cultured play and ability to read the game.

Sir Alf Ramsey was, I am assured, as positive a right-back as he was a manager, and on the left flank I have Roger Byrne, whose fame as a footballing defender has kept his name alive long after his tragic death in the Munich air crash.

I considered Gordon Banks and Peter Shilton for my goalkeeper, but decided on Pat Jennings because I remember Tottenham fans telling me there has not been a more reliable goalkeeper.

He is the final piece in my jigsaw. It is a team that perhaps lacks a midfield anchorman and ball winner, but it would be very entertaining to watch.

WHAT THE PLAYERS SAY...

It was not only Jurgen's skill and finishing ability that took the eye, it was also his astonishing work-rate. He ran his socks off in every game he played and never tried to take an easy passage through any match. **– GERRY FRANCIS**

There is not a weakness in Jurgen's game. He is strong in the air, has two good feet and can finish with power and accuracy. There are few players who can match him for creating goals from apparently impossible situations. **– GARY MABBUTT**

I doubt if any player has made as great an impact on the game in just one season as Jurgen did. He was a joy to play with and was a completely unselfish team player. Some of his goals were out of this world. **– TEDDY SHERINGHAM**

The charismatic German scored 20 goals in 41 Premiership games for Spurs and excited the crowd whenever he touched the ball.

Eric Cantona

Born: Marseille, France, 24 May 1966.

Honours: Eric created a unique record by winning League championship medals with three different clubs: Nimes, Leeds United and Manchester United. But it was while playing at Old Trafford that his fame transcended football.

He made headlines of the wrong sort in the 1994-5 season when he received a record suspension and court sentence for attacking a supporter during a match. But it was for his footballing deeds that he won idol-status in England, although in France his international appearances were restricted because of his unpopularity with the French hierarchy.

Before arriving at Leeds, he had stormy associations with Auxerre, Martigues, Marseille, Bordeaux, Montpellier and Nimes. But following his move to Manchester United for £1.2 million in 1992 he found the platform on which his stunning skill was allowed to flourish. He became captain and main orchestrator of the United team that dominated the Premiership. He was also prominent in United's FA Cup triumphs of 1994 and 1996, including scoring the winning goal that defeated Liverpool two days after he had collected his Footballer of the Year award.

He astonished the world of football by announcing his retirement at the end of the 1996-7 season.

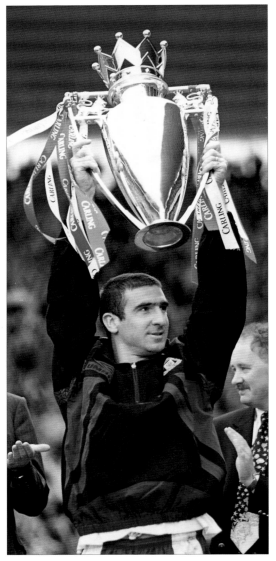

Cantona lifts the Premiership trophy after guiding Manchester Untied through another successful League campaign in 1995-6.

This was my year

I am very proud of my Footballer of the Year award because it proves that I was noticed. It was a long year, but ultimately a very beautiful one. There have been many experiences that enriched me and made me a more understanding and perhaps more tolerant person. It was a great joy for me to play with a team for which I have enormous respect, and together we have proved that we are deserving of the mantle of champions.

I wish to emphasise that the award was not for me as an individual but for the entire Manchester United staff. I am particularly indebted to manager Alex Ferguson and coach Brian Kidd, and I share the award with them. Also I wish to mention the Manchester United supporters who have always been very important to me. They have been instrumental in making me play with total commitment.

There are those who do not perhaps think I am worthy of the award, and thankfully in what is a free democracy they are entitled to their opinions. It is not my intention to talk about the incident at Crystal Palace. That is now confined to the wastebin of history. I prefer to remember the sweeter moments, especially winning the Premiership. Two days after receiving my award I was fortunate enough to score the goal that won us the FA Cup. These are the moments that I prefer to contemplate when asked about my experiences at Old Trafford.

I have listened to lots of good and well-intentioned advice from people whom I respect at Manchester United, and I have tried to do the things that are expected of me. Football is a beautiful game and I hope that I have made a contribution that is in keeping with this concept.

I would like to sign off by wishing good health to everyone in the world. That is the most important thing, not the money or the adulation. It is health and peace that matter above all else.

My Dream Team

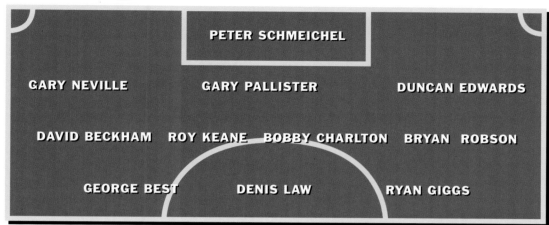

PETER SCHMEICHEL

GARY NEVILLE   GARY PALLISTER   DUNCAN EDWARDS

DAVID BECKHAM   ROY KEANE   BOBBY CHARLTON   BRYAN ROBSON

GEORGE BEST   DENIS LAW   RYAN GIGGS

I have confined my selection to an amalgamation of Manchester United players past and present. Some of those, of course, I did not see play. But during my stay at Old Trafford I have heard much about exceptional players of the past and have had the advantage of seeing them on video. My team is selected with style and panache in mind, which is a Manchester United prerequisite.

I have great confidence that Peter Schmeichel is the right choice as goalkeeper. We have played together many times and I consider him one of the finest players I have seen in what is a very difficult and specialised position. He has the ideal physique for his job and makes an intimidating barrier for any player coming towards him with the ball at his feet.

The two Garys, Neville and Pallister, are well proven at the highest level and I know they will be very sound and reliable in a back line of three. My third choice is Duncan Edwards, a player whom I know only from the many tales I have been told by people who saw him play for Manchester United before his premature passing in the cruel Munich air disaster. My understanding is that he was a colossus who could play in virtually any position.

David Beckham will play wide on the right where he can cause most concern to the opposition with that cultured right foot of his. He is one of the brightest young players in the world. Alongside him will be Roy Keane, whose

Cantona, a League championship winner with three different clubs, guides United to victory in the 1994 FA Cup final.

competitive and inspirational performances always made the rest of us in the Manchester United team raise our game.

Nobody could select a Manchester United team without including Sir Bobby Charlton, whose fame travelled far beyond British boundaries. I have witnessed enough of his performances on film to know that he will be the ideal playmaker in midfield and with the added responsibility for coming through as a support striker. It was a privilege to get to know Sir Bobby, a wonderful ambassador for the beautiful game of football.

WHAT THE PLAYERS SAY...

All Eric had to do was give one of those winks of his and it made you feel ten feet tall. There has never been a player quite like him. He could bring the best out of his team-mates by his performance.

– DAVID BECKHAM

Eric never had a lot to say for himself, but his actions spoke louder than words. His presence was enough to lift us and put the opposition under pressure. I feel privileged to have played with him.

– STEVE BRUCE

Cantona had an aura about him that gave him a cloak of mystery to go with his magic. The Old Trafford fans used to chant 'There's only one Eric Cantona'. I don't think anybody could argue with that. He was a one-off. **– DAVID PLEAT**

. . . .

Bryan Robson completes the midfield unit. I played with him enough times towards the end of his outstanding career with United to appreciate his asset to a team. He had a balanced mixture of power and skill, and could make a team function better by his forceful contribution.

I am assured by everybody who was around at Old Trafford during the George Best years that he was a player who could be mentioned in the same breath as the likes of Pele, Platini and di Stefano. He becomes an automatic selection alongside another legendary Manchester United player from the 1960s, Denis Law, whom I gather from the film action I have seen of him had astonishingly quick reactions. Finally, I select Ryan Giggs whose pace and skill out on the left wing will give another dimension to the attack. Hopefully I have picked a Manchester United team for all seasons.

Interviews compiled with the valued assistance of the Manchester United manager Alex Ferguson.

1997

Gianfranco Zola

Born: Sardinia, 5 July 1966.

Honours: Gianfranco was born in the month that England won the World Cup, so perhaps he was destined one day to play in the English league. It was when Napoli signed him in 1986 as an understudy to Diego Maradona that his career blossomed after he had laid the foundations with minor clubs Nuorese and Torres. He eventually took over Maradona's No. 10 shirt and gives Maradona credit for teaching him many of the tricks with which he confounds defenders.

His goals and passes helped Napoli win the Italian championship in 1990 before a £1.4 million move to Parma in 1993. He replaced Roberto Baggio in the Italy side and was a key player in the Parma team that won the UEFA Cup and European Cup Winners' Cup.

Gianfranco, standing just 5ft 5in tall, became disenchanted at Parma and he jumped at the chance to join Chelsea for £4.5 million in November 1996. The move revitalised his game, and it was his stunning goal that beat England in a World Cup qualifying match at Wembley.

The lifestyle of family man Zola could not be more different from that of his idol Maradona. A teetotaller, he quickly settled into a new London home with wife Franca and children Andrea and Martina, and he loves nothing better than playing Beethoven on his piano.

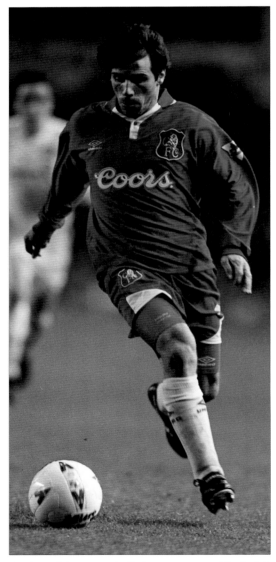

Gianfranco Zola won over the Chelsea supporters and the football writers in his first eventful season at Stamford Bridge.

This was my year

My first season in English football was just unbelievable and the memories of it will live with me for ever. It was very important that I should help Chelsea win something after the player-manager Ruud Gullit had put so much faith in me, and our victory in the FA Cup final against Middlesbrough was unforgettable. To be part of the wonderful occasion was fantastic. I have never known anything quite like the atmosphere of a Wembley final.

Two days earlier I had been honoured by the Football Writers' Association with their award as the Footballer of the Year. It was an overwhelming experience. I felt humble when I looked at the names of the great players who had won it before me, and when I realised that I had won the vote ahead of such exceptional players as Juninho, Ravanelli and Alan Shearer.

I was singled out, but I must say I could not have achieved so much in my first season without the great team effort by everybody at Stamford Bridge. I was lucky to settle very quickly into the Chelsea team and in Mark Hughes found the perfect partner.

The beautiful statuette, which I will cherish all my life, was presented to me by Mister Football himself, Sir Stanley Matthews. He is a god in the game and I was almost speechless not only to meet him in person but also to find myself sitting alongside him. We had a long talk about football past and present, and I found that he was completely up to date with everything that is happening in our great game. He told me that he used to play for just £20 a week. Today he would be worth all the money in the Bank of England.

I was overjoyed to have my father at the awards ceremony. It was his first visit to England and, like me, could not believe that the legendary Stanley Matthews was to make the presentation. It is something that I will never forget.

My Dream Team

RAY CLEMENCE

GEORGE COHEN   JOHN CHARLES   BOBBY MOORE   TERRY COOPER

BRYAN ROBSON   BOBBY CHARLTON

STANLEY MATTHEWS   KEVIN KEEGAN   GEOFF HURST   CHRIS WADDLE

WHAT THE PLAYERS SAY...

You can tell that Gianfranco was an understudy to Diego Maradona because there is something of the great man's magic in his game. He can turn a game in a split second with an incredible bit of skill.

– DENNIS WISE

Gianfranco is very difficult to mark because he is so inventive. He makes his small physique work for him by clever footwork and creating space for himself in confined spaces.   **– GARY MABBUTT**

I feel that he has helped bring the best out of me with his support play. He is always in the right place at the right time, either to make or take a pass. He is a magnificent player.   **– MARK HUGHES**

My first choice was a player who is still known throughout the world even though I was not born when he played his last match. I refer, of course, to Sir Stanley Matthews, who is up there with Pele, di Stefano and Maradona as one of the great masters of football. He will play on the right wing and will also captain the team because just by being on the pitch he will earn the respect of his team-mates.

For my goalkeeper I have selected Ray Clemence, who made a big impression when playing in the outstanding Liverpool team of the 1970s that was so dominant in Europe and which I often watched on television as a wide-eyed schoolboy. Clemence was what I would describe as a typical English goalkeeper, calm and very brave and making his saves with a minimum of showmanship.

You cannot grow up in Italian football without being aware of the legend of John Charles. The old pros still talk in wonder at his performances for Juventus alongside Omar Sivori. They say that when he headed the ball he was so powerful it would go like a rocket.

He will play in central defence partnered by Bobby Moore, who every football fan knows was one of the greatest defenders of all time. My full-backs will be George Cohen and Terry Cooper. I know about Cohen because I have always been interested in the England team that won the World Cup in the month that I was born. Cooper, I have often been told, was one of the most exciting of all attacking full-backs.

There is another legend in midfield in Bobby

Charlton, who represents all that is best about English football. I have seen enough film of him in action to know that he could pass and shoot as accurately as anybody who has ever played the game. Alongside him will be a Manchester United star from a later generation in Bryan Robson, who managed the Middlesbrough team that Chelsea defeated in the 1997 FA Cup final. I was enormously impressed by the dignity he showed in defeat. This used to show in his game as the driving force for both United and England.

Kevin Keegan is a player, like Clemence, that I first noticed in Liverpool's 1977 European Cup winning team, and the fact that later he twice won the European Footballer of the Year award with Hamburg says all that needs to be said about his ability.

He will play as a supporting striker to Geoff Hurst, who scored the unforgettable hat-trick in the 1966 World Cup final. Helping Stanley Matthews create the goal-scoring chances with his dribbling runs down the left wing will be Chris Waddle, who is one of the finest controllers of the ball the game has seen. My substitute will be Gary Lineker, which shows how strong my team is if he can only get a place on the bench. He had a magnificent 1990 World Cup in my home country, and looked then to be as sharp a finisher as there is in the world.

Zola, whose 1996-7 season was transformed following his £4.5 million move from Parma, celebrates after scoring in Chelsea's 6-2 win over Sunderland.

Genius Best the players' favourite

Welsh giant John Charles, who made his name in Italy at Juventus, was as talented at centre-half as he was as a hot-shot centre-forward.

Scotsman Denis Law, the first British £100,000 player, was a demon in the penalty area but only made the substitutes' bench.

Best, who was voted Europe's top player in the same year as he won the Footballer of the Year in 1968, pipped Bobby Charlton.

George Best emerged as the Player of Players in the dream teams selected by our golden heroes. The idol of Manchester United was included in 30 of the 43 teams selected by winners of the FWA Footballer of the Year award. His Old Trafford team-mate Bobby Charlton was pipped into second place, with 28 selections.

Bobby Moore, included in 23 teams, was third in the popularity poll. He lines up alongside John Charles (18 votes) at the heart of the defence in our Team of Teams, with Danny McGrain (13 votes) and Ray Wilson (16) linking up at full-back.

Gordon Banks, the goalkeeper winner ahead of Pat Jennings with 19 votes, joins Moore, Wilson and Charlton as the fourth member of England's 1966 World Cup winning side.

Duncan Edwards, who died following the 1958 Munich air disaster, lives on in the memory of many and was selected in 17 of the teams. Wing wizards Stanley Matthews (17 votes) and Tom Finney (16) both win a place in the Team of Teams,

with Kenny Dalglish (17) the most modern of the players selected.

There are seven Englishmen, two Scots a Welshman and an Irishman in the final selection. Denis Law (14 votes), Jimmy Greaves (13), Jennings (11), Roger Byrne (9) and Bryan Robson (8) win places on the substitutes' bench.

Seven of the team were Footballer of the Year award winners, which cancelled out a possible vote each: Gordon Banks, Bobby Moore, Bobby Charlton, Stanley Matthews, Kenny Dalglish, George Best and Tom Finney.

This is a team for all seasons: Golden Heroes.

Dream Team roll-call

George Best (30 votes), Bobby Charlton (28), Bobby Moore (23), Gordon Banks (19), John Charles (18), Stanley Matthews (17), Duncan Edwards (17), Kenny Dalglish (17), Tom Finney (16), Ray Wilson (16), Danny McGrain (13), Denis Law (14), Jimmy Greaves (13), Pat Jennings (11), Roger Byrne (9), Bryan Robson (8),

The Team of Teams

GORDON BANKS

DANNY McGRAIN   **JOHN CHARLES**   **BOBBY MOORE**   **RAY WILSON**

BOBBY CHARLTON   **DUNCAN EDWARDS**

STANLEY MATTHEWS   **KENNY DALGLISH**   **GEORGE BEST**   **TOM FINNEY**

SUBSTITUTES' BENCH: Denis Law, Jimmy Greaves, Pat Jennings, Roger Byrne, Bryan Robson

The ones who got away

Authors Dennis Signy and Norman Giller asked a cross section of players, past and present, to nominate the players who they felt were unluckiest to miss out on a Footballer of the Year award. These, in order of popularity, were the top 20 nominations . . .

1. JIMMY GREAVES

The Artful Dodger of the penalty area, Greaves scored a record 357 First Division goals with Chelsea, Tottenham and West Ham, and had a brief excursion into Italian football with AC Milan. Tottenham bought him from Milan in 1961 for £99,999, deliberately not burdening him with the tag of British football's first £100,000 player. His 220 League goals remain a Spurs record. Capped 57 times by England, he netted 44 internationals goals – a total beaten only by Bobby Charlton (49 goals in 106 matches) and Gary Lineker (48 goals in 60 matches). He has become one of the best known of all TV sports personalities.

2. DENIS LAW

He made his League debut with Huddersfield Town at the age of 16, and two years later became Scotland's youngest ever international. His transfer to Manchester City for £55,000 in 1960 was then a British record. Torino bought him for £100,000 in 1961, and the following year Manchester United paid £115,000 to bring him home. He scored 171 League goals for United in 309 matches before winding down his career with Manchester City. Famous for his razor-sharp reflexes, he scored a record 30 goals in 55 appearances for Scotland. He was voted European Footballer of the Year in 1964.

3. ALAN BALL

The youngest of England's 1966 World Cup heroes, he played for Blackpool, Everton, Arsenal, Southampton and Bristol Rovers. He was a midfield schemer with atomic energy, and a fiery temperament that matched his red hair. His precise passing was a key factor for the Everton team that won the League title in 1970 when he formed an outstanding midfield trio with Howard Kendall and Colin Harvey. He skippered Everton, Arsenal and Southampton and also captained England six times in his 78 appearances. Ball has managed Blackpool, Portsmouth, Stoke, Exeter, Southampton and Manchester City.

4. JOHNNY HAYNES

During 18 years with Fulham, pass master Haynes set two club records – 159 goals in 598 League appearances. He played 56 times for England, and was captain in 22 of the matches which included the 1962 World Cup campaign. His international career ended after he damaged a knee in a car smash. He scored 18 goals for England, including a hat-trick against Russia in 1958. Haynes became the first £100-a-week footballer in Britain following the lifting of the maximum £20-a-week wage in 1961 after the Italians tried to tempt him abroad. He held his final passing-out parade in Durban City.

5. TOMMY LAWTON

The 'Head Master' of football started with Burnley, and in 1936 at 18 joined Everton for £6,500, then a world record for a teenager. Lawton succeeded Dixie Dean as Everton centre-forward, and won a League championship medal in 1938-9. After the war he played for Chelsea (1945-7), Notts County (1947-52), Brentford (1952-3), Arsenal (1953-6), Kettering Town as player-manager, and then returned to Notts County for a brief spell as manager. He scored 231 goals in 390 League matches, and 22 in 23 for England. Lawton netted another 24 goals in 22 wartime internationals.

6. JACKIE MILBURN

From a famous North-East footballing family, 'Wor Jackie' Milburn plundered 179 League goals for Newcastle and was the idol of Tyneside for more than a decade. He helped Newcastle win the FA

Jimmy Greaves, who scored a record 357 First Division goals

Tommy Lawton, the "head master" who led the England attack.

Geoff Hurst, the hatrick hero of the 1966 World Cup final.

9. WILF MANNION

Mannion made his debut for Middlesbrough at the age of 17 and, despite the loss of five years to the war, scored 99 League goals in 341 games for the Teesside club. Nicknamed 'Golden Boy', he completed his League century during a swan-song season with Hull City. Capped 26 times by England, he was a skilful, elusive inside-forward who could dribble defences to death or catch them unawares with a sudden precise pass. He was a creator of goals as well as a stunning finisher in his own right, and is considered by many to have been the greatest player ever to wear a Middlesbrough shirt.

10. COLIN BELL

Coach Malcolm Allison nicknamed him 'Nijinsky', which captured his thoroughbred talent and his amazing capacity for running marathon distances at sprint speed. He was equally effective as a schemer or support striker and did the work of two men as if he had an extra lung. Bell started with Bury, and was transferred to Manchester City for £45,000 in 1966. He scored 117 League goals in 394 games for City, and 25 in 82 games with Bury. Capped 48 times by England, he formed a feared trio with Francis Lee and Mike Summerbee during an era when City matched their Manchester rivals United in the chase for honours.

Cup three times in the 1950s, scoring three goals at Wembley. Milburn started as an inside-forward, then switched to the right wing and finally settled into the centre-forward position. He wore the No. 9 England shirt ten times and the No. 7 shirt three times and scored 10 goals in international matches. He later managed Ipswich Town before becoming a respected football writer for the News of the World.

7. GEOFF HURST

Hurst will always be remembered as the man who scored an historic hat-trick for England in the 1966 World Cup Final against West Germany. He helped West Ham win the FA Cup and European Cup Winners' Cup, and scored 180 League goals for the Hammers and 22 for Stoke before winding down his League career with West Bromwich Albion, for whom he scored two goals in ten appearances. His goals haul for England was 24 in 49 matches. He became player-manager of Telford United, then managed Chelsea until April 1981 and was a member of Ron Greenwood's England training team.

8. RAICH CARTER

Horatio Carter's career straddled the Second World War, and during it he struck up one of the most memorable of all partnerships as inside-right to wing wizard Stanley Matthews.
He started his League career with Sunderland and captained them to the League championship and FA Cup. Carter teamed up with Peter Doherty to steer Derby County to the FA Cup in 1946. Later, as the 'Silver Fox', he became player-manager of Hull City, helped Cork City win the Irish FA Cup in 1953, then became a manager with Leeds, Mansfield and Middlesbrough. He was capped 13 times and netted 216 League goals in 451 matches.

Colin Bell, a thoroughbred player who was nicknamed Nijinsky.

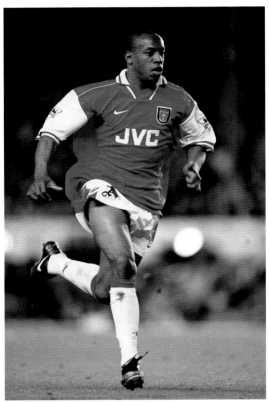

Ian Wright, who is in shooting range of the Arsenal Club record.

John Charles, equally at home at centre-half or centre-forward.

11. IAN WRIGHT

A late starter with Crystal Palace, Wright came from non-League football desperate to make up for lost time. He scored 89 goals in 229 League games for Palace before moving across London to Arsenal where he quickly established himself as a Highbury idol. A quick, powerful and highly emotive player, he started a goal chase that took him within shooting range of Cliff Bastin's long-standing club record of 150 League goals. He made his England debut while with Palace and became a regular in Glenn Hoddle's squad as understudy to first-choice centre-forward Alan Shearer.

12. PETER SHILTON

He was so outstanding as a 17-year-old goalkeeper that Leicester City decided they could let England`s 1966 World Cup hero Gordon Banks move on to Stoke. Shilts went on to succeed Banks between the posts for England and Stoke, and won a record 125 caps. He left international stage after helping England reach the 1990 World Cup semi-finals. His peak years were with Nottingham Forest when he was a key man in the team that won the European cup two years in succession. He later had a successful spell at Southampton. Winding down his marathon career with Orient in 1996-97, he set a record when making his 1000th League appearance.

13. JOHN CHARLES

'The Gentle Giant' was an idol in three countries – Wales, England and Italy. He was equally accomplished at centre-half or centre-forward, and was a powerhouse for Leeds United, Juventus, Roma and Cardiff City after a second spell at Elland Road. At 18, he was the youngest player capped by Wales, for whom he scored 15 goals in 38 appearances. He was adored at Juventus, where he had a magnificent partnership with Argentine artist Omar Sivori. There are many good judges who rate him the greatest British-born player of all time.

14. LEN SHACKLETON

Rejected by Arsenal because he was considered too small, Shack launched his great career with his local club Bradford Park Avenue. He was snapped up by Newcastle United after just seven games for what was then a huge fee of £7,000, and on his debut scored six goals against Newport. Two years later he signed for Sunderland for £20,000. Capped five times by England, he scored 126 goals in 34 League games. He would have won many more caps but for continual clowning that turned the establishment against him. But the fans loved his humour and his stunning skill and dubbed him the Clown Prince.

15. ALLAN CLARKE

Nicknamed 'Sniffer' because of his ability to sniff out the half-chance, Clarke plundered goals for Walsall, Fulham, Leicester and Leeds before becoming player-manager of Barnsley. He briefly returned in 1980 as manager of Leeds where he had his peak years during which he scored 110 First Division goals in 273 matches (1970-9). His total League goals collection was 224. He scored 10 goals for England in 19 international appearances. Clarke had the killer instinct in front of goal, could score with either foot and was a master at creating space for himself in the crowded penalty area.

16. RAY WILSON

A stylish left-back, Wilson travelled the football roundabout with Huddersfield, Everton, Oldham and Bradford City. He was a key man in England's 1966 World Cup winning team, partnering George Cohen in one of the finest full-back pairings in English football history. Capped 63 times by Alf Ramsey, he was a tenacious tackler and one of the pioneers of overlapping play. He helped Everton win the FA Cup in 1966, just a few weeks before returning to Wembley to play a major part in the World Cup triumph. At the end of his outstanding career, Wilson settled into a contrasting life as a funeral director.

17. STAN MORTENSEN

'Morty' survived a wartime bomber crash to become a legendary striker, scoring 197 League goals for Blackpool in ten seasons. It was for his FA Cup exploits that he was most renowned. In 1948 he scored in every round including the final, but Blackpool lost to Manchester United. Three years later he was a runner-up against Newcastle, but made no mistake in 1953 when he netted the only FA Cup final hat-trick at Wembley in the game that became known as the 'Matthews Final'. He played 25 times for England and scored 23 goals. He wound down his career with Hull and Southport, and managed his beloved Blackpool.

18. MARTIN PETERS

A gentle executioner, Peters was once described by Alf Ramsey as a player ten years ahead of his time. He was never fully appreciated by the majority of fans, but any pro will tell you he was a class player who was a master of positional play. He stole through defences to plunder 169 League goals with West Ham (70), Tottenham (46) and

Rodney Marsh, a clowning entertainer with QPR and Manchester City.

Glenn Hoddle, who passed with honours for Tottenham and England.

Norwich City (44) before briefly joining Sheffield United in a coaching and then managerial capacity. Best remembered for his England exploits, he was capped 67 times, and scored 21 goals, including one in the 1966 World Cup final.

19. RODNEY MARSH

A magician with the ball at his feet, Marsh was one of the most creative forces to emerge in English football in the post-war years. The fans loved him, but quite a few coaches tended to resent him because of his refusal to conform to their rigid plans. He was a one-off who believed in doing things his way. He took his considerable skills to the United States after amassing 169 League goals with Fulham (27 in two spells), Queens Park Rangers (106) and Manchester City

(36). He was capped nine times by England but never won the full trust of England managers because he was such a free spirit.

20. GLENN HODDLE

Now famous as the England coach, Hoddle was a master passer who illuminated many matches with spectacular goals. He was a thoroughbred performer for Tottenham before continuing his career with Monaco where injuries continually handicapped him. The winner of successive FA Cup winner's medals with Tottenham in 1981 and 1982, he collected 53 England caps despite the common accusation that he was a 'luxury' player. He was a specialist at free-kicks and his right-foot shots were always deadly accurate. Hoddle started his managerial career with Swindon before taking over at Chelsea.

The top transfers

Danny Blanchflower.

Ian Rush.

Alan Shearer.

1940s

PLAYER	FROM	TO	DATE	FEE
Eddie Quigley	Sheff Wed	Preston	Dec. 1949	£26,500
Johnny Morris	Man Utd	Derby County	Mar. 1949	£25,000
Bobby Langton	Preston	Bolton	Nov. 1949	£22,250
Alf Ramsey	Southampton	Tottenham	May 1949	£21,000
Len Shackleton	Newcastle	Sunderland	Feb. 1948	£20,050
Tommy Lawton	Chelsea	Notts County	Nov. 1947	£20,000

1950s

PLAYER	FROM	TO	DATE	FEE
Albert Quixall	Sheff Wed	Man United	Sept 1958	£45,000
Mel Charles	Swansea	Arsenal	Mar 1959	£40,000
Cliff Jones	Swansea	Tottenham	Feb 1958	£35,000
Jackie Sewell	Notts Co	Sheff Weds	Mar 1951	£34,000
Trevor Ford	Sunderland	Cardiff	Nov 1953	£30,000
Danny Blanchflower	Aston Villa	Tottenham	Dec 1954	£30,000

1960s

PLAYER	FROM	TO	DATE	FEE
Allan Clarke	Leicester	Leeds	Jan 1969	£165,000
Allan Clarke	Fulham	Leicester	June 1968	£150,000
Martin Chivers	Southampton	Tottenham	Jan 1968	£125,000
Denis Law	Torino	Man United	July 1962	£116,000
Alan Ball	Blackpool	Everton	Aug 1966	£110,000
Tony Hateley	Aston Villa	Chelsea	Oct 1966	£100,000
Denis Law	Manchester City	Torino	June 1961	£100,000

1970s

PLAYER	FROM	TO	DATE	FEE
Andy Gray	Aston Villa	Wolves	Sept 1979	£1.469m
Steve Daley	Wolves	Man City	Sept 1979	£1.4375m
Trevor Francis	Birmingham	Nottm Forest	Feb 1979	£1.18m
Laurie Cunningham	West Brom	Real Madrid	June 1979	£950,000
Ray Wilkins	Chelsea	Man Utd	Aug 1979	£825,000
Michael Robinson	Preston	Man City	June 1979	£756,000

1980s

PLAYER	FROM	TO	DATE	FEE
Chris Waddle	Tottenham	Marseille	July 1989	£4.25m
Ian Rush	Liverpool	Juventus	June 1987	£3.2m
Ian Rush	Juventus	Liverpool	Aug 1988	£2.8m
Gary Lineker	Everton	Barcelona	June 1986	£2.75m
Mark Hughes	Man United	Barcelona	May 1986	£2.3m
Gary Pallister	Middlebrough	Man United	Aug 1989	£2.3m

1990s

PLAYER	FROM	TO	DATE	FEE
Alan Shearer	Blackburn	Newcastle	July 1996	£15m
Junihno	Middlesbrough	Atletico Madrid	July 1997	£12.5m
Stan Collymore	Nottingham Forest	Liverpool	June 1995	£8.5m
Dennis Bergkamp	Inter Milan	Arsenal	June 1995	£7.5m
Stan Collymore	Liverpool	Aston Villa	May 1997	£7m
Fabrizio Ravanelli	Juventus	Middlesbrough	July 1996	£7m
Andy Cole	Newcastle	Manchester United	Jan. 1995	£7m